Media Talk

Spoken Discourse on TV and Radio

University of
Chester

Y

'd   3hr

OL
STER
PUS

EDINBURGH UNIVERSITY PRESS

© Andrew Tolson, 2006
Edinburgh University Press Ltd
22 George Square, Edinburgh

Typeset in Monotype Apollo
by Koinonia, Bury, and
printed and bound in Great Britain
by The Cromwell Press, Trowbridge, Wilts

A CIP record for this book is available
from the British Library

ISBN 0 7486 1825 2 (hardback)
ISBN 0 7486 1826 0 (paperback)

Contents

Acknowledgements

The forty-three transcripts that comprise the empirical material for this book were (with one exception) collected over a ten-year period from 1995 to 2004. During that time I taught courses on Media Talk at Queen Margaret University College, Edinburgh, and at De Montfort University, Leicester. I am very grateful to the students on those courses who made many valuable suggestions about programmes to analyse and brought their own materials into classes. In particular I am grateful to Rebecca Lawson for her observations on *Big Brother*.

Also during this period I have been a member of the Ross Priory Seminar on Broadcast Talk. Earlier versions of some chapters have been presented as papers at that seminar, and I am most grateful for the critical comments and advice I have received. In some ways, it is invidious to single out individuals, but helpful comments and observations on previous versions of the contents of this book have been received from: Trudy Haarman, Ian Hutchby, Peter Lunt, Stephanie Marriott, Greg Myers, Kay Richardson, Paddy Scannell and Joanna Thornborrow. I have had conversations with Espen Ytreberg on the approach taken in Chapter 8, and Helen Wood has made some particularly useful comments on Chapter 9. I owe a special debt of gratitude to Martin Montgomery who has been a key supportive influence on this work from start to finish.

Colleagues in Edinburgh and Leicester have contributed to the academic context within which this book has been written, particularly Jim Bee, Richard Butt, Stuart Price, Tim O'Sullivan and Jeanette Steemers. I have had particularly stimulating conversations with Shaun Moores on some of its theoretical aspects.

Finally, I am grateful to Sarah Edwards at Edinburgh University Press for her faith in this project, and to Jenny Millar for providing the supportive environment in which it was completed.

Part One
Approaches to Media Talk

1 Introducing Media Talk

1. This book

This book examines the talk we hear on radio and TV. It looks at styles of programme presentation, commentary, dialogue, interview and debate. Its primary concern is with the way forms of talk, in different programme genres, are designed to appeal to overhearing audiences. As such, its main focus is on 'conversational' media talk which either addresses the audience directly, or attempts to engage the audience in 'quasi-interactive' relationships. Such talk often appears to be 'live' (even when the programme has been recorded) and relatively unscripted (though usually some sort of pre-planning is apparent). This book is not concerned therefore with the overtly scripted dialogue of fictional programming such as forms of drama, including soap opera and situation comedy. Nor is it dealing with the very interesting and developing culture of new media, where 'chat' has become a hybrid form of spoken and written communication.

The first reason for paying close attention to these forms of talk on radio and TV is that they are fundamental to the way these media work. As far as radio is concerned, this is an obvious point, but it has also been recognised that talk is a key aspect of television, both in its engagement with audiences and in the audience response. However, because of its disciplinary and theoretical roots, the study of talk has been relatively neglected in the development of media studies. The main emphasis has been on visual culture, and radio has long suffered from being a relatively 'forgotten' medium. Where the verbal dimension has been discussed, the main focus has been on propositional content, often characterised, in one way or another, as 'ideological'. This book, however, investigates media talk as verbal interaction. It is concerned with the ways participants in radio and TV programmes interact with each other in such a way that viewers and listeners, after a fashion, interact with them. Sometimes defined as a 'double articulation' (Scannell 1991) there is a communicative dynamic at the heart of broadcasting which this book seeks to explore.

This book is located within a growing research interest in the study of broadcast talk. For about twenty years now a body of academic work has grown around the investigation of broadcast talk as mediated verbal interaction. Prominent in this field has been the work on the news interview of Heritage, Greatbatch and Clayman (particularly Clayman and Heritage 2002); and also the studies of radio phone-ins and talk shows carried out by members of the Ross Priory group (Hutchby 1996; Tolson 2001a). A pioneering collection of essays included discussions of interviewing and DJ talk, together with an initial definition of the theoretical interest in broadcast talk (Scannell 1991), and there have been other significant contributions (Livingstone and Lunt 1994; Fairclough 1995b). To date, however, the study of broadcast talk has been rather disparate, with much of it confined to specialist academic journals. It is a further aim of this book to present an overview of the field and to trace its key lines of development.

To this end, the book is structured in two parts. Part One, consisting of the first two chapters, offers a general rationale and introduces a methodology for the study of media talk. The present chapter develops the observations just made about the relative neglect but importance of this area for understanding the culture of broadcasting. Some reasons why media talk might be of interest to students of spoken discourse are also introduced. Chapter 2 then presents a discussion of selected key concepts derived from discourse analysis which can be applied to the study of media talk. These concepts are derived from three main approaches to the analysis of spoken discourse: Conversation Analysis (CA), Pragmatics, and what has come to be known as 'Interactional Sociolinguistics'. In Chapter 2, key concepts and methodological protocols are applied to the analysis of news interviews.

Part Two offers a series of case studies of different forms of media talk. These range from news and current affairs, through sports and DJ talk, to ubiquitous and mundane forms of 'ordinary talk'. The principal aim of Part Two is to explore various genres of programming with respect to the main forms of talk they employ. With every genre, however, the main emphasis is on development and innovation, as radio and TV programming is faced with an increasingly competitive environment in which to attract its target audiences. For this reason, each chapter contains newly published material, with examples derived from an archive assembled over ten years, since 1995. The transcripts are offered here as a resource and stimulus for further analysis, for I am sure I have not exhausted what can be said about them.

However, the last three chapters in particular do a little bit more than simply explore generic developments. The study of ordinary talk in talk shows, celebrity interviews and reality TV begins to point to an additional critical reason for the interest in media talk. It is not just that talk is fundamental to the way broadcasting works, or that innovations in forms of talk are of intrinsic interest. It is that there is a contemporary culture of talk which is both cultivated and catered for by mundane forms of broadcasting. This is part of what Frances Bonner calls 'ordinary television' (Bonner 2003).

A major feature of the contemporary environment is programming which features 'ordinary' people talking in ordinary ways – and, as I also argue, celebrities 'being ordinary'. Here being ordinary involves the performance of ordinary talk, and indeed in many programmes that is principally what it involves. The conclusion to the final chapter, therefore, offers a tentative argument as to why there should be such an interest today in ordinary people doing ordinary talk on radio and TV. My suggestion is that this connects with a profoundly moral engagement with the 'presentation of self' in everyday life.

2. Overcoming the barriers

There are, I think, two main practical considerations which, together with a more theoretical point, have created barriers to the study of media talk. The first reason is to do with the way media studies has sought legitimacy as an academic subject. In many universities, this claim to legitimacy has entailed a primary focus on film, or more generally on visual culture (photography, video etc.). Sometimes this has been seen to complement the more traditional study of art and literature; and in this connection it has been possible to insist on the significance of 'film culture', with its fairly long history and its canon of 'classic' films. By comparison, broadcasting seems to be a poor relation. The products of TV and radio seem transitory and ephemeral and at best their consumption is a routine form of leisure. Some interest might be afforded to some TV 'classics' (usually forms of drama) and experimental video, insofar as these too illuminate the analysis of the visual, but there are limited things one could say about a broadcast interview, or a TV talk show, from this kind of perspective.

Secondly, however, it is not just a matter of cultural prestige (or snobbery). There is also the very practical question of how the study of audio communication might be developed. Where the focus is on visual culture, there are well-established methodologies for the analysis of 'signs' and 'film language', to which all media studies students are introduced. But, as far as sound is concerned, the disciplinary tools are not so readily available. For the untrained, music appears dauntingly technical, and today it seems, in addition, a knowledge of electronics is required. With speech, there are methods for conversation and discourse analysis, but these require media students (and their teachers) to take some steps into another discipline. In essence, the second problem for the study of media talk is that it is, necessarily, an interdisciplinary activity. Genuinely interdisciplinary work is demanding, but also, as we shall see, it has its rewards.

In addition to these practical problems, there has also been a theoretical difficulty for the study of media talk. For as media studies has developed, particularly in Britain, with a strong influence from 'cultural studies', its primary focus on visual culture has adopted a particular theoretical perspective. In essence, this perspective has investigated media texts for their cultural influence, on the basis of an initial analysis of 'meanings' (denotations/connotations) or 'ideologies', and the subsequent (though less frequent) analysis of audience response ('decoding'). A great deal of debate then hinges around whether the 'preferred readings' identified by academic critics correspond to the interpretations, or the uses, of media texts by audiences. Of course what I am offering here is a sketch of an extensive theoretical tradition, but it will do for the present purposes: for my point is that this 'interpretive' cultural studies paradigm is very different from the perspectives of conversation and discourse analysis.

As we shall see, these perspectives analyse speech not in terms of what it is *saying*, but what it is *doing*; or, more precisely, what it is doing when it says what it says. As one of the originators of this approach (J. L. Austin) put it, it is 'how to do things with words'. Here, 'doing' is understood, not as making (ideological) statements, but as initiating social actions which, crucially, invite interactions. In the first instance, to talk is to form relations with others (co-participants, interlocutors, audiences) and only on that basis can we go on to make claims, propositions, or statements about the world. Moreover (and as we shall see this is an absolutely basic point), the primary social relations constituted through talk do not require analysts to make 'interpretations'. It is true that in some forms of 'critical' discourse analysis there is some recourse to theoretical speculation, but in principle the interactions made possible by talk can be empirically observed in recorded examples of data. The participants themselves, in their behaviour, reveal the relevant patterns and structures.

I am aware that the previous two paragraphs are extremely condensed and possibly contentious, but by the same token I hope they whet the theoretical appetite. They are intended to indicate that the study of media talk is not only about recuperating a neglected area; it also, to some extent, involves a challenge to a prevailing orthodoxy in media and cultural studies. This point was established some years ago by Martin Montgomery, in a pioneering analysis of DJ talk (1986b), where he argued that the talk of presenters on mainstream pop radio 'foregrounds the interpersonal' over the 'ideational'; in other words, the primary focus of the talk is on building a relationship with the audience. In this medium what is said about anything is pretty much inconsequential, or rather, it is primarily designed to support the interactive focus. A polemical version of the implications of this point has also been articulated by Paddy Scannell (1989, 1991), who argues that the shift from critical interpretation to discourse analysis changes our view of what broadcasting is about – from a largely negative critique of ideology in the media to a more open minded (he would say positive) focus on building communicative relationships.

In the rest of this chapter I want to take this approach further by looking at the main theoretical issues that arise in the study of media talk, and indeed which make it a subject worth studying. These issues can be approached from the two perspectives that make up this interdisciplinary field. First, we will consider media talk from the point of view of media studies, and what it can add to that discipline. Secondly, we will turn to the potential interest from spoken discourse analysis, where, as we shall see, the study of broadcast talk raises some challenging questions.

3. Talk and the media

Despite its primary orientation towards the visual, there has been some recognition in media studies that talk is a significant aspect of broadcasting. Oddly, however (though this is understandable given the history of the subject), this recognition has not really focused on its obvious point of reference, which is radio. Rather, this has been formulated as a point about television, considered in relation to the other main audiovisual medium, the cinema. In his influential discussion of the differences between these media, John Ellis (1982) argues that cinema, as a type of theatrical experience, privileges the visual 'gaze' – visuality, we might say, is in dominance; whereas TV is constantly talking to us. On TV, the visual element is less detailed, less spectacular, and domestic conditions of reception make it a focus for the 'glance' rather than the 'gaze'. Correspondingly, our attention is mainly grabbed by sounds, for instance jingles and signature tunes, or by talk which speaks to us directly.

Other commentators have also highlighted the significance of talk for television, particularly its mode of direct address (Morse 1985; Corner 1995). For his part, Ellis has more recently broadened this perspective to encompass the general development of sound recording, but again his analysis comes to focus on television's mode of address, specifically its 'illusion of liveness' (Ellis 2000: Ch. 3), a key concept to which we shall return. However, in the perspective adopted here, talk is central to *broadcasting*, on radio as well as television: for instance, music on radio seems to require the constant accompaniment of DJ talk, and live events on TV (sports etc.) simply cannot proceed without commentary. In the direct form of address, the first person of the broadcasting institution ('I' or 'we') talks to the audience in the second person ('you') often with a view to constructing a collective identity ('us'). In cinema, such direct address is limited to specific genres such as comedies, or musicals where songs are performed 'for us' outside the narrative space. But in broadcasting directly addressed talk is pervasive and built into the fabric of its presentation.

Why is this? As previously indicated, the conventional argument focuses on the domestic environment, both in negative and in positive ways. The basic suggestion is that broadcasting is rather like a domestic utility: it is constantly 'on tap', available at the touch of a button. As such, it blends in with the domestic life that surrounds it, either competing with other activities or often accompanying them. The negative take on this is that, because it is so easy to switch off, broadcasting is under constant pressure to engage our attention, to keep us listening and watching, by 'buttonholing' us, in Ellis's phrase (1982: 132). In contrast, the more positive argument, which has been put most forcefully by Paddy Scannell (1989, 1991, 1996), is that the onus is then on broadcasters to speak to us in ways we want to be spoken to, in ways which enhance our domestic environments and do not detract from them.

In part, Scannell bases his arguments on historical research carried out at the archives of the BBC. Together with his colleague, David Cardiff, he investigated the formation of broadcasting policy at the time (in the 1930s) when radio was establishing itself as a domestic medium (Scannell and Cardiff 1991). Of particular interest here was a growing realisation in the BBC Talks Department that certain forms of talk might be alienating the radio audience. In their own homes, people did not want to listen to lectures or sermons, and they did not want to be 'talked down' to. On the contrary they expected to be spoken to in friendly terms, and in 'ordinary' (i.e. not too 'posh', not too formal) speech. In the 1930s the BBC also experimented with different ways of making talk more dramatic: direct address to the microphone was supplemented with forms of dialogue, interview and debate, where listeners could hear a diversity and an exchange of voices (Cardiff 1980).

Scannell's positive conclusion from this research extends beyond the study of particular forms of talk, to more general arguments about the contribution of broadcasting to modern 'public life' (Scannell 1989). In Britain, starting in the 1930s, public service broadcasting has constructed a common culture, incorporating an annual calendar of shared national events (sports, religious festivals, royal occasions etc.) and widely enjoyed 'sociable' programming, often involving ordinary people as participants (quizzes, game shows, human interest documentaries). These are embedded in the daily lives of audiences, partly through practices of scheduling, but also in the ways they are 'talked about', which the accessible discourse of these programmes aims to encourage (Scannell 1996). In my view these arguments are insightful and challenging, even though they digress into philosophical speculation at times. Particularly where they are grounded in historical examples (for instance, in the account of 'sociable' forms of radio programming in the 1930s–1950s) these arguments invite us to consider the profound and central place of broadcasting in modern everyday life.

4. Three key concepts for Media Studies

At this point then, building partly on Scannell's historical work, I want to identify three key concepts in the study of media talk. These are pivotal, not only because they sum up much previous work in this area, but also because they provide a bridge between the empirical study of talk and the wider social considerations to which Scannell alludes. All these concepts extrapolate from the basic point that media talk needs to be 'friendly' to its audiences – listener-friendly we might say. The first two points have been generally discussed and should not appear too controversial. However, my third point is taking previous work into new areas, which will be illuminated by subsequent chapters, but where further research is also needed.

4.1 Interactivity

The first concept defines what is implicit in much of the previous focus, in television studies, on direct address. It also links with Scannell's history of programming policy at the BBC, with its long-held belief that audiences should be active listeners. In the early days of BBC radio, it was thought that active listening, as distinct from general, uncommitted 'hearing', could be encouraged by manipulating schedules (though this was the antithesis of scheduling as we understand it today). It was thought that by scheduling programmes at different and unpredictable times, the radio audience, equipped with the *Radio Times*, would be forced to make conscious decisions about when, actively, to listen. No doubt this was the case, but it became clear in the 1930s that the cultivation of active listening could also be achieved in other ways. One was to make more extensive use of those forms of talk which are designed to provoke listener response and which in that respect can be defined as 'interactive'.

As a basic and very simple illustration of this concept let us consider a very mundane point: that the introductions to many programmes on radio and TV involve a greeting of some kind ('good evening', 'hello. welcome to the show'). Why is this? It is not, strictly speaking, necessary – and would seem to be something of an optional extra for more formal programmes, like the news. Clearly it is an aspect of broadcasting's direct address, but there is crucially more to it than that. Conversation analysts define greetings as an example of the 'adjacency-pair' principle – simply that, in ordinary conversation, some utterances conventionally expect a response (questions also expect answers in this way). If the expected response is not forthcoming speakers will attend to that fact, indicating in one way or another that some breach of the normal exchange pattern has occurred. This 'attending to', demonstrable in speakers' subsequent behaviour, is an example of the type of empirical evidence which this approach takes as proof of its analytical claims. So the greeting can be defined as an interactive device in ordinary conversation in so far it typically initiates an exchange. But what about its use in broadcasting? This raises an interesting issue.

How does a greeting work in broadcasting where it cannot be returned by the listener or viewer? Is this use of the interactive device just a sham, a kind of simulated friendliness intended to disguise the fact that this is one-way communication? Or, at the other extreme, do some viewers sit at home returning those greetings to the faces on their TV sets? Certainly there is some evidence of this sort of behaviour (see Morse 1985), but let us consider a third option. What might be a more plausible explanation, for this simple example, is that the talk constructs a place for *potential* interaction, whether or not it is taken up in practice. The listener or viewer is placed by the talk in a 'quasi-interactive' situation (Thompson 1995), and this terminology does not need to carry the negative implication that it is thereby disguising something. It might simply be a way of reaching out to the active listener, provoking a basic form of active listenership, as part of the general preference in broadcasting for direct address. It also, however, links with an important discussion of the wider social impact of broadcasting to which we shall return.

4.2 Performativity

The second point, which is also illustrated by the work of Scannell and Cardiff, is that mediated quasi-interaction should also be understood, in principle, as a type of *performance*. What the historical research shows is that the new practices of broadcast talk, pioneered in the 1930s–1940s, did not initially 'come naturally' – on the contrary they had to be learnt. In particular, broadcasters had to discover effective ways of communicating through a microphone. This was partly a technical matter of adopting the right tone of voice for an intimate medium; but also some of the earliest broadcasters who were unused to this situation commented on the particular problem of communicating with an audience you couldn't see. On one level, any form of public talk is a performance, as anyone who has delivered a speech or a lecture will know. But at least in these public contexts, where the audience is co-present, it is possible to adjust the performance to accommodate perceived reactions. Somehow, when those reactions are absent, performativity becomes even more of an issue – more self-conscious and reflexive.

For an example of mediated performance, let us consider another very basic form of media talk, the interview. When people are involved in broadcast interviews they are not just engaged in the kind of conversational practice where questions expect answers. This adjacency-pair principle is built into interviews, for if a question is asked and there is no answer, this becomes noticeable. But interviews are more than conversations between participants; they are manifestly and obviously conducted for the benefit of the 'overhearing audience' (Heritage 1985). How is this apparent? We can detect it in the ways interviewers frame and follow-up their questions (and this will be examined further in Chapter 2). But performativity is also demonstrated by the obvious and simple fact that, by comparison with ordinary conversation, interviewees talk too long. They are not only expected to answer the question, they are also expected to elaborate. In this situation a one-word or even a one-sentence answer will not do. Interviewees know they are required to speak to two audiences, not only to an immediate co-participant but also to the unseen audience 'out there'. And as far as the latter is concerned, the pressure is on to 'come across', in other words, to perform.

This can be a daunting prospect! Novice interviewees often find it nerve wracking. But it is here that another basic issue can be defined; for clearly this is a peculiar kind of performance which is not entirely reducible to a type of acting. To pick up on our previous point, this is a type of mediated performance which is also potentially 'interactive'. Now consider the very peculiar situation one finds oneself in: in this context two contradictory demands seem to be placed on speakers. On the one hand they are on display, rather like actors, for an audience (to which, unlike stage actors, they have no access). On the other hand they are expected to speak to, or for, that audience in a listener-friendly (and not actorly) manner. How do you interact with someone who is invisible and silent? How indeed do you perform (as opposed to just do) 'friendliness'?

4.3 Liveliness

One general precondition for an answer to these questions is suggested by my third concept: 'liveliness'. As in popular parlance, on radio or TV you have to 'look lively'. This is not a concept to be found in Scannell's work, or in the wider literature on broadcast talk, for I have invented it – but it is intended to define a phenomenon which the previous literature describes. It also explains why scholars are typically more interested in some kinds of talk than in others. It comes back to what we mean by performances which are like acting in some ways, but are not 'actorly'. The key point here is that, unlike dialogue in a play, the most interesting forms of broadcast talk have a feel of spontaneity. As in most interviews, the speech seems to be made up on the spot and is, to some extent, at least potentially, unpredictable. Implicit in this point, and an area that urgently requires some research, is the status of the script in many types of broadcasting. Of course scripts exist and programmes couldn't function without them; but 'liveliness' is most effective when the determinacy of a script is concealed.

'Liveliness' is a pun on 'liveness', a widely recognised defining feature of broadcasting (Feuer 1983; Corner 1999; Ellis 2000). Originally, for technical reasons, all broadcasting was live. Now the majority of programmes are recorded, but many of these pretend to be live, suggesting that the principle of 'liveness', for whatever reason, is indispensible. In media studies, there are several definitions of liveness: one refers to time – the times of production and reception are simultaneous, 'happening now'. A second theory emphasises the difference between photographic and electronic images; where the former provide documentary records, the latter consist of live signals. These are relevant technical points, but it is interesting that Ellis's recent discussion suggests that the key issue may not be technological, so much as 'rhetorical': much broadcast talk insists on its 'liveness' even where this is patently not the case. The following quote relates this to the points we have made so far:

> Programmes adopt the rhetoric of liveness without being literally live. Presenters still adopt the stance of direct address. Not only do they look directly into the camera and adopt a casual person-to-person form of speech, they also use all the indicators of co-presence. They talk of 'now' and 'today', 'here' and 'we'; they use the present tense. They use all those speech indicators whose meaning is context-dependent in order to orient themselves as speaking in the same moment of time as their audience hears them ... The presence of a live audience (live that is, at the point of recording) will help to ensure that the 'illusion of liveness' is maintained, of course. But the truly remarkable feature of this pervasive television practice is the willing participation of the viewer in this situation. (Ellis 2000: 33)

In this passage, however, Ellis only covers half the story. He shows how the illusion of liveness is sustained by direct address and by the use of 'deictic' language (the context-dependent references to time and space which are a feature of co-present conversations). His example is the long-running (but now discontinued) television dating-game show *Blind Date* where the format required a recorded timescale that couldn't possibly correspond to its apparently live, weekly scheduling. But this is only half the story because Ellis has not considered the other principal illusion of this show, namely, that the contestants appeared to be speaking their own words. In actual fact, when they replied to the questions posed by the 'picker', their answers had been scripted for them, and to the viewer it was certainly apparent that these answers were pre-formulated (and therefore the questions must have been known in advance). But somehow this did not equate to performing roles in a script. Our awareness of a script was displaced by the apparent spontaneity of performances which, to repeat, were not perceived as 'acting'.

Further peculiarities of *Blind Date* are discussed more fully below (in Chapter 2); here I want to concentrate on the general point. I want to emphasise that 'liveness' is not a technological, or even a just a 'rhetorical' phenomenon – in addition, it is a feature of performances which are perceived (in my terms) as 'lively'. To use a term from discourse analysis, much of the talk we hear on radio and TV seems to be 'locally occasioned', by a record that needs to be introduced, a goal that has been scored, a question that needs to be answered. In this sense it seems to be a spontaneous construction rather than a scripted dialogue, just like real-life conversation. Apart from those genres which announce themselves as dramas (which for this reason do not feature strongly in the analysis of broadcast talk) elsewhere on TV and radio people perform not as actors, but as 'themselves'. Their performances then engage our attention as if they were conversations with which we could potentially interact.

Again, this point is illuminated by Scannell's historical research. In the 1930s there were as many challenges facing the producers of scripts as there were for the performers behind the microphone. Initially it was felt that scripted dialogue was necessary in case speakers, unfamiliar with the demands of live broadcasting, 'dried up'. It was also judged necessary to script some working-class speakers for fear of what they might say publicly. At the same time, however, particularly where ordinary people were involved, it was preferable that these scripts should reflect the patterns of everyday speech. So it is often the case, when you listen to radio from the 1930s and 1940s that this scripted speech sounds unnatural; the scripted approximation of everyday speech is not 'ordinary' enough. Gradually it seems that broadcasters have learned to adopt a lighter touch, but why this is the case is an interesting (and open) question. It may be, as Scannell claims, that the post-war 'populist' consensus was more open to a diversity of public voices. Alternatively, as the example of *Blind Date* suggests, it may be that scriptwriters have become more adept, and the participants, who are now entirely familiar with the conventions of popular broadcasting, know 'instinctively' how to perform.

Taken together, I suggest that these three concepts – interactivity, performativity, liveliness – provide a fruitful starting point for the analysis of media talk. They begin to define the very peculiar nature of broadcast communication: principally, that it speaks to an absent audience as if it was co-present (at least in time) and in 'lively' ways as if it was spontaneous and interactive. But the fact that the audience is absent (though studio audiences have an interesting role to play) and unable to respond directly (though phone-ins and other interactive devices are increasingly common) transforms that communication from conversational interaction into performance. What challenges that poses for the analysis of spoken discourse will be the focus for the final section of this chapter. In my next section I want to widen the discussion to consider briefly some of the social and cultural ramifications of the argument so far.

5. Media and modernity

The three key concepts introduced in the previous section not only serve to illuminate some of the peculiarities of broadcast communication. They also, as we shall see in this section, connect with important arguments in contemporary sociology and cultural studies. Again, some of Paddy Scannell's work begins to make these connections, particularly where he discusses ways in which conversational and interactive forms of broadcast talk are embedded in routine practices of everyday life (Scannell 1996). The key connection here is the link between the ways broadcasting speaks to us, and the ways in which media use punctuates daily existence. For instance, if the news invites us to listen and watch at regular times, in speech forms which emphasise its liveness and immediacy, do we correspondingly regulate our lives to respond to these invitations? Indeed do we at times 'talk back' to the face on the screen as it talks to us? As we have already mentioned there is American evidence to suggest that some of us might; but the main sociological thesis is couched in more general terms.

This thesis has its roots in a cultural phenomenon which was first documented in America in the 1950s, when television (but not broadcasting) was still in its infancy. It is famously defined by Donald Horton and Richard Wohl in their (1956) account of 'para-social interaction':

> In television, especially, the image which is presented makes available nuances of appearance and gesture, to which ordinary social perception is attentive and to which interaction is cued. Sometimes the 'actor' – whether he is playing himself or performing in a fictional role – is seen engaged with others, but often he faces the spectator, uses the mode of direct address, talks as if he were conversing personally and privately. The audience, for its part, responds with something more than mere running observation: it is, as it were, subtly insinuated into the programme's action and internal social relationships and, by dint of this kind of staging, is ambiguously transformed into a group which observes and participates in the show by turns. The more the performer seems to adjust his performance to the supposed response of the audience, the more the audience tends to make the response anticipated. This simulacrum of conversational give and take may be called *para-social interaction*. (Corner and Hawthorn 1993: 156)

Now it should perhaps be recognised that Horton and Wohl themselves supplied no empirical evidence of their central claim about audience response. They also opened the door to suggestions that such responses, were they forthcoming, might be part of an unfortunate tendency for some socially inadequate individuals to substitute para-social interaction with media figures for real social relationships. But the key thesis, as expressed above, does not need to take this pathological turn. It can be interpreted as a sociological argument, in two parts, which raises questions for further research. The first part of the argument notes, as we have noted, that TV (broadcasting) talks to us in 'conversational' ways that invite our response. The second part then proposes that the individual audience member takes on a group identity in this process (and this is also implicit in my use of 'us' in the previous sentence). The research question would then involve investigating how audiences do in fact respond, without prejudging, as the above quote tends to do, that an immediate response is automatic.

From the point of view of some current sociology, Horton and Wohl's argument is interesting because it connects with aspects of 'modernity'. For these sociologists (Giddens 1990, 1991; Thompson 1995; Moores 2000) modernity is a term which defines certain general aspects of lived experience in modern societies (as distinct from pre-modern, traditional communities) and it points to the social factors which produce those experiences. For instance, in modernity, knowledge communicated through face-to-face interaction is extended by knowledge derived from media sources; and our daily lives are increasingly dependent on 'expert systems' (such as computer networks) of which we have limited understanding. Our 'situated' world is extended in time and space by the availability of media, which both expand and threaten our cultural horizons. 'Para-social interaction' can be regarded both as an extension of this process and, in part, as a compensation for it (Moores 1995). Clearly we now live in worlds inhabited not just by people we've met, or alternatively heard about; there are also people we somehow 'know' by virtue of their media appearances. Some of these people appear as 'personalities' and even as 'media friends' (Meyrowitz 1985) who we think we can trust to interpret an uncertain world on our behalf.

There is much sociological argument here which we must gloss over in this context. However, one key point, as Shaun Moores puts it, is that in modern societies, everyday social interaction partly revolves around and incorporates a 'mediated interaction order' (Moores 2000: Ch. 8). Here the para-social relationships fostered by broadcasting are part of the general cultivation of mediated relationships with absent others (through tele-communications, computers etc.) which allow for the development of 'intimacy at a distance'. But this is not something that just affects us as individuals; as Horton and Wohl also emphasise it contributes to the growth of new forms of group identity. Members of the audience for live TV events (or those which present themselves as live) imagine themselves to be sharing this event with others, and the talk with which they are addressed encourages this. This is similar to Benedict Anderson's argument that reading a daily newspaper fosters a sense of national 'imagined community' shared with other readers one has never met (Anderson 1983).

These points connect with two further issues of central importance for current sociology and cultural studies which are also brought into particular focus by the study of media talk. The first of these issues is the question of cultural identity in a mediated world which is extended and diverse. Again, there is much to gloss over here, but the key question concerns the negotiation of identity in the face of a range of cultural influences (Rutherford 1990; Hall and du Gay 1996). As far as media talk is concerned we can distinguish between two levels of influence. First, there is the long-recognised fact that identities are ascribed to audiences in the ways they are addressed (e.g. as belonging to a nation, a family, a gender etc.). More generally, however, personal identities are increasingly targeted by public discourses, particularly through the promotional discourse of advertising. Through broadcast talk, the personal, private space of the home is invaded by public messages couched in the friendly terms of 'intimacy at a distance', and, in particular, audiences are addressed in 'conversational' terms as potential consumers (Fairclough 1989, 1994).

Subsequent chapters in this book will provide illustrations of this point: that 'friendly' interactive forms of talk must also be understood as targeted in these ways. There has to be a critical perspective here, which is sometimes missing from Scannell's arguments, concerned as they are to emphasise the positive contribution of broadcasting to 'public life'. If, as he claims, broadcasting has extended 'communicative entitlements', making it possible for more people to talk publicly in diverse ways; it is also quite possibly the case that we have become more sceptical about what they are saying. The friendly face of the broadcaster might not be responded to automatically in a positive way (cf. Horton and Wohl) where this is perceived to be selling us something. What particularly is brought into question here is the 'authenticity' and 'sincerity' of performances with ulterior motives.

A further debating point, in many such discussions, concerns the quality of the contemporary 'public sphere' (Garnham 1986; Dahlgren 1995). For all its apparent friendliness and intimacy, it must be remembered that broadcast talk is public talk, for indeed it is a public performance. One of its functions is to mediate between the world of public affairs, carried out by public figures, and the private, domestic sphere – by translating the former into terms intelligible by the latter. In so doing, a further issue concerns its presentation of public discourse. As is widely discussed in contemporary journalism, there is much concern, particularly at election times, that public issues are being oversimplified to sustain audience ratings. By speaking through its 'simulacrum of conversational give and take' it may be that broadcast talk is guilty of trivialising and/or 'dumbing down'.

Sometimes (though not usually in journalistic commentary) this critical perspective is informed by the theories of the German social philosopher, Jürgen Habermas. In his view, a healthy public sphere is vital to democracy because it makes possible, through reasoned debate, the formation of informed public opinion. Obviously in modern societies the public sphere is not limited to meetings and gatherings; it is mediated through broadcasting and the press, where a central issue concerns the forms of this mediation. To what extent is reasoned debate possible in broadcast talk which targets its audiences as consumers? Habermas is particularly worried that the contemporary public sphere has been overtaken by publicity, manipulated by a cynical public relations industry, employed by those striving to maintain a positive image in the 'public eye'.

Close, empirical attention to forms of media talk is able to illuminate this question, and indeed all the social and cultural issues identified in this section. How is para-social interactivity encouraged by the strategic employment of particular forms of talk? In this practice, what kinds of cultural identity are promoted, by being 'talked-up' as it were? To what extent is the discursive world of broadcasting committed to 'communicative entitlements' or alternatively to promoting a consumer culture consistent with its commercial imperatives? What kinds of talk circulate in the contemporary public sphere? To be sure, there are limits to what the analysis of media talk can achieve: it is more concerned with the structures of public discourse than with the complexities of audience response. We are certainly not about to add to the journalistic speculation about the cynicism of the electorate in an age of 'sound-bites' and 'spin-doctors'. What we can achieve, however, is a much clearer sense of how contemporary public discourse speaks, and how it attempts to engage with diverse target audiences.

6. The analysis of spoken discourse

The previous two sections of this chapter have considered some ways in which the study of talk can illuminate aspects of broadcast communication and the place of broadcasting in the modern world. We will return to these points throughout this book, where the empirical studies (Chapters 3–9) are designed to explore them further. At this point, however, it is necessary to turn our attention to this book's second contributing discipline: discourse analysis. Hopefully there will be some readers whose main interest is not in what the study of media talk can do for media studies, but rather what contribution this can make to the analysis of spoken discourse. In exploring this topic, our primary focus on broadcasting must be extended to engage with perspectives derived from discourse analysis – to which the rest of this chapter, and the next, are devoted.

Let us again begin with fundamentals and attempt to clarify what, precisely, is the nature of the interest in 'talk' from a discourse-analytical point of view. On this basis, we can then go forward to examine what might be particularly interesting, in this perspective, in the study of media talk. This seems a reasonable strategy; but immediately we encounter the connected problems that, within this discipline, there is a diversity of approaches and consequently, no single, overarching definition of 'discourse' as such.

To deal with the second problem first, a key theoretical issue hinges around whether the term, 'discourse', can be used in the plural. Where it can, the concept is topic centred: in this definition it refers to established ways of speaking about particular topics, or, in stronger versions, constituting what these topics are. We might say that, in our society, there are, for example, particular discourses of crime, or sexuality, which specify what can normally be said about those topics or alternatively what might be classed as deviant or taboo. This usage bears close affinity to the term 'ideology', seen as conceptual frameworks which define social practices. It is not, however, the usage which is most prevalent in spoken discourse analysis. For these purposes (and for the purposes of this book) 'discourse' is a singular noun which refers to 'language-in-use' (Cameron 2001). It builds on the understanding of linguists that what is required to communicate in social situations is more than a knowledge of language per se. There are general principles and protocols that govern how we know how to *speak*.

Even if this second definition is accepted, however, a further problem is that there are different approaches to these principles and protocols from a variety of starting points. To some extent, these approaches are the product of divergent philosophical perspectives with different attitudes to the interpretation of data. In essence, some approaches insist on the highly empirical, data-driven analysis of speech events (such as Hutchby and Wooffitt 1998) where others are prepared to allow some theoretical discussion of wider social influences (such as Fairclough 1989, 1995a). We will mention these differences where they are materially relevant, but for the present purposes it is more productive to introduce a set of approaches which are (more or less) complementary and applicable to the analysis of media talk. Conversely, the study of media talk is of interest to these approaches mainly because it is such a peculiar phenomenon.

As will be explained in the next chapter in more detail, our first approach has its roots in a form of sociology known as 'ethnomethodology'. Here, the basic interest is in the way social order is reproduced 'from below', by social actors themselves, and not simply imposed by social structures or institutions. Actors are said to display a predisposition towards orderliness both in the way they interpret social situations and perform social actions which are oriented to the anticipated responses of others. This predisposition is reciprocated in social interaction and so, in this view, social order is a mutually achieved practical accomplishment by members of society. As far as talk is concerned, ordinary conversation clearly betrays this predisposition, as participants co-construct orderly, interactive speech events. In particular, a remarkable basic fact, even in multi-party conversations, is that participants take turns at speaking in reasonably orderly ways, as if somehow everyone knows when it might be their turn to speak.

The ethnomethodological understanding of ordinary conversation has been principally developed in a field of study known as Conversation Analysis (Hutchby and Wooffitt 1998). Having described some of its general features, such as turn-taking, some practitioners of CA have turned their attention to institutional talk (Drew and Heritage 1992). Here, the initial interest has been in what ways institutional constraints overdetermine the basic principles of social interaction, so that we know for instance, in some contexts, that the professionally qualified participant is expected to take the lead. In classrooms, courtrooms, clinics etc., the lay person's turn to speak is when they are spoken to. By the same token questions, when asked of pupils by teachers, have preferred answers (the evidence is provided by teachers' 'follow-up' turns); and a sequence of questions, as in the legal interrogation of a witness, will betray a predetermined logic lacking in everyday talk. Institutional routines are talked into confirmation in these ways. And this approach has been adopted for the study of media talk: quite clearly, for example, the news interview, is a particular species of institutional communication, where it is expected that one person will ask questions of another who is supposed to supply answers (Heritage and Greatbatch 1991; Clayman and Heritage 2002). At the same time the questions asked are governed by institutional conventions such that the interviewer should appear, in principle, to be 'neutral'.

So far perhaps, so good – and we will consider the quite extensive CA literature on the news interview later. What we will also examine, however, are two further points of interest. The first is that, by comparison with other kinds of institutional talk, media talk often seems to be rather flexible. In fact some CA accounts of the news interview are too strict in their prescriptions, for even this relatively formal situation allows for some variation. For instance, it is not entirely unknown for interviewees to ask questions, for interviewers to interrupt, and even for question-answer sequences to be transformed into other forms of talk such as arguments, or humorous banter. No doubt these variations sometimes occur in other kinds of institutional talk, as asides to the main business (such as the preliminary pleasantries that might occur when a patient visits a doctor). In media talk, however, apparently increasingly, these variations are part of the main business because they contribute to making the talk 'entertaining'.

A second area of interest then begins to extend this basic observation to pick up on some of the points made earlier about the peculiarities of broadcasting. From a discourse-analytic perspective, a particular challenge is posed by the paradox that here we have an institutional form of talk which is, nevertheless, highly 'conversational'. It does not always draw a neat line between its practices and those found in ordinary conversation – indeed, for the reasons outlined in section 2 above, these boundaries are often intentionally blurred. The paradoxical nature of this is where we find forms of talk which are not conversations as such, but where conversational features are exploited for institutional reasons. This connects with that other peculiarity of media talk, namely, the key dimension of *performativity*. It makes a profound difference to the analysis of spoken discourse when we take account of the fact that there are not just two, but three, even four, sets of participants (presenter, co-participants, studio audience, domestic audience) where what is exchanged in the studio is always a performance for the overhearing audience.

Furthermore, in Western societies we have been socialised into bringing certain expectations to ordinary conversations. Over and above the basic orientation to orderliness described by CA, there are principles we bring to the interpretation of utterances. Specifically, there are ways we make judgements about the import of utterances where the intention might not be entirely clear, or when what is meant requires some interpretation of what is said. Some general principles for making these interpretations are outlined in a second contribution to spoken discourse analysis known as 'Pragmatics' (Cameron 2001: Ch. 6) and here the basic point is that we approach conversation with the general assumption that this is a 'co-operative' activity.

To some extent, co-operativeness is apparent in orderly turn-taking, but in Pragmatics this extends to our interpretation of what those turns are doing and what they were intended to do. It is suggested that we presume, unless there are very good reasons to think otherwise, that turns at speaking are intended to be relevant, to convey truthful information, and to be generally 'felicitous' – that is, appropriate to the situation. In particular, we expect people to speak in ways they would like to be spoken to, and with a modicum of politeness. Where these presumptions are in doubt, we seek clarification, and where they are not fulfilled we seek reasons why. There is a general ethics of conversational practice which people are expected to abide by and, if they do not, they are held accountable.

The problem in applying this approach to broadcast talk is not that these principles do not apply, but rather the principle of performativity makes their application more complex. Take the interview format, for example: this is a situation where questions are supposed to produce answers, but, as we have already seen, these answers are often longer than is normal for ordinary conversation (they are 'extended turns'). Sometimes, there are parts of such an answer where the relevance can be doubted or, even, where we are not sure the question has been answered at all (Harris 1991). To what extent does our awareness of such evasiveness raise ethical questions, when for instance we also know that this is not an ordinary conversation but a public performance in a confrontational news interview? At what point does acceptable and even amusing defensive strategy give way to the negative judgement that an answer is 'economical with the truth'? The point is that we may ask these questions about media talk just as we ask them about ordinary conversation but the grounds on which we make our judgements are not the same.

In these kinds of ways, therefore, media talk presents a particular set of challenges to spoken discourse analysis. It is a form of institutional talk, which is nevertheless, in some respects, 'conversational'; and it is a situation where conventional pragmatic judgements are complicated. 'Conversation-ality' is given a further twist by the constraints and opportunities for public performance. However, the great advantage of taking spoken discourse analysis into these territories is that there is a conceptual framework and methodological approach on which to draw. As we conclude this chapter it will be useful to point to the key methodological resources we have available.

As has been mentioned a couple of times in this chapter, discourse analysis sets great store by its highly empirical focus. The most rigorous version of this is to be found in CA, but generally all forms of discourse analysis work closely with empirical materials. Speech is recorded on tape, and there are well-established protocols for doing transcription (a list of transcription conventions used in this book is provided at the end of this chapter). Transcription not only represents the spoken dialogue, but also attempts to capture relevant interactional and para-linguistic features (such as pauses, overlapping speech, stress patterns etc.). The result is data which has the form, not so much of a 'text' (like the script for a play) as a practical notation (similar to a musical score). It is an attempt to grasp the multi-dimensional minutiae of spoken interaction (Hutchby and Wooffitt 1998). In this respect, however, one of the great advantages of studying broadcast talk is that the data is not affected by the circumstances of its recording; it is already, as it were, 'on the record' as publicly available talk.

There is, however, a more fundamental methodological point on which CA, in particular, insists. It is not just that there is a preference for 'naturally occuring' and accurately transcribed data; it is also that this data, in principle, provides its own epistemological guarantees. This is achieved by what is known as the 'next turn proof procedure' (Hutchby and Wooffitt 1998) whereby, in the organisation of the responses to prior turns, partici-pants demonstrate what is salient as far as they are concerned. Their interactive display is available to empirical observation, which, while it may require further explanation, does not initially rely on the analyst's own interpretation. For example, it is in the response of the interviewer to an interviewee's prior turn that we can judge whether or not this has been taken as a satisfactory answer or, alternatively, that further follow-up questions or 'probing' might be necessary. Just a moment's pause, an intake of breath, or a minimal response ('mm', 'hmm') is enough to display participants' understandings of how a speech event is developing.

Here, however, we discover a further resource for the analysis of media talk. This has been largely ignored in previous work, but it will make a major contribution here (especially in Chapters 4 and 7). As we have noted, what some media talk makes available to the analyst is not just the behaviour of participants, but also the responses of a studio audience. Audience participation has become a major feature of some influential formats where the 'theatrical' boundary between performers and audience has been crossed (Carpignano, Andersen, Aronowitz and Difazio 1990). More generally, even for traditional genres (game shows, chat show interviews, studio debates) audience reaction constitutes a significant resource. It can provide the 'next turn proof' precisely in those performative areas where conventional pragmatic judgements are uncertain. When is an insult impolite, or when is it meant to be funny – or both, as one recent analysis (Montgomery 1999) of a popular British talk show, *Mrs Merton*, has demonstrated? It is the audience reaction that frequently provides the clue. This is to build into the analysis of broadcast talk a principle developed some years ago by Max Atkinson, in his well-known work on political speeches (Atkinson 1984). What works most effectively in this context is 'clap-trap', or the rhetorical provocation of applause.

In these ways, spoken discourse analysis has particular methodological strengths. It is resolutely empirical, and it is able to demonstrate, not simply insist on, the quality of its evidence. This is probably why it is so refreshing when introduced into media studies or, in contrast, is particularly challenging to traditional analytic approaches. As we began by pointing out, the study of broadcast talk is notable for its rejection of traditional forms of textual interpretation: it does not offer 'critical readings' of texts, however buttressed these may be by the latest social theory. Even less is it concerned with making judgements (positive or negative) about the value of particular media texts. What is interesting, in the analysis of broadcast talk, are the very mundane, routine practices of spoken interaction which occur on radio and television and speak out to intersect with the ways we live our everyday lives. Just like ordinary conversation, media talk is interesting because it is so unremarkable: it is about what these media are really *doing* when they say what they say.

Appendix: Transcription conventions

( )   If empty, indicates unclear portions of text.

[bold]   Description of non-verbal behaviour or visual information.

[ ]   Back channel behaviour which does not amount to a turn at talk.

(1.5)   Length of pause in seconds.

(.)   Pause of less than .5 seconds.

=   Indicates that utterance follows immediately on previous utterance, or is latched to separate parts of a continuous utterance by the same speaker.

[Indicates the point at which overlap with another speaker begins.

>....<   'More than' and 'less than' signs indicate that the talk they encompass was spoken noticeably quicker than the surrounding talk.

word-   Hyphen indicates word has been cut off sharply.

word   Underlining indicates stress given to word or syllable.

WORD Uppercase letters indicate increased volume.

sho::w Colons indicate lengthening of vowel sound.

.   Terminal falling intonation.

,   Brief pause ('list' intonation).

?   Rising intonation.

!   Excited intonation.

.hh   Audible intake of breath.

hh   Audible exhalation.

heh   Laugh token.

hhhhh Extended laughter. Where appropriate for the analysis, the length of the laughter response in seconds is indicated in parentheses.

xxxxx Applause. Where appropriate for the analysis, the length of the applause in seconds is indicated in parentheses.

Note also:

• As indicated above, conventional punctuation marks such as full stops and commas are to be taken as markers of intonation and not of syntax.

• Transcriptions are given in a form consonant with the level of delicacy appropriate to the analysis at hand.

2   Analysing Media Talk

1. Introduction

In the previous chapter, we considered three key features of broadcasting which are highlighted by the study of media talk. Media talk needs to be interactive because it needs to capture the attention of its audience and Horton and Wohl's concept of 'para-social interaction' has become the first of several attempts to characterise the peculiar nature of this interaction where the audience is located at a spatial, and sometimes temporal, distance. Accordingly, as these authors also began to recognise, there are performative features in media talk, professionally developed, which often serve to minimise the experience of distance. At its most basic, though the speaker on TV or radio may be talking to an audience of millions, it sometimes seems as if the speech is personal, directed at an individual viewer or listener. Also, as some of Ellis's work, in particular, emphasises, possible perceptions of temporal distance between the recording of a programme and its transmission are often disguised by the apparent 'liveness' of the broadcast event. As I have discussed, I want to explore this phenomenon here in terms of the *liveliness* of broadcast talk, which somehow convinces us of its liveness even when we know it has been recorded.

So we now face the question of how to conduct this exploration. How can we begin to analyse the mechanisms of interactivity and the techniques of lively performance in media talk? As Chapter 1 has also indicated, we will be involved here with a methodology of spoken discourse analysis, defined as 'language in use'. The virtues of this approach have been introduced as a particular insistence on close attention to detail, where talk, or 'conversation', is recorded and transcribed according to strict protocols. Such an approach is able to demonstrate that the strategies of talk it identifies are attended to by the participants themselves, and are not simply interpretations of the data made by the analyst. It is crucial therefore that our approach to analysing media talk follows the same strict methodology, which it is the purpose of this chapter to introduce.

There is now a growing introductory literature on 'language in use', and its contributory disciplines. I do not intend, therefore, to offer another

24

general introduction here. Suffice it to say that readers with an interest in discourse analysis, as applied to different varieties of spoken discourse, might well begin by consulting Cameron (2001) and also the overview offered by Jaworski and Coupland (1999), where an emphasis on the diversity of approaches to this type of discourse analysis is also demonstrated by their selection of contributions to *The Discourse Reader*. In this book, however, we are not so much concerned with spoken discourse in general, but more particularly with broadcasting, where it takes particular (and sometimes peculiar) forms.

If we restrict our focus to broadcasting, as previously defined, we will be especially interested in what discourse analysis has to say about verbal interaction. We will be looking at the performance of speech in 'ordinary conversation' but more particularly at its transformation and redeployment in this particular institutional context. To prepare for this, it is the aim of this chapter to provide a selective introduction to those approaches to spoken discourse analysis which I take to be crucial to further analysis of media talk, namely: Conversation Analysis (CA), Gricean Pragmatics (as previously touched upon) and what has come to be known as 'Interactional Sociolinguistics'. Subsections of this chapter will summarise key concepts in each approach, as defined by previous work, but also these will be illustrated by original extracts from TV news interviews.

2. Conversation Analysis

2.1 Ethnomethodology

As mentioned in Chapter 1, CA is best understood as a branch of sociology, with its roots in the enterprise known as 'ethnomethodology'. The theoretical origins of this enterprise are founded on a basic, indeed classic, sociological question: namely, how can we account for the existence of that thing we call 'society', defined (in some views) as a systematic, and even functional, organisation, which reproduces itself over time? The ethnomethodological 'take' on this question is that social order can be understood from the point of view of the member of a society, the social 'actor'. And here, to put it very simply, we are not programmed, or conditioned, to act in socially acceptable ways (with non-compliance simply being labelled as 'deviance'); rather, social actors have their own understandings of what counts as socially appropriate, and they find ways of checking these out against the perceptions of fellow actors. Socialisation can be understood, not so much as the internalisation of pre-given social 'norms', rather as a continuous process of negotiation, an 'intersubjective' activity, where members of social groups collectively determine the boundaries of socially acceptable behaviour.

One interesting question which then arises concerns the ways social actors behave when they perceive such boundaries are transgressed. No doubt there is a variety of possible courses of action: individuals or groups may be subjected to physical violence, or they may be disciplined through judicial processes etc. However, the more routine social practice, which particularly interests ethnomethodology because it is so mundane, is the activity it calls 'accounting': the production of 'accounts' in situations where individuals are held 'accountable' for their behaviour. This pheno-menon was empirically demonstrated in the well-known 'breaching experiments' carried out at Harvard University in the 1960s, where Harold Garfinkel instructed his students, in particular social contexts, to transgress the norms of everyday social interaction (Garfinkel 1967). For instance, one experiment involved students introducing into everyday conversations a particularly pedantic line of questioning, of the 'what do you mean by that?' variety: 'what do you mean you had a flat tyre' etc. (for a useful summary, see Heritage 1984). Such questions, or such an approach, soon gave rise to annoyance in co-participants, because it could be assumed that this was breaching the common knowledge that 'goes without saying'. In that context, the questioners might be taken to task, invited to explain themselves, and to offer an *account* of why they were asking such obvious questions.

Very shortly we will observe that this breaching experiment finds an interesting echo in some forms of media talk. In news interviews, for example, 'want do you mean by that?' can be a legitimate question, but equally interviewers are sometimes taken to task for their particular line of questioning. In Garfinkel's ethnomethodology, however, what the breaching experiment demonstrates is the intersubjective negotiation of order in everyday life, to which individuals are expected, more or less, to conform. It might also be suggested that verbal interaction is one of the most fundamental ways in which such 'orderliness' is negotiated (though there are also, of course, non-verbal codes of behaviour) and, on this basis, Harvey Sacks and his colleagues at UCLA in the 1960s began to investigate the conduct of 'ordinary conversation'. Their investigation was initially focused on the fact that such conversation is indeed remarkably orderly, and, where the expectation that it will be so is in some way breached, participants themselves attend to such breaches, account for them, and in many cases attempt to 'repair' them.

2.2 Adjacency

Though it is capable of a highly nuanced account of the management of ordinary conversation, introductory summaries of CA usually focus on its three basic insights concerning adjacency, turn-taking and sequencing (or the existence of predictable sequences for performing conversational acts). The notion of *adjacency* was introduced in Chapter 1 (in the section on interactivity). It is basically an elementary observation that some kinds of utterance expect an immediate and appropriate response: such that questions require answers, a command or 'summons' expects a response, and recipients of greetings (such as 'hello', 'hi', 'good evening' etc.) are expected to return the greeting, or at least acknowledge it. To fail to conform to such expectations is to transgress this conversational norm, to appear (perhaps) rude, or, at the very least, to get into a situation where repair work is necessary or an account is produced ('I'm sorry I didn't hear you'; or 'not just now, I'm too busy' etc.).

In the next two subsections, we will examine the use of the first two forms of adjacency in media talk, but, to begin with, let us first consider the rather interesting depolyment of greetings. As we have previously noted, it is standard practice for presenters of radio and television programmes to address the audience directly ('hello and welcome to the show') thereby encouraging its 'quasi-interactive' involvement. However, in some types of programming (but not others) greetings are also exchanged between participants, in a routine, but also rather strange, way. For example, on British television, over a period of twenty years, we became familiar with this formulaic exchange of greetings:

```
Transcript 1
Host:        Hello number one. What's your name and where do
             you come from?
Contestant:  Hello Cilla, I'm James and I come from Liverpool
             [audience applause]
```

Here of course, the host is Cilla Black, and the programme was the long-running dating game show *Blind Date*, an internationally successful format. Here is another version of this use of greetings:

```
Transcript 2
CB: Thank you. Hello and welcome back. Well let's find out about
    our three girls, Helene, Diane and Nadia. Come on
    [Cilla traverses the stage: audience applause and cheers]
    Well(.)he:llo Helene
H:  Hello Cilla
CB: You look gorgeous in that sexy outfit
H:  Thank you
```

In Transcript 2 we can see that the use of greetings by the presenter shifts from address to the TV audience, to an exchange with a contestant, who (as in ordinary conversation) reciprocates. But the interesting point of course is that, in this context, this exchange is not 'ordinary' at all. For Cilla, one assumes, has already met Helene prior to the recording of the show and, similarly, she already knows the identity of 'number one' in Transcript 1. In other words this is a 'staged' greeting, where Cilla is not greeting the contestant (or asking the question to number one) on her own behalf. Rather, she is greeting the contestant for the purposes of the show, on his or her first appearance in front of the audience. Cilla is adopting the audience's perspective and position, which is also apparent in 'let's find out about *our* three girls'. Equally, however, the contestants exchange these greetings with Cilla; they don't say 'hello audience' or words to that effect (though in this show they sometimes looked at the studio audience as they spoke). They speak to Cilla, in her role of greeting contestants and asking questions on the audience's behalf.

The issues involved in these formulaic extracts are absolutely fundamental to media talk. Crucially, as we have previously observed, it is 'conversational' in so far as it makes use of features of ordinary conversation, but it is not 'ordinary conversation' as such. For one thing (as noted in Chapter 1) there is a suspicion that, for all their apparent 'liveliness', these exchanges are scripted. But that aside, the key point is that the 'conversation' is performed for an audience and the greetings are a kind of simulation. The role of the presenter is to mediate between the participants and the audience, in the studio theatre and at home ('welcome back').

Greetings, of the sort described above, however, do not occur in all forms of broadcast talk. They primarily occur within the formats (quiz and game shows, some forms of talk show) which Scannell (1996) describes as 'sociable'; though they may be beginning to extend to other formats as these become more 'conversational'. Traditionally, greetings have been noticeably absent from the format discussed by Heritage, Greatbatch and Clayman (henceforth collectively referred to as Heritage et al.) as the 'news interview'. Since their work is a major application of CA methodology to media talk, it is now necessary to consider it in some detail. It also brings into focus the second main preoccupation of CA, namely, the practice of turn-taking.

2.3 Turn-taking

As previously noted, CA has found the 'orderliness' of ordinary conversation to be its most remarkable feature. We can now appreciate how the ethnomethodological roots of CA might have foregrounded this issue, which is most evident in turn-taking, in multi-party conversations. Here there is the potential for chaos, with everyone trying to speak at once, but in fact a set of rules are followed which minimise this possibility. Harvey Sacks and his colleagues described these as a 'simplest systematics', a set of rules which Cameron outlines as follows:

1. Current speaker selects next speaker
   Or if this mechanism does not operate then ...
2. Next speaker self selects
   Or if this mechanism does not operate then ...
3. Current speaker may continue

(Cameron 2001: 91)

In short, participants in ordinary conversations seem to have a mutual understanding of how to accomplish turn-taking as an orderly procedure. Clearly this is very much in line with the 'intersubjective' approach to social order taken by ethnomethodology.

But in this connection we need to recognise two further points, both of which are highly relevant to some forms of media talk. First, it is not the case that this mutual accomplishment is always neat and tidy. Even though speakers know these rules, it is not unusual for turns at talk to overlap, with two (or more) people speaking at once. Normally in such situations, where the overlap is perceived as problematic, some forms of 'repair' work will ensue, and one speaker will be permitted to take the 'floor'. However, there are also situations where speakers compete for the floor, for instance, where (at point 2 in the 'systematics') two or more speakers self-select. Related to this, it is also, of course, possible to interrupt the current speaker. In both such instances, overlap is sometimes extended and intensified until all but one of the rival competitors for the floor give way.

Secondly, it is a very interesting question how (again at 2 above) the next speaker identifies an opportunity to self-select. If a current speaker fails to nominate a next speaker, there must be moments in the talk where the next speaker feels it is possible to start a turn without seeming to be interrupting. CA calls these 'transition relevance places' (TRPs) and suggests that the mutual accomplishment of order in turn-taking is possible because speakers are monitoring the conversation for possible TRPs. How these are identified is a complex matter, involving perceptions of intonation, grammatical structure and some sense of semantic completion. One important theorist, Mikhail Bakhtin (1986), suggests that speakers have some sense of the 'finalisation of an utterance', which he relates to the 'speech genre' being used. Certainly we usually know when someone has come to the end of a story, or a joke, but, as we will see very shortly, it is not always as straightforward as that.

However, the starting point for Heritage and Greatbatch's (1991) discussion of the news interview is that the turns at talk, in this context, are institutionally predetermined. The participants have 'pre-allocated roles', where it is the responsibility of the interviewer (IR) to ask questions and interviewee(s) (IE) to provide answers. One might assume therefore that, unlike ordinary conversations, since the turntaking is non-negotiable, news interviews will proceed as particularly orderly events.

And in this the participants are additionally helped by the existence of conventions, developed over the years, for the conduct of news interviews. Heritage et al. discuss the transition from deferential to more 'probing' styles of news interview familiar since the 1950s. In these formal events, IRs package their questions in relatively complex structures of 'question delivery', consisting of prefatory statements as well as questions as such. The IE knows that a question is coming, so will wait for that as a likely TRP, but the interviewer's preface will also provide some prior orientation as to what the question will be. For their part, as we have noted, IEs are expected to produce much more than one-word answers. The institutional require-ment, for this type of verbal performance, is a 'multi-unit' extended turn, where the IE is given space to elaborate.

Such conventions characterise news interviews, like some other similar varieties of 'institutional talk' (legal cross-examination, for example) as relatively formal speech events. The expected exchange of turns, in the prescribed manner, is supported by norms governing public behaviour and politeness. However, as Heritage et al. also point out, the prescribed conventions can also be exploited by participants, to introduce a further level of interactional dynamics. Essentially, this is where 'probing' news interviews start to become adversarial. For example, the prefatory state-ments by IRs may contain implications that the IE feels obliged to contest. The question itself may be leading the IE down a path which he or she wishes to avoid. In such cases the conventional system for turn-taking still tends to prevail, but having provided their answers, and using the multi-unit possibilities available to them, IEs sometimes proceed to attack the presuppositions of the question, or attempt to shift the topical agenda (Greatbatch 1986). Heritage et al. also show that there are occasions where IEs are prepared to interrupt the question delivery, or even attempt to 'turn tables' on the IR by asking questions themselves.

Arguably, the more adversarial the news interview becomes, the greater is its potential for entertainment. Heritage et al. do not make much of this, but it is clear that some contemporary 'current affairs' programming operates with a double agenda where public information is packaged in dramatic and sometimes amusing, 'lively' interchange.[1] However, in one important essay Heritage (1985) does give a detailed account of a strategy used by news IRs to heighten the level of dramatic tension. This is what he calls (following an earlier paper by Garfinkel and Sacks) the practice of 'formulating'. In the turn which follows an IE's answer, the IR may not immediately proceed to another question, but instead reflect back on that answer 'summarising, glossing, or developing the gist of an informant's earlier statements' (Heritage 1985: 100).

In the news interview, 'formulations' are used in a way which again takes us back to the first principles of broadcast talk. For the IR (typically, but we will look at some exceptions later) does not respond, react or seek further clarification in a personal capacity. News IRs do not normally react to news in the manner typical of ordinary conversation, where personal reactions (surprise, shock, horror) are conveyed by third-turn receipts known as 'newsmarks' ('Oh really', 'Oh my goodness', 'How exciting' etc.). In ordinary conversation, the newsmark serves to indicate that the information is indeed news for the recipient and moreover that he or she has some personal investment in that fact. But news IRs do not react to news in this way; their stance is different from that taken in ordinary conversation. For the formulations they produce, and indeed the questions they ask in the first place, are produced on behalf of the audience. This is the same principle, though in a very different format, as that which obtains when Cilla Black greets the contestants on her game show. As Heritage puts it, the talk produced by all participants in news interviews is not just for each other, but also, and primarily, for the 'overhearing audience'.

Transcript 3 provides an illustration of this principle at work. It is taken from what Heritage et al. call a 'panel interview', where several IEs (here four) are involved. This interview took place on 20 November 1995, on the BBC programme *Newsnight*, immediately following a notorious interview given by the late Princess Diana, on another BBC current affairs programme, *Panorama*. In that interview she had confirmed her personal unhappiness in her marriage to Prince Charles, and had confessed that she, as well as he, had had adulterous relationships. On the *Newsnight* programme, the IE, Jeremy Paxman, began by asking a politician, Nicholas Soames (introduced as a 'good friend of Prince Charles'), to comment:

Transcript 3

```
    JP:  Well now we're going to explore some of the implications
         of that interview. First off erm Nicholas Soames you're a
         good friend of Prince Charles presumably he was sitting
         watching it tonight what do you think he'll have
 5       made of it?
    NS:  Well I have no idea and I certainly couldn't erm speak
         for the Prince of Wales (.) but er for my own part as an
         interested observer I found some of it to be er toe
         curlingly dreadful (.) but some of it I found er a
10       portrayal of a desperately unhappy and sad marriage and
         I think that what needs to happen now is for a line to
         be drawn under all this and for people all people of
         good will and good sense to wish that both the Prince
         and the Princess of Wales will find happiness in their
15       lives in whatever way they choose to pursue it.
    JP:  Has Prince Charles ever indicated to you what the
         Princess of Wales said he'd indicated which was that he
         did not wish to be king?
    NS:  Never. And I think what the Princess said with great
```

```
20          respect to her position was absolute nonsense.
     JP:    He's never given you the slightest ink[ling?
     NS:                                         [Never. And I
            simply do not recognise it as being the case.
     JP:    And when she says that she recognises she will never be
25          queen what do you make of that?
     NS:    I I couldn't possibly comment (.) I simply don't know
            what she means by that.
     JP:    The picture that she paints of er the harassment the
            oppression the mail interception the characterisation
30          as mad by Prince Charles' household do you recognise
            that?
     NS:    No I don't and I really do think that some of this was
            er really trying to stretch er people's imagination (.)
            Er I I simply don't recognise it as being such and all
35          all that comes through is of this tremendous sadness
            terrific complications great unhappiness and er I don't
            know what you call it but a period of of obviously
            unhappiness that led to instability and mental illness.
     JP:    But you presumably are one of the people she called the
40          enemy
     NS:    Well I I hope not but I I can't account for what the
            Princess was talking about when she referred to to to
            those matters for example like mail interception I mean
            I simply don't know what she's talking about and about
45          telephones being tapped and all that it really is sort
            of the advanced stages of paranoia.
     JP:    So she's made it all up she's para[noid
     NS:                                       [I I've simply no idea
            (.) but it seems to me the advanced stages of paranoia.
```

These opening exchanges, from the *Newsnight* programme contain several classic features of news interview talk, some of which we will discuss later. For the moment, let us dwell on the fact that Jeremy Paxman's interviewing technique is basically founded on the protocols described by Heritage (1985). In particular, he does not express his own perspective on this 'news', nor does he personally react to the statements of Nicholas Soames. Rather, he is more concerned to 'probe' the IE for further information. He partly does this by asking questions (lines 5, 16–18, 24–5, 28–31) but one of these questions (line 21) is clearly a *prompt* following the IE's previous, and somewhat cursory, answer. However, some further IR turns could scarcely be classified as 'questions' at all. The IR utterances on lines 39–40 and 47 fall into the category of formulation defined by Heritage as the *inferential elaborative probe*. Such utterances follow the IE's answer by seeking to thematise an implied inference (line 39–40) or to commit the interviewee to a categorical, and thus more controversial, version of his position (line 47). In this, they 'formulate' the IE's answer for the benefit of the overhearing audience. At the same time they introduce an adversarial manner into these proceedings which is (mildly) unco-operative.

In each case, it is the 'next turn proof' procedure which supports the analysis. For instance, in lines 41 and 48 we can observe that the IE initially 'disaffiliates' with the prior formulation (though it is partially recycled in line 49). Furthermore, we observe that moments of problematic turn-taking occur on lines 21–2 and 47–8. The overlap of turns here, where the IE interrupts the IR's prior formulation, indicates to us that it is problematic for him. Interruptive overlapping talk in a news interview of this kind is often a sign of 'trouble'.

Another such indicator is the noticeable pause (.). On three occasions here the IE produces an answer followed by a pause, which might, in some contexts, be construed as a TRP. Here, however, the next speaker, in terms of the 'simplest systematics' described above, does not self-select. The current speaker is then obliged to continue, perhaps unwillingly, but partly driven by the expectation that he should be producing multi-unit turns (which by line 32 he is again prepared to do). The fact that this IE, between lines 19 and 27, displays a noticeable reluctance to produce extended turns, allied to other features of his verbal performance such as the hesitation and the stuttering, relates to another level of analysis we will consider shortly. For the moment, however, let us conclude this introduction to turn-taking by observing once again that a CA-inspired analysis of this kind is both empirically driven and highly detailed in its approach to the dynamics of verbal interaction.

2.4 Sequencing

A third key concept in CA is that of the 'sequence', or more precisely, verbal interaction as a sequential activity. Here it is recognised that features of orderly interaction such as adjacency and turn-taking are not simply rules to be followed, rather, they have a strategic potential which is 'locally occasioned'. That is to say, particular uses of these features are related to perceptions of context; but for CA 'context' is understood to be a developing social event, and not simply an a priori definition of a situation. Clearly, participants in news interviews have prior expectations of the pre-allocated roles they are expected to fulfil. What they actually say, however, and particularly the behaviour they display, is oriented to an understanding of the sequential development of the event in which they are currently engaged.

Accordingly 'sequences' can be defined as developing patterns of inter-action, running across several turns, which are reflexively monitored by participants. In the CA literature, however, there seem to be two versions of this concept. In one version, CA is interested in we might call 'mini-rituals' of verbal interaction, which are so routine and orderly they might almost seem to be scripted. For example, a great deal of attention has been given to the opening and closing of telephone calls, where a familiar pattern of exchanges is almost invariably followed, determined in part by the peculiarities of this technology. Secondly, however, some types of sequence are less formulaic, and their consequences are less predictable. Indeed, in one example we will consider the type of sequence evident in the exchanges is only intelligible in retrospect: the prior turn can only be understood as a particular turn-type in the light of what follows it.

Both these perspectives on sequencing inform Ian Hutchby's work on radio talk (Hutchby 1996). This provides a detailed analysis of the talk produced on a familiar type of radio phone-in, where listeners are invited to contribute opinions on topical issues. Hutchby's main interest is in the way such statements of opinion serve as the basis for extended sequences of argument between the caller and the host. Also, however, he makes some observations on the way the openings and closings of calls to the radio phone-in are institutionally managed.

Once again it is a matter of recognising that, whilst it may be 'conversational' in some respects, broadcast talk differs from ordinary conversation. As far as the openings of calls is concerned, a key difference lies in the way identifications are made, which then affects the whole sequence of opening moves. We can illustrate this difference by comparing and contrasting Hutchby's data with the classic discussion of openings of telephone calls by Emmanuel Schegloff (1968, 1986). For example:

```
Transcript 4
(Hyla and Nancy are teenage friends)
 1.         (Ring)
 2.  Nancy: H'llo?
 3.  Hyla:  Hi:,
 4.  Nancy: Hi::.
 5.  Hyla:  How are yuhh=
 6.  Nancy: =Fi:ne how er you,
 7.  Hyla:  Oka:[y,
 8.  Nancy:     [Goo:d
 9.         (0.4)
10.  Hyla:  .mkhhh[hh
11.  Nancy:       [What's doin'
                   (cited in Hutchby and Wooffitt 1998: 97)
```

Schegloff's analysis of this extract suggests that the exchange of greetings between Nancy and Hyla is embedded in a more complex pattern of adjacency which has the following structure: (1) Summons–Answer (lines 1–2) where the answerer's first 'hello' is a response to the telephone ringing; (2) Identification–Recognition (lines 2–4) where the two parties mutually recognise each others' voices – but note that in many telephone calls it is necessary for the participants to identify themselves explicitly; (3) Greeting–Greeting (lines 3–4) which develops into an extended greeting sequence (lines 5–8) followed by the pause; and then finally (4) a move to establish the purpose of the call, which it is incumbent on the caller to supply. The caller is always then in the position of being accountable for the call, and has to say something in response to the question (in line 11) which justifies having made it.

However, as Hutchby shows, in radio phone-ins the first two moves in this sequence are unnecessary. The host already knows the identity of the caller (this having been supplied by production staff) and the caller, being also a listener, understands the purpose of the show. The result is a curtailed opening sequence where (1) the identity of the caller is *announced* by the host and (2) greetings are exchanged. In Hutchby's data, the caller then proceeds immediately without further prompting to state an opinion about the topic which is the focus of the programme. There is no doubt, in this institutional context, what the purpose of the call might be. The four-part opening sequence of an ordinary telephone call has thus, in the radio phone-in, been reduced to two, as follows:

```
Transcript 5
(1) Host:    Kath calling from Clapham now good morning
    Caller: Good morning Brian. Erm: I (li-) I also agree that thee
            .hh telethons are a form of psychological blackmail now
            (.) .hhh Be:cause… ...

(2) Host:    On to Philip in Camden Town. Good morning.
    Caller: Yeh guh morning Brian. (Erm (.) Really what I wanted to
            say was that I'm fascinated by watching these
            telethons ...
                                            (Hutchby 1996: 45-6)
```

Equally, as Hutchby also demonstrates, the quite lengthy closing sequences characteristic of ordinary telephone calls (where parties mutually negotiate an ending) is not necessary for the radio phone-in, where the host, unilaterally, has the power to terminate the call.

All of which might seem fairly mundane – though we will encounter some variations on this pattern in Chapter 5. What becomes significant, however, is Hutchby's observation that the opening sequence is just the first in a series of four 'phases' in a call where: (1) the first phase (as above) involves announcements and greetings; (2) the second phase involves an extended turn in which the caller states an opinion; (3) the third phase requires the host to argue with that statement, which may be followed by 'a relatively free exchange of speaking turns in which the host and caller discuss, or, much more frequently, dispute the issue in question' (1996: 15); until (4) in his final turn, the host initiates a closing (which may, but does not necessarily, include a minimal closing exchange – 'thank you' etc.). Crucially then, in the radio phone-in, not only does the host always have the final say, but also it is the host, in phase 3 of the sequence, who introduces the argument. What the caller has to say is invariably treated as 'arguable', and what Hutchby has to say about this is interesting.

There are two points. The first point is that 'argument' here is understood as an interactive accomplishment. No doubt the caller, in stating an opinion, makes 'an argument' as a series of propositions – but the participants only start to argue with each other where the arguability of the opinion is established by the host. This perspective takes argument to be a sequential effect: in fact it is an 'action–opposition' sequence in CA terminology. It is at this point that the participants understand themselves to be 'having an argument' for the purposes of this programme (though callers to the show, being listeners, must also know what to expect). Their subsequent 'relatively free exchange' of turns will therefore be strategically orientated to this fact, and performed, as they must be, with the overhearing audience in mind.

Secondly, however, this sequence always positions the host in the opposing role, or the 'second position' as Hutchby puts it. This means that the caller's first position is always vulnerable; and Hutchby goes on to argue that the sequence of turns itself contains an in-built imbalance of power. Here power is not simply given to the host by virtue of his institutional status; it is accomplished through the action–opposition sequence which invariably puts the caller on the defensive. Hutchby goes on to show that there are formulaic strategies available to the host, such as 'you say X but what about Y?', in which his turns are packaged to display this power. For their part, callers' turns are obliged to take this sequential effect into account. To defend an opinion, in the face of such 'confrontation', is to assume a position of resistance.

The talk radio programmes we will look at in Chapter 5 of this book suggest that Hutchby's format is not universal. In particular it is possible to engage in forms of argument which are not confrontational. However, the main point here is to observe again that sequences of talk can follow strategic, as well as ritualistic, patterns. Participants are required, not simply to follow the 'simplest systematics' of turn-taking, but also to design their turns with a sequential position in mind. Sequencing is particularly significant in media talk because it is so institutionally circumscribed. The pre-allocated roles of game show contestants, news interviewees and phone-in callers predetermine the kinds of contributions they can make. Equally how the hosts, presenters or interviewers handle their discursive power is always on the agenda, and, as Hutchby demonstrates, this is a power that reaches right down to the local management of turns.

3. Pragmatics

With its focus on features such as adjacency, turn-taking and sequencing, CA has explicated some of the structural constraints that govern verbal interaction. In principle, it is content to describe these features of conversational behaviour and is not inclined to speculate further about participants' intentions or motives. In practice, however, even in work inspired by the CA approach, it is not unusual to encounter inferences about the meaning of aspects of interactive behaviour for the participants involved. In fact we have seen this already, in Heritage's discussion of the 'unco-operative' formulation. It is true that the empirical evidence for this is contained in the next turn (e.g. where the IE disaffiliates with the prior formulation). At such moments, however, it is also clear that speakers are monitoring the talk, not just for sequential structure or for TRPs, but also for the meanings it contains. Similarly, Heritage shows that some formulations are regarded, not as hostile probes, but as the 'co-operative recycle' of IE propositions.

We have observed that in some aspects of his behaviour in Transcript 3, Nicholas Soames displays a reluctance to elaborate. When he does, towards the end of these exchanges, begin to produce multi-unit turns, he displays a certain nervousness and hesitation. Now there could of course be various reasons for this. Perhaps NS is nervous about appearing on TV, but this is unlikely given that he is a politician. Perhaps he has an incurable stutter, but he doesn't display this in other contributions to this panel interview. There may be an aspect of this which has something to do with social class, for NS is also a member of the English aristocracy (his grandfather was Winston Churchill) and there is a form of what we might call aristocratic 'self-presentation' which involves stuttering on occasion (Prince Charles does this too). However, for reasons which we will now begin to explore, it is also possible to conclude that NS finds this topic, and what he is invited to say about it, problematic. In particular, he has no real evidence to support his speculations.

To explore this issue, we need to dip our toes into the sub-discipline of discourse analysis known as Pragmatics. Again, this will be highly selective, and I will simply introduce elements of this approach which serve to illuminate the study of media talk. Pragmatics is interested in the way meanings can be inferred from conversational acts. Here then, an inter-subjective social order does not just revolve around the cut and thrust of turn-taking, it is an activity which involves mutual interpretation. This becomes particularly evident when we consider that, in much ordinary conversation, more is meant than is actually said. To give just one example – though for many more see Levinson (1983) and Schiffrin (1994) – the statement 'boys will be boys' is literally meaningless; in fact it is a tautology.

However, when uttered by a woman to another woman about a man of their mutual acquaintance, it carries a certain (sarcastic) import.

Parties to conversations where such utterances are produced recognise a meaning in what is said. In Pragmatics, this meaning is known as an *implicature*. This is a mutual inference drawn from the production of this utterance, in this context, and with perhaps a certain tone of voice. On this basis, Pragmatics then seeks to explicate how it is that we are able to make such inferences. Our starting point must be that we assume that this statement is intentional – the speaker who produces it intends that its recipient understands the implicature. Conversely, if she is to interpret this utterance successfully, the recipient also must recognise the intention. This mutual reading of intentions assumes a basic level of co-operation in ordinary conversation, according to H. P. Grice, the American philosopher who invented this branch of Pragmatics.

In this mutual exchange of inferences, many of which lie beneath the surface of literal meaning, ordinary conversation displays what Grice calls a 'co-operative principle'. In particular, this involves a code of ethics. Participants must have confidence in co-participants if they are to read their intentions. Participants must speak to others to encourage, or at least make possible, mutual understanding. They must not intentionally mislead or confuse co-participants, because to do so would break the co-operative principle and would prevent the implicatures being inferred. To this end, Grice produced a set of conversational *maxims* to which, he argued, participants in ordinary conversations are mutually orientated:

1. **Quantity**: make your contribution as informative as is required for the current purposes of the exchange. Do not make your contribution more (*or less*) informative than is required.
2. **Quality**: do not say what you believe to be false. Do not say that for which you lack evidence.
3. **Relation**: be relevant.
4. **Manner**: avoid obscurity of expression. Avoid ambiguity. Be brief (avoid unnecessary prolixity). Be orderly.
   (Cameron 2001: 75, adapted from Grice 1975; my addition in italics)

Let us immediately observe the applicability of this code to the news interview in Transcript 3. If he is not careful, NS is in danger of transgressing, or 'flouting', the maxim of Quality. Indeed he is invited to do this by the IR, when he is invited to speculate on the reactions of Prince Charles, for which (unless he has just spoken to him on the phone) he cannot possibly have any evidence. NS signals his refusal to go down this route by rephrasing the question in a stronger version, where the invitation to speculate is glossed as 'speaking for' Prince Charles. The unacceptability of this, given the maxim of Quality, is used as a justification for shifting the agenda. Furthermore, at the end of the interview, NS becomes noticeably hesitant on the topic of 'mental illness'. There are various reasons for this to which we will return, but one of NS's tactics here might be described as a 'Quality disclaimer'. He is not sure whether there is evidence of paranoia (and, by implication, he is not qualified to say so) but in the end he's prepared, with some hesitancy, to make this suggestion.

Grice's argument is that maxims are assumed to be operating by parties to ordinary conversation. So, when a speaker says something which seems to be irrelevant, co-participants, assuming that the maxim of Relation is operating, and that the speaker intends it to be so, will search for some possible relevance in the utterance. When speakers provide more information than is normal (Quantity) it will be assumed that there is an intention to this (e.g. they are issuing detailed instructions). If a speaker is talking for too long (Manner) it may be because they think they have a good story to tell. But if no good reason can be found, and particularly if a speaker is judged to be intentionally flouting the maxims, then he or she can be held to account: why did you make that irrelevant point? Why are you lying to me?

A couple of caveats need to be introduced here. The first is that Grice's 'co-operative principle' with its maxims does not assume that, in common-sense terms, all talk is co-operative. Of course speakers can engage in heated argument, even personal abuse, but what the co-operative principle assumes is that this, however uncomfortable, is nevertheless intelligible to co-participants. It can be read as intentional, and it is intended to be recognised as such. In this sense, some conversation is 'co-operatively unco-operative', in that the intelligibility, even of hostile behaviour, should be apparent.

Secondly, however, I also want to develop the point introduced in Chapter 1, that careful consideration needs to be given to the application of these maxims in broadcasting. The co-operative principle does apply to media talk, as a fundamental principle of all communication, but again we need to remember that we are not dealing with 'ordinary conversation' as such. Participants in news interviews are interacting with each other, and inferring implicatures in each other's statements – but they are also, of course, staging a performance. On a mundane level, as we have noted, this means that judgements of Manner will differ from ordinary conversation: the multi-unit turns expected in interviews do not conform to the maxim that speakers 'be brief'. More subtly, because this is a performance, and because the performance is public, pragmatic accountability is both more explicit than in ordinary conversation and more highly charged. In news interviews, for example, participants seem to have a heightened orientation to Grice's maxims to which they explicitly or implicitly draw attention. For example, if this was a private conversation, NS might get away with a statement which lacks proper evidence, but he has to be especially careful not to flout the maxim of Quality on TV.

To illustrate these points, and to explore further the relevance of Gricean Pragmatics to broadcast talk, let us now turn our attention to Transcript 6. This is an extract from a news interview on the BBC programme *Panorama*, recorded in April 1984. It features Sir Robin Day, then the BBC's principal interviewer, and the Prime Minister of the day, Margaret Thatcher. At this point, the interview had lasted over forty minutes, covering various topics (for in those days *Panorama* staged such lengthy news interviews as set-piece occasions). But as his penultimate topic Day introduced a controversial matter. The Prime Minster's son, Mark Thatcher, apparently had business interests in the Gulf state of Oman at the same time as she was leading a trade delegation to that country. Was she aware of this? Was there a danger of her exploiting her public position for personal, or at least familial, gain? Observe here the way that Day interrogates Mrs Thatcher (he was himself trained as a barrister) but note also how his behaviour in line 54 provokes a particularly strong response:

```
Transcript 6
     RD:  On another matter (.) Prime Minister what is your
          reaction to the view of Mr Peter Shore, the shadow
          leader of the House (.) that there are still questions
          about the Oman contract and your son Mark which you have
          a public duty to answer?
 5   MT:  Well he's had the relevant answers, the House has had
          the relevant answers. He may not like the answers but
          erm that's not my fault.
     RD:  But the relevant answer he says he hasn't had, and other
10        people say also (.) that er you haven't answered the
          question as to when you were in Oman (.) did you know of
          your son's financial interest in the Cementation bid?
     MT:  I answer for what I do. I have answered for what I do. I
          have said perfectly clearly it was up to Oman to whom
15        they allocated this right to negotiate and debenture the
          contract. I don't mention the names of particular British
          companies and didn't on that occasion. I said it is
          vitally important, I believe, that the business comes to
          Britain. I have answered fully for my role. The
20        business did come to Britain, that business and a lot of
          other business in the rest of the Gulf. Now (.) what are
          they saying I did wrong? Did wrong in getting business
          for Britain, some four hundred companies? What are they
          saying I did wrong, batting for Britain? I shall go on
25        batting for Britain.
     RD:  Were you at any time advised or warned by your officials
          about a possible conflict of interest between your public
          duties and your son's private interests?
     MT:  As I have indicated in the House on many occasions I was
30        advised to raise the matter of the whole university
          contract with the government of Oman.That I did. I did it
          I believe very forcefully, because I wanted the business
          to come to Britain. The business did come to Britain,
```

```
       some four hundred companies are involved. I am
 35    sorry that the Labour Party doesn't like the business
       coming to Britain. I'm very sorry, but I shall go on
       trying to bat for Britain, getting more business for
       Britain. And on that tour I got contracts worth hundreds
       of millions of pounds=
 40 RD: [Well let me
    MT: [=and scarcely a week goes by now without my being asked
       to back up the demand, to back up the representations
       that British companies are making to try to get business
       overseas. Because competitors' governments back them.
 45 RD: Let me ask you one more question on this matter=
    MT:    [mm
    RD:    [=er because you've made your position clear on it. Can
       you give the public, the people, an assurance that if
       all the facts were disclosed about this matter, there
 50    would be no evidence of any impropriety on your part and
       no breach of the rigorous standards we all expect from
       people in public life?
    MT: I believe that is correct.
    RD: Then why not publish all the facts?
 55 MT: Because the facts will be published in due course of
       time but you know full well when the thirty year records
       come [of course=
    RD:   [oh
    MT:                    =they will of course they will but you
 60    know as well as I do Sir Robin that discussions between
       heads of governments are confidential (.) and what do
       you think, are you really suggesting that I should have
       confidential discussions with other heads of government
       that I should break confidentiality that I should break
 65    confidentiality on commercial contracts? Are you really
       suggesting, is the Labour Party really suggesting that
       that's the way for Britain to behave (.) that that's the
       way to get contracts for Britain? Are they really
       suggesting that the right way for the head of a British
 70    government is to breach confidentiality? What they're
       complaining about is that as a result of work that the
       British prime minister did, did correctly, did on advice
       from government departments, did on advice from the
       relevant departments work came to Britain. They haven't
 75    been able to say that a single thing (.) which I did (.)
       was wrong. Not a single thing. The work came to Britain.
    RD: [What they have what they have said what they h- (.)
       What they have said=
    MT: [It was the government of Oman who decided to whom it
 80    should go
    RD:                    =that is wrong is that you
       refused to say whether you knew that your son had a
       financial interest.
    MT: I answer for what I do. [Sir Robin what are you=
 85 RD:                         [Okay well we're going we won't
    MT:                                    =what
```

```
                 are you alleging that I did wrong?
          RD:    I'm not suggesting anything. I'm just putting to you the
                 questions which they say you have not answered and we'll
    90           leave it there.
          MT:    You're acting as a postman.
          RD:    [Let us leave it there.
          MT:    [Yes
```

Both Heritage and Greatbatch (1991) and Hutchby (1996) point to a variety of ways in which IEs and callers can 'turn the tables' in adversarial situations. For example, IEs sometimes comment on the questions they are asked, or they object to prefatory statements in the question delivery. There are also instances where news IEs and callers to phone-ins turn the tables by asking questions. In the news interview especially, this is a departure from the IE's pre-allocated role. Heritage et al. claim that such occurrences are rare, but it is my impression that they were becoming more common precisely at the time, in the 1980s, when their primary research was done. Robin Day himself commented on the increasingly confrontational tactics adopted by interviewees such as Margaret Thatcher.

But what occasions the confrontation between Day and Thatcher in Transcript 6? We will begin by observing that in the turns which begin on lines 55 and 84 MT questions RD's neutrality, committing him to making suggestions and allegations. The exchange which begins on line 84 is particularly interesting: for MT firstly resists RD's interruption (on line 85 he initiates a closing move on this particular topic), and then in response to his defence of his position (lines 88–90) MT herself reformulates that in derogatory, which might even say insulting, terms (line 91). From around line 59, in the common parlance MT 'kicks off' – but what provokes this? In the discourse-analytical perspective adopted here it is not necessary to speculate on psychological motives, we can instead simply concentrate on the way this response is interactionally intelligible. We can investigate this by tracing the way it is 'locally occasioned' by signs of trouble as the interview proceeds.

For Day's question in line 54 is clearly *a question too far*. This is evident in the fact that he has announced that the previous question will be his last on this topic, to which MT assents with the minimal response ('mm') in line 46. In the light of his production of a further question, RD's question delivery in line 45 appears in retrospect to be disingenuous. How far this is a deliberate ploy is debatable. If RD had known in line 45 that this was not going to be his final question, then again he could be accused of flouting the maxim of Quality (saying what he knows not to be true). However, it is more likely that the further question, in line 54, is working as a prompt, in response to MT's far too brief (for these purposes) answer in line 53. The prompt clearly works, but in unexpected ways, evident in RD's expression of personal surprise (the 'oh' receipt in line 58). Perhaps because of this, MT is put in a position where she can draw an implicature from RD's line of questioning, that he himself has a personal axe to grind.

Is MT correct to infer this implicature – despite RD's explicit statements to the contrary? Let us grant that in his role as IR, RD does not have a personal opinion on the topic in question; but what he does demonstrate in this extract is some frustration with the *Manner* of MT's answers. This is evident in his 'oh' receipt, but also it is previously apparent in line 40 where RD seems to interrupt MT. Actually, on the tape, line 39 is hearable as a possible TRP, but MT clearly has not finished. Her continuation in line 41 retrospectively gives RD's intervention (line 40) the force of an interruption. It also, however, confirms an increasing feeling that in the lengthy answers that begin on lines 13 and 29, MT is displaying a degree of 'prolixity' (she is talking too much). This is obviously a tricky judgement because IEs are expected to produce extended turns, but there are two points which support it.

What do we make of MT's answers to RD's initial question? First of all, there could be no clearer example of political evasiveness (Harris 1991) as MT shifts the agenda of the question. Furthermore, she does this in a very blatant way, according to Greatbatch's scale of strategies for agenda-shifting (Greatbatch 1986). A less marked strategy would be to produce a minimal answer to the question prior to an agenda shift, or, having initiated that shift, to ultimately return to the question which has been asked. MT, however, performs neither a 'post-answer' or 'pre-answer' agenda shift, nor does she account for why she will not answer this question. She simply pursues what Greatbatch calls an 'alternative track' (in terms of what she does, not what she knows) though she packages this in a way which recycles the key word: 'answer'. A minimal level of apparent relevance is thus preserved.

Having initiated the agenda shift, MT then embarks on an extended turn. This becomes increasingly rhetorical, with its repetition of key words 'business' and 'Britain' embedded in a rhetorical question-and-answer sequence which culminates in the cricketing metaphor 'batting for Britain' as its punch line. This may be fair enough, for politicians do make speeches, and RD waits for the punchline as an anticipated TRP. He interrupts, however, on line 40 after MT has produced another dose of the same rhetoric. Clearly the argument is not advancing, and in its lengthy repetition might be judged to be stretching the maxim of Manner. That, plus its questionable relevance in the first place, possibly provokes RD's intervention on line 40.

As it develops then, this interview becomes increasingly problematic for both participants. These problems are visible in the data, in the overlapping turns, the question delivery and the minimal responses, well before the 'turning of tables' takes place. They can be traced to strategies employed by the IE, particularly agenda-shifting and rhetorical repetition, which give rise to possible inferences in the light of Grice's maxims. Of course we will never have access to the inferences actually made by the participants, but we know that they are being made, that they follow the 'co-operative principle' and that, in this light, MT might well have been judged to be 'economical' with the truth.

However, again we should recall that this is a public occasion where the pragmatics are more complex than those which obtain for ordinary conversation. Though MT displays prolixity and RD disingenuity, arguably both these experienced participants know that some of this is to be expected in such a public, adversarial situation. Grice's maxims apply and they are invoked, but not simply to make moral judgements. Or rather, we might say, moral judgement is being used as a strategy, in a kind of language game which is also a public performance. MT is holding RD accountable for his line of questioning as a strategy to avoid answering the question. He knows that she intends this, she knows he knows (and we, the audience do too) so paradoxically the co-operative principle is being observed even as some of its maxims are being tested to the limit.

4. Interactional Sociolinguistics

In some recent introductions to discourse analysis (Schiffrin 1994; Jaworksi and Coupland 1999; Cameron 2001), there are chapters or subsections on an area known as 'interactional sociolinguistics'. This field is more diverse than CA and Pragmatics, and it is not always clear where its boundaries lie. It has some affinities with a more traditional approach to the 'ethnography of speaking', which takes an anthropological interest in the cultural knowledge required to function as a competent member of a 'speech community'. In its 'interactional' form, however, this often becomes a more specific focus on cross-cultural differences, and the potential for mis-communication between speakers from different cultural backgrounds. For example, work has been done on problematic interactions between speakers of English from different ethnic communities, and on potential sources of misunderstanding associated with gender (see Cameron 2001: Ch. 8, for an accessible summary). We will note the relevance of such issues, where appropriate, in this study of media talk; but we will start with a hugely influential theorist whose work, though included under this heading by some, cannot really be described as a 'sociolinguist' as such. This is the work of the American sociologist, Erving Goffman, which, crucially, introduces the *performative* dimension of verbal interaction.

4.1 Footing

As we have seen, in Transcript 3 the IE, Nicholas Soames, adopts a strategy to avoid answering the IR's first question. This involves reformulating the question in a stronger version (speaking *for* the Prince of Wales) which would be problematic on Quality grounds. NS then shifts the agenda to speaking for himself: 'for my own part as an interested observer'. Now, the veracity of his own opinion cannot be doubted, and indeed it is not challenged by the IR, Jeremy Paxman. In this move NS is also exploiting a communicative strategy described by Goffman (1981) as a shift of 'footing', which here has to do with the question of on whose behalf one might legitimately speak. A similar issue, though with the opposite effect, is apparent in the footings adopted by news IRs, and made explicit in Transcript 6 by Robin Day. In their institutional roles IRs do *not* speak on their own behalf, for they are not the originators of the questions they ask.

In his influential essay on footing, Goffman was interested in the complexities of participation in acts of communication. He observed that these complexities take us beyond a notion of everyday communication as interaction between two unitary entities, 'sender' and 'receiver'. The 'participation framework' for communication is more complicated than that. For instance, as far as receivers are concerned, there is a difference between the intended recipient of an utterance (or the 'ratified listener') and the 'eavesdropper' to an exchange between others. Eavesdroppers are on an unratified recipient footing which may be less legitimate and even uncomfortable. This carries interesting implications for the position of the 'overhearing audience' of broadcasting to which we shall return (in Chapter 6).

Speaking too is a complex process involving the employment of different footings. To begin with, Goffman suggests, we must recognise that this is a multidimensional activity, involving an *animator*, an *author* and a *principal*. The animator is the source of the speech (usually, though of course not necessarily, a person); the author is the originator of the words being spoken and the principal is the entity on behalf of which the speech is being made. The different footings taken up by speakers involve the exploitation of relations between these dimensions of speaking. In everyday speech, most of the time, speakers animate words of which they themselves are the authors and (like NS) they speak on their own behalf. In Goffman's terms, they engage in 'fresh talk' where animator, author and principal coincide. However, a moment's reflection will confirm that this is not always the case: it is perfectly possible to animate the words of others (e.g. by quoting, or animating another author's script); also it is possible not to speak for oneself, but on behalf of a wider entity (such as an institution or a political party).

In Transcript 6, RD makes it clear that he is not the author of his questions and that he is not speaking for himself. This is the 'neutral' footing which comes with this pre-allocated role (Clayman 1992). Note, however that, in this analysis, 'footing' and 'role' are two quite different concepts – for it is possible to be in this role (as a social position) and still utter the odd personal statement ('I'm not suggesting anything'). Nevertheless the neutral footing not only demands that RD recycles other peoples' statements and questions, it also requires him to do this on behalf of the audience. This is most explicit in lines 47–52, and I shall argue later that it is very significant that RD defines the audience here as a 'public'. The 'we' in line 51 clearly aligns the IR with the audience in these terms: 'we all' are members of 'the public' and RD is speaking for us, in his capacity as a 'public service' broadcaster.

His work on 'footing' is an example of Goffman's interest in everyday speech as a kind of performance. Thus far, we have seen that CA primarily focuses on the accomplishment of (orderly) interaction, whilst Pragmatics offers a framework for mutual interpretation. The interactional sociology of which Goffman was a pioneering exponent takes a 'ritualistic' view of social interaction in which participants are invariably playing, and not simply occupying, social roles. Shifts of footing constitute one such type of 'play', and the dramaturgical metaphor here is significant. Like the ethnomethodologists, Goffman was primarily interested in the inter-subjective resources for accomplishing social interactions. His particular take on this, however, was a focus (derived from phenomenology) on the notion of the 'self'. The self is an identity assumed by a person, rather like a mask, which is projected and performed in interactive encounters with others (Goffman 1959).

In the case studies which follow this chapter, I will be suggesting that there is much more to media talk than the fulfilment of pre-allocated roles. There is, to use the popular idiom, a question of how people 'come across' within these roles, in the light of their constant scrutiny by the overhearing audience. We have previously touched on this point in our discussion of Horton and Wohl, where it is recognised that TV performers construct identities to engage with the audience. Horton and Wohl define these identities as 'personae', and subsequently the concept of 'personality' has been seen to be central to the conduct of broadcasting (Langer 1981; Tolson 1991). In my view, Goffman's work is particularly useful for exploring this performative dimension, particularly where, in many contexts in contemporary broadcasting, there is an injunction to 'come across' as 'oneself' (see Tolson 2001c and Chapters 8 and 9 below). More generally, the 'personae' adopted by performers on radio and TV can be seen as professionalised versions of the identities we all project in everyday life.

4.2 Face

As Goffman (1967) also pointed out, a key factor in the maintenance of identity in everyday life is our attention to the question of 'face'. This is Goffman's term for what we might call self-esteem, or a sense of self-worth, which is constantly at risk in social interactions. Here, it is possible to 'lose face', or conversely to 'save face', in situations which are potentially threatening. Goffman argues that there are two kinds of 'face', positive and negative. Positive face is the need to be well liked, to have one's positive sense of self endorsed by others. Negative face is the desire to avoid trouble, or situations which might involve stress, or unwanted obligations.

Goffman's concept of face has been adopted and extended in discourse analysis through Brown and Levinson's (1987) work on 'politeness' (key extracts from both sources are reproduced in Jaworski and Coupland 1999: Chapters 18 and 19). Utterances which are potentially damaging to a co-participant's self-esteem are known as 'face threatening acts' (FTAs). These can be performed in two ways, either 'on record' (where they are explicit) or 'off record' (where they can be inferred through implicature). In addition, they may be stated 'baldly' or they can be mitigated by 'redressive action'. Clearly a 'bald on record' FTA is the most threatening kind; but generally, in ordinary conversation, because there is a preference for politeness (and remember that Grice's co-operative principle is assumed to operate) speakers opt for strategies of indirectness and mitigation.

At this point, the interest in face and politeness begins to focus on a range of features of spoken discourse which are discussed across all of its contributory perspectives. Where the principle of politeness is in place (and Brown and Levinson argue that it is universal) spoken discourse is, as it were, 'packaged' with the face of other parties in mind. To illustrate this, let us take one further look at Transcript 3, and, in particular, the seemingly nervous, hesitant behaviour of Nicholas Soames. Previously we have accounted for this by reference to Grice's maxim of Quality, suggesting that NS may be hesitant to say things for which he lacks evidence. But to state that the Princess of Wales is suffering from paranoia is also to stretch the boundaries of what it is polite, in public, to say. Indeed the fact that this is a public event puts a particular premium on the politeness principle, for there are now two senses in which this suggestion is 'on record'. The fact that it is a public statement adds particular force to the fact that it is explicit, in Brown and Levinson's schema. Observe then, the way NS packages this utterance:

```
Transcript 3 (extract)
NS: Well I I hope not but I I can't account for what the Princess
    was talking about when she referred to to to those matters for
    example like mail interception I mean I simply don't know what
    she's talking about and about telephones being tapped and all
    that it really is sort of the advanced stages of paranoia.
```

The use of items like *I mean* and *sort of* is referred to in discourse analysis as 'hedging'. Hedges 'mitigate' or lessen the force of utterances: it makes a difference to say 'sort of ... paranoia' because this makes the controversial claim less categorical (and indeed makes it less likely that the Princess will sue for slander). That, plus the stuttering hesitancy, suggests that NS is alive to the possibility that this could be seen as an insult. In this context, 'I mean' is also a hedge used to lessen the force of his argument. It is also very interesting because it is a way of packaging the argument interactively for the response of his co-participant. When we hear 'I mean' attached to an argument we are less likely to contradict it because the hedge makes it clear that this is a personal perspective (the 'animator' is also on the 'author' footing). To take issue would then be to threaten the positive face of the person making the argument.

Connected to this, we will also note in passing a feature of ordinary conversation known as 'sympathetic circularity' (see Montgomery 1986a: 110). Here utterances are packaged in such a way that they seem positively to invite a response from the listener, typically by the insertion of items such as *you know, know what I mean?*, or tag questions at the end of statements: 'that's typical of her *isn't it?*'. Such devices often provoke minimal responses from their recipients ('mm', 'uhuh' etc.) demonstrating mutual affiliation, as well as an invitation for the speaker to continue. It has been claimed by some sociolinguists (Bernstein 1971) that sympathetic circularity is a feature of working-class, idiomatic speech, in its presumption of a shared social world and set of values ('common sense'). Because it presupposes agreement, *know what I mean?* is very difficult to contradict. We might also expect that such affiliative features are unlikely to occur in the formal, adversarial context of a news interview and indeed they are absent from Transcripts 3 and 6 (but not from the more 'conversational' styles of news interview we will consider in the next chapter).

At any rate, when we begin to look at this 'packaging' element in the delivery of turns, we become sensitised to a whole level of discourse practice which can easily be overlooked. In spoken discourse, there is a liberal use of words like *well, I mean, sort of, oh* and *er*. It is too simple to reduce these to the notion of 'fillers', employed by speakers to retain the floor while they think of what to say next. They may sometimes have this function, but they also operate as 'discourse markers' which regulate the interactive impact of an utterance. Discourse markers are detachable from the point of an utterance; that is, their removal does not change the literal meaning but it does affect the interactive force. Hedges serve to mitigate that force, particularly when 'face' is at stake – as do the more formal phrases uttered by NS such as 'with great respect' and 'it seems to me'.

Of course it may also be the case that speakers do not intend the impact of their statements to be mitigated. In this respect, we might observe the marked absence of any hedging when, in Transcript 6, MT produces a derogatory comment on RD's role and footing (line 91). Here, presumably, there is an intention to produce a 'bald on record' FTA, to which the IR, noticeably, does not respond. In Transcript 3, we can also observe that NS packages no less than five of his responses (lines 23, 26, 34, 44 and 48) with the adverb 'simply'. To say 'I *simply* don't know' is to attempt to foreclose further argument or questioning. It is the categorical version, carrying the implication that the answer is complete and unequivocal. A linguistic term that is sometimes used to define this 'packaging' of utterances, whether in weaker or stronger versions, is *modality*. The modality of statements can be made more or less categorical, through the use of discourse markers and other grammatical features such as verb forms and adverbs, such as 'simply'.

In all of this, the key points again are that spoken discourse is highly interactive and, as Goffman understood, personal identities are at stake. Verbal performances are calibrated, whether politely or deliberately hostile, towards the identities of a speaker's 'self' and of other parties to a conversation. Running through all this, however, is a further overarching principle discovered in ordinary conversation by the practitioners of CA. We have said that there is a preference for politeness, and that 'bald on record' FTAs are rare, other than in unusual, ritualised contexts (Labov 1972). CA has demonstrated a more general point, that in ordinary conversation there is a 'preference for agreement' (Hutchby and Wooffitt 1998: 43–6). That is to say, second turns are generally designed in terms of the 'preferred response' to a prior turn, where it can be said that a particular type of response would normally be expected. Where these expectations are not met, and the preferred response is not forthcoming, then this will be marked in the discourse (by pauses, hesitations, discourse markers and the like). Generally speaking, in ordinary conversation, 'co-operativeness' is the norm.

4.3 Frames and Genres

Towards the end of his (April 1984) interview with Mrs Thatcher, and immediately following the heated exchange in Transcript 6, Robin Day initiated a change of topic. He raised the question of MT's personal ambitions as leader of her party. Here's how that topic develops:

```
Transcript 7
    RD:  Mrs Thatcher do you intend to lead the Conservative
         Party into the next election in say '87?
    MT:  I hope so.
    RD:  Because if you do that and let's say that the next
5        election is in the autumn of 1987 do you realise then
         that you would have been, held the office of Prime
         Minister for a longer, for the longest continuous period
         of this century and possibly long before that?
    MT:  Yes.
10  RD:  Eight and a half years and you'll be [six
    MT:                                       [Not very long
    RD:  Eight and a half years.
    MT:  Yes it's not very long if you look back to other times
    RD:  And you'll be sixty two. You still think you want to go
15       ahead at the next election?
    MT:  Yes. I shall be a very fit sixty two. You might be a
         little nearer that than I am but you feel all right?
    RD:  hhh forgive me if I don't answer that question Prime
         Minister, towards the end of this interesting interview.
```

In a previous discussion of this extract (Tolson 1991) I suggested that what was going on here might be understood in terms of the concept of *genre*. I was interested in the increasingly common practice of shifting between different types of speech (formal/informal; serious/humorous etc.) in the same discursive context. For instance, I was aware of the prevalence of banter between guests and hosts in celebrity talk shows of that period (in particular *Wogan, circa* 1984–5), and Transcript 7 seems to indicate that even a formal news interview might contain moments of 'chat'. Clearly we have to recognise that various strategies are available to IEs when they pose questions to IRs, and some of these are not simply confrontational. Nor does the reaction of RD to MT's question in lines 16–17 suggest that this is simply out of order. The humorous exchange here gives the news interview another level of apparently spontaneous entertainment. I still think the concept of genre is relevant, but now I want to introduce this via another concept derived from the work of Goffman.

In *Frame Analysis* (1974) Goffman argues that participants in social interactions are always faced with the question 'what is going on here?'. He is interested in the transformations of experience that occur when what we thought was going on turns out not to be the case, such as the con-trick or 'fabrication', or when something we thought was serious activity turns out to be playful. This is discussed in terms of a shifting of *frame*, where this concept refers to our understanding of the type of activity in which we are engaged. Less radical than a complete break of frame is the notion of 'key-shifting' within a frame, a notion which Goffman defines as follows:

a set of conventions by which a given activity, one already meaningful in terms of some primary framework, is transformed into something patterned on this activity but seen by the participants to be something quite else. The process of transcription can be called keying. A rough musical analogy is intended. (1974: 43–4)

I now want to suggest that this notion of 'keying' can be applied not only to news interviews but also to many other forms of media talk. A news interview is the 'primary framework' which the participants in Transcripts 6 and 7 understand themselves to be accomplishing in their pre-allocated roles. From time to time, however, a key-shift occurs within this frame, which might be defined as 'getting personal'. This key-shift can take different inflections: it can be confrontational (as in Transcript 6) or it can be playful (as in Transcript 7). The normative approach to news interviews taken by Heritage and Greatbatch would suggest that 'getting personal' is transgressive behaviour and they would point to the fact that the IR, in his capacity as manager of this event, prefers not to answer MT's question, and tries to move on (Transcript 7: lines 18–19). However, close analysis shows that RD does in fact respond, momentarily, with a chuckle (hhh). The primary framework for the interview has not therefore been broken, but a brief shift of key has occurred.

Much the same sort of point was made by the Russian literary theorist, Mikhail Bakhtin, who was writing several years prior to the development of interactional sociolinguistics. In his essay 'The Problem of Speech Genres', Bakhtin (1986) argues that all speech communication is generically defined, but also that speech genres can be 're-accentuated'. He makes a distinction between relatively formal and restricted speech genres (of which the news interview might be an example) and more informal, open conversational practices. Even the formal speech genres can be re-accentuated, in, for instance, 'nuances of intonation' which 'express the speaker's individuality' and where, for example, formal speech can carry 'parodic-ironic re-accentuation'. However, Bakhtin's discussion of the genres of everyday conversation is particularly interesting and insightful:

In addition to these standard genres, of course, freer and more creative genres of oral speech communication have existed and still exist: genres of salon conversations about everyday, social, aesthetic, and other subjects, genres of table conversation, intimate conversations within the family, and so on. (No list of oral speech genres yet exists, or even a principle on which such a list might be based.) The majority of these genres are subject to free creative reformulation ... But to use a genre freely and creatively is not the same as to create a genre from the beginning: genres must be fully mastered in order to be manipulated freely. (1986: 80)

There are two points to be drawn from this quotation. The first is the general point about generic 'mastery' and 'manipulation'. Here, though he is dealing with similar issues, Bakhtin takes a slightly different approach to that taken by Goffman. Whereas Goffman's first question is about understanding and defining the primary frame, Bakhtin is interested in how, from the perspective of the speaker, this can be creatively and strategically 'reformulated'. It is a short step from this to suggest that verbal performances (where, as Goffman emphasises, self-identities are at stake) will inevitably involve some orientation to the rules of the game, or speech genre, being played. This is very pertinent to media talk where speakers are concerned, not just with their co-participants, but with coming across as an effective 'player' for the overhearing audience. As we have seen, MT is prepared to engage in face-threatening activity in order to manipulate the news interview to her advantage.

Secondly, however, Bakhtin's comment about a 'list' of speech genres is intriguing. In fact Bakhtin himself was not averse to starting such lists, as indicated here in his distinction between 'salon', 'table' and 'intimate' conversations. The relevance of this for media talk is that it connects with our primary point: though it is institutional, because of the way it is obliged to address its audience, media talk is also highly 'conversational'. It routinely makes use of the speech genres of ordinary conversation, including those mentioned by Bakhtin, but these are institutionally transformed and strategically manipulated by participants. Some of these genres include: stories, jokes, gossip, chat, witty repartee, banter, teasing and flirting, and of course selling and promoting all kinds of 'products' (including oneself, as a 'personality').

In this book, we will regularly encounter speech events in which we can observe the conversational re-accentuation of institutional frames. What many professional participants are particularly skilled at doing is introducing the genres of everyday conversation into the performance of their pre-allocated roles. It is what speakers achieve within the institutional constraints that matters – their shifts of footing and key, and their re-accentuation of genres. An institutional format (such as news interview, current affairs debate, DJ talk, talk show) thus provides a primary framework for the credible, entertaining and, above all, 'lively' performance of talk, which, to repeat, must have an interactive and interpersonal orientation. It is, in Bakhtin's terms, 'dialogical', which is to say, formulated with an addressee in mind.

Indeed, I think we might give the penultimate word in this chapter to the remarkably prescient Bakhtin. As you read this quotation, consider its particular relevance for broadcasting, with its 'double articulation' to two addressees, including the overhearing audience.

An essential (constitutive) marker of the utterance is its quality of being directed to someone, its *addressivity* ... This addressee can be an immediate participant-interlocutor in an everyday dialogue, a differentiated collective of specialists in some particular area of cultural communication, a more or less differentiated public, ethnic group, contemporaries, like minded people ... and so forth ... All these varieties and conceptions of the addressee are determined by that area of human activity and everyday life to which the given utterance is related. Both the composition and, particularly, the style of the utterance depend on those to whom the utterance is addressed, how the speaker (or writer) senses and imagines his addressees, and the force of their effect on the utterance. Each speech genre in each area of speech communication has its own typical conception of the addressee, and this defines it as a genre. (1986: 95)

In these terms then, the various forms of talk to be heard on radio and TV have a particular generic structure targetted at a 'typical conception of the addressee'. This dialogical perspective, which Bakhtin was the first to enunciate, will inform our analysis in the case studies that follow.

Note

1. Actually extended formal 'news interviews', of the sort described by Heritage et al. in the 1980s, no longer occur in regular news bulletins. They have survived as a feature of longer news and current affairs programmes (such as BBC2 *Newsnight*, Channel 4 News) where selected news items are followed up by further analysis and debate.

Part Two
Case Studies

3   News Talk

1. Introduction

The previous two chapters have introduced key concepts and methodological principles for the analysis of media talk. On the whole, because this is where the bulk of the pioneering work was done, the focus of attention has been on 'news talk', especially the format defined by Heritage et al. as the 'news interview'. However, before we proceed any further, it will be helpful to recall two caveats in our discussion of this work. The first of these is that the news interview format is rarely found in contemporary news bulletins; set-piece interviews consisting of a series of turns are more a feature of news magazine or current affairs programmes. Secondly, as we have already seen, in this context the *frame* of the interview is not as tight, or as 'normative', as Heritage et al. suggest. It is possible for the news interview to contain a variety of speech genres, from political speech making to conversational banter.

In this, and the chapters that follow, we will be looking at developments in media talk which have become increasingly apparent since the 1980s. We will see that some of the classic formats have been modified, particularly in response to institutional and cultural changes. A proliferation of channels with increasing competition for target audiences, and a corresponding search for new formats containing cheap-to-produce 'lively' talk – all this has transformed the landscape of media talk. Nowhere has this been more apparent than in the 'news interview', which is now much more than a format for the probing cross-examination of public figures. Indeed some contemporary news interviews raise really basic questions about what is meant, today, by the concept of 'news', and how we are expected to relate to the information contained in news bulletins.

These questions are not only brought into focus by news interviews, for they also relate to different styles of news presentation, which we will go on to consider. However, let us begin our exploration of contemporary news talk by retaining some continuity with the previous chapter, starting with a news interview which as an exceptional case, proves one of its basic rules.

2. Generic instability

Queen Elizabeth, the Queen Mother, died at 3 p.m. on Saturday 20 March 2002, aged 101. Because of her great age this event was not, of course, entirely unexpected, and it was widely known that the BBC had been working on its coverage (codename: 'operation lion') for several years. As is routine for such events, normal schedules were to be suspended, to make way for a rolling news programme, containing a pre-constructed documentary as well as live news and comment. Of course, it is a sign of the enormity of a news story (elite death or major catastrophe) that 'liveness' is still used in this way; the status of the event is confirmed by a sense of bearing collective witness to its occasion. What is also sometimes controversial in such coverage, however, is the question of what it is appropriate to see and to say. There is the problem of public intrusion on private grief and, where coverage is live, unscripted and unedited pressures are placed on broadcasters to produce appropriate forms of talk.

I have to say that when I turned on my TV at 5.45 p.m. that evening, I was expecting the BBC's coverage, with all its pre-planning, to be a model of slick professionalism. Instead, the first hour was faltering, and widely criticised. A furore broke out in the British press, led (for its own purposes) by the *Daily Mail*. Peter Sissons, the programme's anchor, was judged to be inappropriately dressed in a burgundy, not black, tie. Another focus for criticism was a live interview, by phone, carried out by Sissons with the Hon. Margaret Rhodes, the Queen Mother's niece. Sissons was accused of being disrespectful, but, as a detailed analysis of the transcript shows, it is more true to say that he was placed in an embarrassing and contradictory situation, apparently compromised by the values of his own profession:

```
Transcript 8
    PS:    For the moment er Daniel thank you I believe we have on
           the (.) phone the Queen Mother's niece Lady Margaret
           Rhodes erm (2.0) L-Lady Margaret erm a-a very sad day for
           the whole nation.
 5 Lady M: It is indeed I think that there has (.) really never been
           anybody who has (.) been held in such a huge amount of
           affection by such an enormous number of people as Queen
           Elizabeth. She was deeply loved (.) by all age groups and
           all kinds of people erm and I think there's a hole now
10         that will be very difficult to fill.
    PS:    W-when did you last see her?
    Lady M: I left at half past three this afternoon.
    PS:    Oh I see were you [were you
    Lady M:                  [I was there all day yeh
15 PS:     You were at her bedside
    Lady M: Yes
           (3.0)
    PS:    [It must have been
```

```
    Lady M: [=But she will just be greatly missed by everybody. She
20          was a wonderful wonderful person
            (1.5)
    PS:     It must have been a very private moment
            (2.0)
    Lady M: Sorry I didn't hear
25  PS:     It must have been a very private moment [Lady Margaret
    Lady M:                                         [Yes it was a
            very moving and very (.) very sad moment but luckily it
            was wonderfully peaceful
            (3.0)
30  PS:     And (.) without wishing to intrude too much who was
            there?
    Lady M: No I-I won't go into that it was just a few members of
            the family but the great thing was that the Queen was
            there.
35  PS:     And (1.5) after (1.5) y-you all came out (.) what
            happened then?
    Lady M: No I sorry I really don't want to go into those sort of
            details I just want to say how much she'll be missed and
            how much she was loved.
40  PS:     I appreciate [that=
    Lady M:              [thank you very much
    PS:                       =but can you just stay with us a moment
            and tell us a little more about what sort of a gap there
            will be in our national life?
45  Lady M: (.) Well I think there will be a huge gap because she was
            interested in so many things erm and had was patron of
            hundreds and hundreds of organisations (.) all of whom
            she helped with her work and all of whom she gave a
            devoted a great deal of attention to. Erm so all these
50          people will miss her hugely.
    PS:     And how how will her passing (.) affect the royal family
            and the way it's perceived [or is it too early to tell?
    Lady M:                            [Well I think that any family
            is sad when their mother and grandmother (3.0) d-dies it
55          it's just a sad-sadness for any family (2.5) particularly
            so for them.
    PS:     It was a (.) a tremendous life.
    Lady M: It was a wonderful life spanning a whole more than a
            hundred years and one can hardly believe that somebody
60          who grew up in the horse age (.) erm has er seen has seen
            people landing on the moon and (.) hh all the things that
            happen now.
    PS:     And as we celebrate th-the life Lady Margaret what will
            what when you recall it what will give you most joy?
65  Lady M: Just her as a person (.) She was just a wonderful a
            wonderful person to know that we'll we'll almost never
            see the like of again. She just was wonderful.
    PS:     Lady Margaret Rhodes=
    Lady M:                     [I think that's really all I need to
70          say (.) thank you
    PS:                       [=we're very grateful for you to come
            on the line like this. Thank you.
```

Whether or not this interview can be judged to be 'disrespectful', it is apparent that it is conducted with a great deal of difficulty. Throughout the interview, a look of embarrassment is etched on Sissons's face, which is confirmed by several features of the talk. There are numerous hesitations, but also lengthy pauses between (lines 17, 21, 23, 29) and during turns (lines 35, 54–5), indicating that what is to follow might be problematic, or in CA terms 'dispreferred'. On a couple of occasions (lines 24 and 37) Lady M's dispreferred responses are mitigated by apologies, preserving a modicum of politeness. Equally, however, she is also prepared to interrupt Sissons (lines 19, 41, 69–70) particularly where it is apparent that her 'thank you's are intended as closing moves. Nevertheless, on the first of these occasions her closing move is rejected by Sissons who, for his purposes, very much wants this interview, however problematic, to continue.

What might these purposes be, that they can override the difficulties apparent in these exchanges? In terms of the standard practices for news interviewing, a very significant event occurs in line 13, where Sissons, the interviewer (IR), produces a news receipt ('Oh I see'). Heritage's (1985) analysis of news interviews insists that such utterances are inappropriate because they cast the IR as a primary recipient, whereas it is his role to elicit information on behalf of the overhearing audience. In this institutional role it is important that the expressions of personal reaction or alignment, which are routinely offered in ordinary conversation, are avoided. Here, however, Sissons reveals that it is news to him that Lady M was present at the bedside. Subsequent press coverage of this incident confirmed that he had not been properly briefed, for on this, the Easter holiday weekend, only a skeletal production team was available. More to the point, however, it is also clear that Sissons views this as a journalistic opportunity where Lady M can add some further detail to the narrative of this sad event.

The most excruciating moments of this interview then occur as Sissons invites Lady M to move from a public to a private terrain. The prompt itself, as a redundant statement of the obvious ('It must have been a very private moment', line 22) attests to the difficulty here. Clearly Lady M has no desire to enter the experiential territory which Sissons, however hesitantly, now wishes to explore. Her initial reaction to the prompt ('Sorry I didn't hear') is capable of two interpretations: it could be a straightforward apology, or it could be a very polite way of saying that she cannot indeed believe what she is hearing. The shifting news agenda is introducing a level of personal familiarity which she evidently wants to resist; and the fact that her resistance is expressed in a hearably aristocratic tone of voice serves to confirm the sense of inappropriateness.

Taking a broader view, I think this is an example of a news interview which has become generically unstable. That is to say, whatever infelicities might have contributed to its production, what is ultimately produced is a clash of speech genres. Lady M appears on the programme as a representative of the family to make a public tribute. Sissons, however, opportunistically, spots a potential scoop: Who was there? What happened next? That this would involve an invasion of privacy which would be impolite and even face-threatening is betrayed by the very bizarre construction of the prompt, which Lady M either does not, or affects not, to hear. In the end, with her steadfast refusal to be drawn down this route, Lady M succeeds in returning to her tribute. But there remains the question of what is driving the journalistic agenda, in moments such as this, to the manifest discomfort of the journalist himself.

3. News as narrative

One place to look for an answer to this question is the type of discourse which is produced when journalists talk to each other. Nowadays news programmes of all kinds contain dialogues, which are not interviews with public figures or institutional spokespersons, but rather exchanges with other journalists working for the same organisation. Foreign correspondents do not simply file reports, they are interviewed in live two-way satellite links. Routinely, they are invited to speculate about what they have just reported. Domestic journalists, either in the studio or on location, do not simply address the audience, they also respond to questions put by the presenter. Typically, the conduct of such 'interviews' is very far from the probing cross-examination of public figures with its more-or-less hostile formulations. For the journalists are on a mutually understood terrain, and, as we would expect, their talk is noticeably more co-operative. Often it becomes a way of investing the facts of a story with 'informed speculation' or even dramatic reconstruction, for the benefit, of course, of the overhearing audience.

On the day following the Queen Mother's death, the BBC's royalty correspondent, Jennie Bond, appeared on the evening news, where she was 'interviewed' by its presenter Fiona Bruce:

```
Transcript 9
      FB:  ... and Jennie Bond is at Windsor. Jennie you've been
           talking to people who were with the Queen Mother in her
           last days, indeed in her last moments.
      JB:  (.) Mm yes that's right. And I think they all knew that
   5       the fight back from the chest infection she got at
           Christmas was going to be a very very long haul, and
           she was getting frailer by the day. Erm in the last few
           days she became very breathless and that was a big '
           problem for her. And also of course she hadn't really
  10       been eating anything more perhaps than soup for a few er
           some weeks. Yesterday morning she was still able to talk.
```

```
           She was er lying in a large armchair and er talking to
           close members of her family. Er, at one point she did ask
           the Queen not to stay erm, the thought is that she knew
   15      at that stage that her life was er ebbing away(.) The
           Queen did return though at a quarter to three and er it
           was with the Queen at her side and other close members of
           her family erm and they were holding hands that she er
           died very peacefully. And I'm told that that peace was
   20      reflected today on the Queen Mother's face. Erm, someone
           who saw her before her body was placed in the coffin said
           she was dressed very beautifully. She had her pearls on
           and her earrings and erm she looked incredibly beautiful.
       FB: And, Jennie, did she have any sense you know, in the last
   25      few days (.) that the end was close?
       JB: (.) Well I think she probably did. Erm, she'd become
           rather reclusive, which was not characteristic at all in
           the last few weeks, she didn't want to see very many
           people. And er, those that she saw said something else
   30      had changed and that she began to reminisce a great deal
           in the way a lot of old people do (.) but it was
           something the Queen Mother erm hadn't done very much in
           the past. She wanted to talk a lot about Princess
           Margaret who died of course just erm seven weeks ago (.)
   35      Erm one other pointer perhaps to the fact that she knew
           the end was near was the day before she died, on Friday,
           she handed out a number of small presents to er very
           close members of her family who are now of course
           mourning her loss.
   40  FB: Jennie, thank you very much.
```

Evidently, the BBC was very keen to broadcast an account of the deathbed scene and, if Lady M was not going to provide this, the task would fall to Jennie Bond. Her account is based on unattributed information from sources close to the event, an interesting linguistic reflection of which is the use of the definite article ('the thought') in line 14. This avoidance of attribution, together with the passive voice ('I'm told') mitigates her authorship of the account; but it also creates a space for Bond to deliver a crucial journalistic requirement. Her account is both a report based on what she has been told and a narrative reconstruction of the scene.

Later we will look at the use of narratives in other forms of broadcast talk. This is not a fully-fledged oral narrative based on personal experience, nor is it an anecdote designed to exemplify the character of a famous person. However, though this narrative is, by comparison, somewhat truncated, it does contain some of the key features of oral narrative, as defined in William Labov's much-quoted model (Labov 1972).[1] Thus, in her first turn, Bond begins by giving some background information ('orientation') to the Queen Mother's state of health and her physical situation. She then, at line 13, proceeds to key events ('complicating action') particularly the absence and then the presence of the Queen. Finally Bond delivers what in Labov's terms is a 'coda': a statement of the climax of the narrative and its main point, the sense of peacefulness. This is reinforced (from line 19) by a description of the deceased's appearance, which takes the form of a rhetorical list of three ('pearls ... earrings ... beautiful', lines 22–3) and which is almost elegiac in its effect.

On closer inspection, however, the import of this narrative is paradoxical. Certainly, on one level, it serves to elevate the event, giving it a poetic quality as a 'moment of history'. On the other hand, however, the event is humanised by a familiar (from novels, films etc.) imagined family scenario. This element of the familiar, even the 'ordinary', is retained through Bond's second turn where the Queen Mother is characterised as a typical old person (line 31). There is an element of this also in Lady M's account (Transcript 8: line 53) where, even though she is not prepared to reveal the details, she is willing to humanise the family, in terms with which 'any family' could identify.

Bond's account, though, is based on second-hand information rather than direct experience or knowledge. With such accounts it is always interesting to examine the way they handle the maxim of Quality, and there are three aspects to this. First, and routinely, journalists defend the quality of such second-hand information in terms of the credibility of their sources: they might not have been there but their sources were, which counts as 'proper evidence' in this context. Secondly, however, where these accounts drift into speculation, which in this extract is almost inevitable following FB's question (Transcript 9: lines 24–5), this can be mitigated by shifts to less-definite forms of modality, here using adverbs like 'probably' (line 26) and the preposition 'perhaps' (lines 10, 35). The shift of modality modifies the speaker's personal commitment to statements of which she is the author.

Overwhelmingly, however, any doubts about the credibility of this second-hand account are dispelled by its apparent plausibility. With its familiar scenario, the narrative lends weight to this, as do commonsense references to 'what everyone knows' about old people. In news talk, such kinds of discourse are crucial in the construction of 'human interest', designed to lend additional colour to the reporting of facts and the delivery of public statements. Where those involved in the events are reluctant to do this, the journalists must step in – and it is noticeable that they do this in the most collaborative of environments where they are on first-name terms with each other and predisposed to produce preferred responses. Such is the force of this preference that Bond can only answer FB's question in the affirmative, even though this takes her into speculative territory. Clearly she is prompted to do this by the delivery of a question which recycles 'the thought' she herself reported in line 14, contains an element of sympathetic circularity ('you know') and, on the friendliest possible terms, addresses her by her christian name.

4. News as gossip

In more extreme versions of this type of journalistic exchange, news talk sometimes becomes a form of gossip. As a speech genre, 'gossip' has received much attention in work on spoken discourse, particularly from analysts interested in language and gender. Gossip has been traditionally defined as a species of 'women's talk' (Jones 1980; Coates 1989) but more recently it has been demonstrated that men too gossip on occasions (Cameron 1997). In this debate, something is at stake in the way gossip is defined: if, like narrative, it can be defined as a speech genre, its characteristics are nevertheless more difficult to define. In fact Cameron argues that gossip cannot be identified simply by its formal features, but also in terms of its content. In her definition it is 'discussion of ... persons not present but known to the participants, with a strong focus on critically examining these individuals' appearance, dress, social behaviour and mores' (1997: 446). In her view, the 'critical examination' is invariably negative, as co-participants form a collective identity which stigmatises those they are criticising.

In news talk, gossip occurs in exchanges between journalists, where previous news, already known to the participants, is up for further discussion. However, because this is produced not just for the participants themselves but also for an audience, it only works if the topic is already in the public domain. The audience must be included in the collective identity being affirmed. In this context at least, however, I would dispute Cameron's claim about the negativity of gossip, for it is also possible for a collective identity to be formed in admiration of the person discussed. Here gossip serves a useful purpose in the construction of fandom, where, for instance, the public appearances and actions of celebrities are routinely scrutinised.

Following her (1995) *Panorama* interview, the performance and appearance of Princess Diana was extensively discussed. We have previously observed how the content of some of her claims was interrogated on *Newsnight*, in classic 'news interview' fashion. However, not all news programmes take this form, nor are they designed for the same target audience. On the following day, another, very different kind of exchange took place on the ITV breakfast news magazine *GMTV*. In fact it took place at 9 a.m., just as the programme was passing from a news orientation to its morning magazine format, hosted by Lorraine Kelly, and targeted at a female audience. But this was still 'news talk' of a kind. From the studio Kelly had a live two-way link to Martin Frizell, then a regular journalist on the programme and subsequently its editor:

```
Transcript 10a
    LK:  Well more of that later on but first (.) well I was glued
         as the Princess of Wales admitted last night on
         television that she'd had an affair with former guardsman
         James Hewitt. So what happens next? Well Martin Frizell
 5       is outside her West London gym. Martin, she hasn't turned
         up this morning has she?
    MF:  Not yet erm (.) Lorraine but we expect she may well do
         because you have to remember she's off to Argentina
         tomorrow and er her routine is that she normally works
10       out before she goes off on a trip so she could still turn
         up this morning we're ever hopeful as you can see we're
         not alone (.) there are several members of her majesty's
         press (.) queuing up here with their ladders from Texas
         and B&Q they've had a field day erm up against the er the
15       fence to peer over and get a picture of her.
    LK:  Indeed I just wonder as a-as a sort of cynical old hack
         yourse:lf Martin. what did you think of it, what did you
         think of her performance and what did the rest of the
         boys and girls behind you think?
20  MF:  I think I speak for most of them >although they probably
         wouldn't say it because they still like to keep up the er
         the er appearance of being a hardened cynic< my jaw
         dropped (.) I'd seen hadn't seen anything like it befo:re
         probably because we'd never actually heard her speak but
25       also, what she was saying. Some of the revelations that
         came across (.) the post natal depression, the bulimia
         confirming everything that was in Andrew Morton's book
         because we (.) took it with a pinch of salt but there she
         was on screen, prime time, admitting it all. And also
30       the que:stions again (.) being a hardened cynical hack we
         had thought well she probably won't be asked about the
         love affairs all those sort of things and she was, and
         she an:swered. It was just the frankness that just
         astou:nded me.
35  LK:  I was, I was the same I was astou:nded about how frank
         she was and actually like you say the kind of questions
         that were ask:ed, because you know what it's like
         normally when you interview someone from the Royal
         Family, you really have got to it's usually they're there
40       to talk about their cha:rity work and nothing else:
    MF:  And al:so as you know Lorraine, er >we all, know those of
         us who work behind this side of the camera< erm appearing
         in front of a lens can be quite difficult. And these
         lenses don't really li:e. I think we would have known if
45       she was putting on on an act and she certainly didn't
         look like she was putting on an act to me.
```

Two principal features define this talk as 'gossip', over and above the precondition of shared knowledge of the person being discussed. The first feature is the high degree of mutual affiliation, which is absolutely the opposite of the neutrality normally displayed in the classic news interview.

Kelly's style of 'interviewing' involves her agreeing with everything an IE says, and she is particularly fond of the minimal response 'indeed'. Sometimes her question delivery doesn't actually deliver a question (lines 35–40) but a statement which recycles a point the IE has made (for example, 'like you say', line 36). In the same way MF recycles a characterisation made of him by LK ('hardened cynic', line 22), which might have been potentially face-threatening, but is of course interpreted as banter, partly because of LK's hedge ('sort of', line 16) and her metaphorical characterisation of the journalists as 'boys and girls' in line 19.

Most apparent, however is the construction of a collective identity between the journalists themselves. In this extract, there is a shifting use of the personal pronoun 'we' by MF, which starts as a reference to himself and his fellow journalists on location, but extends to encompass LK herself, as a fellow broadcaster. Here 'we' (who work on this side of the camera) 'would have known if she was putting on an act' (lines 44–5). This collective identity is further reinforced by a second feature of gossipy talk; its use of colloquialism and common cultural reference. There are two levels to this: first, there is the use of colloquial idiom in common circulation – 'my jaw dropped' (lines 22–3), 'pinch of salt' (line 28). But there is also an ironic characterisation of the profession, using terms like 'hack', reference to popular chains of DIY superstores, and the disingenuous label 'her majesty's press' (lines 12–13) which presumes a co-participant capable of reading its multiply ironic implicatures.

All of which raises an interesting question. To the extent that this talk is dedicated to mutual affiliation between members of the same profession, there is a danger of it setting up a barrier to the overhearing audience. There is a danger that the journalistic 'we' might become exclusive – for the audience of course would not have interviewed the Royal Family or worked behind the camera. But in fact MF starts to mitigate this effect in line 41, in the shift from 'you' (directed at Lorraine) to 'we all', which clearly is designed to explain to the audience what working behind a camera is like. But then, as these exchanges develop, a further interesting series of shifts occurs:

```
Transcript 10b
    MF: We were here yesterday morning watching her going in:to
        the gym and she must have known it was going to get a
        good reaction because she she almost skipped in she
50      bounded in smiling and she left as well smiling as well.
        And then last night we got some pictures of her last
        night at this fashion charity do for the cancer charity.
        She turned up there looking absolutely stunning, smiling,
        apparently er she was having a wonderful time to all
55      those people who were there she was mixing with Mickey
        Rourke and the wonderful supermodels too she thoroughly
```

enjoyed herself and waived and smiled to the cameras as
she left as well again [LK: mm] waiving to the cameras
which she talked about last night on the interview saying
60   they had given her such a hard time.
    LK: Indeed. There wa:s one omission and that was that we
        didn't hear anything and nothing was asked about Will
        Ca:rling. Were you surprised by that?
    MF: (0.3) No, although I thin:k she almost alluded to it
65   where she talked about erm the men who come across her
        door at Kensington Palace er the trouble that they seem
        to get into (.) and that's why she was saying she was
        qui- I think quite happy being on her ow:n there because
        of the trouble that men get into but, I mean (.) let's
70   forget about the Will Carling thing we had enough didn't
        we?
    LK: [hhh indeed
    MF: [the Hewitts, the Gilbey, the Oliver Hoare, it was all
        explai:ned
75 LK: It certainly was. Do we know what Cha:rles was doing
        where he was watching it or indeed any reaction at all
        from that camp?
    MF: Yes he was watching it at Highgrove last night the
        country home that he and Diana used to share (.) and of
80   course that was where Camilla held er held court so many
        times which really infuriated Diana, led her into that
        rampage of bulimia as she told us last night. He was
        watching it at Highgrove (.) and then in the middle of
        the night he left Highgrove to a railway halt, a siding
85   in Gloucestershire erm quite a dramatic scene got on to
        the royal train there in the dead of night, nobody else
        around boarded it quietly and it's taken him now down to
        Cornwall this morning where in just one hour's time it's
        his first public appearance since this came out he's
90   actually erm, at a fish er a fish quay in Newlyn.
    LK: Very glamorous for him Martin thank you very very much
        indeed thank you.

When, in line 51, MF starts to talk about last night's pictures of the Princess,
the clips are shown on the screen. Interestingly, what seems, as a live two-
way, to be developing spontaneously, turns out in part to have been
planned. As was mentioned in previous chapters, the question of the
scripting of 'liveness' is raised by some contemporary forms of media talk.
But also of course this allows the audience to see these images for
themselves; they are now included in the journalistic account. When LK in
line 61 produces another collective 'we', this is clearly not exclusive to
journalists but extends to include anyone who has heard the interview. And
when MF in lines 70–1 refers to 'we' who 'had enough didn't we?', is this
just a tag question addressed to LK, or is it, as it were through her, a
statement about all of us who avidly consume celebrity gossip and scandal?

I have previously argued (Tolson 2001b) that this kind of news talk is in the business of constructing a 'communal' identification between broad-casters and their audience. It presumes that 'we all' share similar interests and (mediated) information. Note here how the 'public sphere' has shifted, from the principle invoked in Transcript 6 by Sir Robin Day. There, the audience was cast as a public judge of statements which it was the responsibility of the IR to elicit. Here, the audience is encouraged into a position of vicarious co-participation in the collective fascination for royalty as celebrity. The 'we' produced by LK in Transcript 10b: line 75, is therefore *both* a reference to journalists *and* to a public knowledge which might be shared by all. MF is then only too willing to supply this, and once again his discourse takes a narrative turn.

We noted, in the previous section, that it is the purpose of narratives in news talk to embellish reports with 'human interest' in ways which at times might be speculative. We also observed, in Transcript 3, that Nicholas Soames refused to go down that route, citing the maxim of Quality in his defence. Here, in the context of gossipy news, MF has no such compunc-tions. Highgrove is characterised in terms reminiscent of soap opera, as the court of Camilla. The actions of Prince Charles are then narrated as a 'dramatic scene' which might be from a movie. It might have been the 'dead of night' but does anybody imagine that the Prince of Wales ever gets on a train with 'nobody else around'? Either by 'nobody else', Frizell is referring to the absence of the press, or he has simply made it up. But in the context of gossipy news, quality of information is not always the point. A 'good story' can be informative, but it can also be entertaining – and sometimes the latter takes precedence.

5. Conversational news presentation

The forms of talk illustrated by Transcripts 9 and 10 are indicative of two, possibly linked, developments in contemporary broadcast news. The first development is the tendency for 'two-way' exchanges between presenters and journalists to dominate the dialogical possibilities of news. As previously noted, extended 'news interviews' of the sort discussed by Heritage et al. now seem to be marginalised in many mainstream news bulletins: the voices of politicians and public figures are reduced to 'sound bites' and ordinary people appear in 'vox-pops' of minimal duration. Otherwise, apart from the longer news and current affairs programming, news talk is virtually monopolised by the broadcasters, talking to each other in ways that display their mutual affiliation.

The second point is then that these kinds of professional exchange are, to varying degrees, open to the possibility of informality. Anchors and journalists are obviously colleagues, they are on first-name terms, and their collective 'we' is supported by shared frames of reference. Their dialogue features colloquial idiom, sympathetic circularity and, at times, possibilities for humour, even banter. Transcript 10 presents an extreme form of this, in what is not, at this time of the day, a conventional news bulletin; but a degree of informality is generally apparent in live two-ways, on far more serious topics (Montgomery 2004). Such developments in news talk echo Fairclough's (1989, 1995b) argument about the 'conversationalisation' of public discourse, which he also extends to news (1995b, 1998). His point is that conversational forms of address are characteristic of 'marketised' public discourses, where the recipient is cast as a consumer. Health authorities, education, even the police, are now in the business of selling their services to potential customers. In the radio news programme (*Today*, BBC Radio 4) that Fairclough analyses, 'conversationalisation' is evident in a highly combative style of interviewing, where the IE (John Humphrys) takes the 'commonsense' perspective of the 'lifeworld'. His speech is highly colloquial, littered with conversational discourse markers (oh, well, right etc.) and in its collective 'we' adopts a populist footing shared with the audience.

In this section, I will suggest that there is much to commend Fairclough's general point, and indeed it is precisely applicable to my example. To fully appreciate this, however, we need to take the arguments about 'conversationalisation' a stage further than he, and other analysts, have left it. Hitherto (and this includes the previous sections of this chapter) attention has focused on the interviews and two-way exchanges which accompany news reports, rather than the presentation of reports themselves. It has been assumed that reports are still introduced by anchors in the traditional style – that is, relatively formal reading from a script – before being passed on, as it were, for further interrogation or speculative comment. In fact, in his work on the live two-way, Montgomery (2004) formalises this distinction (with my addition in italics):

Table 3.1

News Report	Live Two-Way
Scripted	Unscripted
Formal	Informal
Unmarked modality	Marked modality
Statements of fact	Statements of possibility
Descriptive	Interpretative
Institutional voice	Personal voice
Monologue	*Dialogue*
Then (past)	Now (live)
Here (studio)	There (in the field)

But in the highly competitive environment of contemporary broadcast news, these distinctions are breaking down. As we have noted, news is packaged in different forms, at particular times of the day, for different target audiences. In addition, new possibilities have been opened up by 24-hour rolling news, on dedicated news channels, both on radio and (in the UK) on non-terrestrial TV. There is not the space here to investigate all these possibilities (and there is scope here for much further study) but we can briefly note three main developments:

1. Extension of the practice of using two presenters (previously a preserve of local/regional TV news, having been imported from the USA) to national TV news bulletins, in the early evening 6–7 p.m. slot. In this format, the presentation of stories may be alternated, or they may be co-narrated, with each presenter taking a successive sentence or segment of the narrative.
2. Greater use of support personnel, or 'secondary presenters' – and not only in their traditional segments such as sports or the weather. The use of multiple presenters and studio personnel offers increasing opportunity for dialogic exchange, including interpersonal banter, and shifts into what Montgomery calls the 'personal voice'.
3. Increasing likelihood, particularly in 24-hour news, that 'breaking' stories will not have been fully scripted, so that presenters are obliged to extemporise over raw, unedited visual footage. As one very suggestive account puts it, this changes the form of representation of news from 'reporting' to an act of 'witnessing' (Carpignano et al. 1990). The discourse of the studio personnel takes the form of commentary on a piece of jointly witnessed live action, just like a sports event, and again it invokes the collective 'we' who share a common position of spectatorship.

Suffice it to say that practices of news presentation are now diverse, ranging from scripted monologue to experiments with various kinds of verbal performance, as they seek to engage with target audiences. To give one illustration of the last point, let us now consider a fairly recent addition to the repertoire of TV news, involving a novel use of the 'secondary presenter'. The BBC, which generally uses this in its early evening, 6 o'clock news bulletins, calls it the 'big screen' presentation. It was introduced in 2001 as a strategy, according to Fergus Walsh, one of its presenters, of making news more accessible. Indeed Walsh describes it as a form which is 'much more conversational than conventional VT'.[2]

It involves a secondary presenter, such as Walsh, standing in front of a graphic display, quite similar to the presentation of the weather. His performance mediates between the viewer and the screen by alternating direct and indirect address, to and from the camera, with occasional hand gestures in the screen's direction. Meanwhile the script, which is a collaborative production by Walsh and other production staff, is addressed to the viewer in a style which is much more direct and personal than a traditional news report. In these bulletins, therefore, rather than the traditional distinction between scripted reporting and unscripted dialogue, we now have a situation where the script itself is moving from a formal to a less-formal, conversational style. In 'big screen' presentations the script has become a hybrid of the two possibilities presented in Table 3.1 – a form of scripted conversationality:

```
Transcript 11
      GA:  So you can save money if you make the effort to shop
           around. Fergus Walsh is here. Fergus is it a complicated
           business changing your supplier?
      FW:  It's really not that difficult George [turns to camera]
   5       So why have millions of people, like me, simply not
           bothered to switch? Well it is a bit confusing the
           electricity supply market was opened up to competition
           four years ago. And there are now more than twenty
           suppliers. It doesn't matter where you live you can pick
  10       any of them. Now even supermarkets are getting in on the
           act. Sainsbury's is signing up customers for both gas and
           electricity promising big savings but shoppers told me
           they were sick of the hard sell.
                        [consumer vox pops]
           So switching really can save money and this is how you do
  15       it. The consumer body Energywatch has a simple guide on
           its website which shows exactly how much you could save.
           If it's easier you can give them a ring on this number.
           Now if you do decide to switch companies you have to
           contact the new supplier and agree a contract. Give your
  20       old electricity supplier twenty eight days notice and of
           course pay any outstanding bills. Remember to read the
           meter the day you switch. That's all there is to it.
           But even the best deals don't reflect the massive falls
           in the real price of electricity. The companies that
  25       generate electricity have slashed what they charge by a
           whopping forty percent. But not all those savings have
           been passed on by electricity suppliers.
                        [expert comment]
           So we've only ourselves to blame here. Most of us could
           have lower electricity bills but it seems we simply don't
  30       have the energy to switch suppliers. George
      GA:  Fergus thank you. Well to the United Nations now. Talks
           have just started on lifting the economic sanctions
           imposed on Iraq ...
```

In broad terms the verbal discourse of the big screen presentation is reminiscent of the characteristic forms of traditional of radio DJ talk (see Chapter 6). That is to say, it uses a highly personalised form of direct address, in which the speaker refers to himself as well as to his audience, and where the 'me' (lines 5, 12) together with the 'you' (used throughout) constitute a collective 'we' of electricity consumers (lines 28–30). A quasi-interactive exchange is offered to the viewer, reinforced by deictic markers of co-presence and, as here, using the screen to reinforce a set of instructions ('this is how you do it'). One routine feature of this quasi-interaction is the 'So ... Well' sequence, where the script answers its own rhetorical question (lines 5–6). It also makes extensive use of colloquial idiom ('the hard sell', line 13; 'whopping forty per cent', line 26) and it is not afraid to resort to the occasional jokey pun ('we don't have the energy', lines 29–30).

This particular big screen presentation followed a report on a review of electricity prices, carried out by a government-appointed watchdog. It was the first item in the bulletin, which, as we can see, preceded a report on the UN debate about economic sanctions on Iraq. It is perhaps not inappropriate to question what this might be indicating about the BBC's sense of its own news priorities. Indeed, by the time we reach Fergus Walsh, it is debatable whether we are still in the realms of 'news' at all, or have strayed into some kind of consumer advice programme. In fact, it would seem that the BBC has been reinterpreting aspects of its public service remit, to provide not only a public sphere of news and current affairs but also a quasi-educative function, which includes advice on consumer rights.

In some respects, this example would seem to offer a classic illustration of the 'conversationalisation of public discourse' in broadcast news. Not only does the big screen use conversational talk, it also uses this news item to reassert what Fairclough (1994) calls the 'authority of the consumer'. Indeed the marketisation of public services (here electricity) is taken as a political given, there is no residual debate about that, and, once again, no politicians are featured. Rather the agenda has shifted to the communal orientation; not, in this case, to a collective investment in celebrity gossip, but to a slightly more mundane interest in how much we all, as consumers, pay for 'our' electricity.

However, in his critical attitude to such developments, Fairclough, at times, takes a dubious theoretical stance. He refers to conversational public discourse as a form of 'ventriloquism', a kind of simulation of the voice of the ordinary person. He suggests that the relation between this simulated version and 'people's real conversation' is problematic (1998: 160), at times amounting to a manipulative strategy of pseudo-democratisation. It is clearly the case that there are political limits to the choices offered to consumers by this BBC news. But at the same time we need to remind ourselves that all broadcast talk is institutional talk, that it is a perform-ance, and, however 'conversational' it may be, it can never be 'ordinary conversation' as such. Nor, for that reason, is it any less 'real' or authentic than any other form of talk; indeed broadcasters like Fergus Walsh claim that they are extending the communicative entitlements of potential audiences.

A more constructive position, I think, will involve understanding the scope, but also the limits, of conversational discourse. To reiterate a very basic point: as far as news talk is concerned what seems to be occurring is a shift, perhaps an oscillation, between two different 'principals' on whose behalf the news is speaking. These are defined in terms of 'interests': there is the 'public interest' as traditionally conceived in public service broadcasting and a focus, as we have seen, for the formal news interview. But there is also a prevalent focus on a new kind of consumer-orientated 'human interest' in ordinary and extraordinary people. Contemporary news talk frequently addresses its audiences on the basis that 'we' all share this human interest, and are therefore avid consumers of the endless diet of speculative talk which the journalists produce to maintain it. But it takes the verbal equivalent of a slap on the wrist, such as that delivered by Margaret Rhodes, to insist that human interest ought to have its boundaries, and that there are necessary limits to the publicly sayable.

Notes

1. Further references to Labov's model for the speech genre of oral narrative are made below, in Chapters 3 and 7. Readers who are not familiar with this work might wish to turn to page 136 where the model is more fully explained.

2. Fergus Walsh was interviewed in 2002 by George Malsbury, a student of media studies at De Montfort University, for a research project on the use of 'big screen' presentations.

4 Political Talk

1. Presidential debate

The first of three debates between the candidates running for the US presidency in 2000 took place at the University of Massachusetts. It was billed as the most formal of the three, with later debates taking a more conversational and 'town hall' format. As such, the candidates were restricted to two-minute contributions on topics nominated by the chair, following a conventional sequence of primary and secondary statements, followed by rebuttals. In the event, as we shall see, these rules were not strictly adhered to. However, there is a further convention in such formal debates that participants should speak 'through' the chair. They should not directly address each other, but should refer to fellow debaters in the third person (though they can speak directly to the chair). Similarly presidential candidates tend to refer to the audience in third-person categories – as voters, taxpayers, or sometimes the 'American people'.

I thought it was interesting in 2000 that, even within these strict parameters, different debating strategies were pursued by George W. Bush and Al Gore. These differences are illustrated by Transcript 12, which contains the second statements by each candidate in response to the first question. The debate began with a question to Gore from the chair, Jim Lehrer, requesting his views on Bush's 'experience'. Gore's response to this involved a blatant agenda-shift on to his own and his opponent's taxation proposals, which Lehrer then 'formulated' in the classical manner, by way of occasioning the second statements:

```
Transcript 12
    JL: So I take it by your answer then Mr Vice-President that
        in your er an interview recently with the New York Times
        when you said that you questioned whether or not Vice-
        President er er Governor Bush was experienced enough to
  5     be president you were talking about strictly policy
        differences.
    AG: Er yes Jim (.) er I said that his tax cut plan for
        example raises the question o-of whether it's the right
```

```
        choice for the country and let me give you an example o-
 10     of what I mean. Under Governor Bush's er tax cut proposal
        (.) he would spend more money on tax cuts for the
        wealthiest one per cent than all of the new spending that
        he proposes for education, health care, prescription
        drugs and national defence all combined. Now I think
 15     those are the wro:ng priorities. Now under under my
        proposal, for every dollar that I propose in spending for
        things like education and health care (.) I will put
        another dollar into middle class tax cuts (.) And for
        every dollar that I spend in those two categories I'll
 20     put two dollars towards paying do:wn the national debt.
        I think it's very important to keep the debt going down
        and completely eliminate it. And I also think it's very
        important to go to the next stage of welfare reform. Our
        country has cut the welfare rolls in half (.) I've fought
 25     hard >from my days in the Senate and as Vice-President<
        to cut the welfare rolls and we've moved millions of
        people in America into good jobs but it's now time for
        the next stage of welfare reform and include fathers and
        not only mothers.
 30 JL: We're going to get to a lot of those - yes go ahead
        Governor
    GB: Well let me just say that er obviously tonight we're
        going to hear some (.) phoney numbers about what I think
        and what we ought to do erm (.) People need to know that
 35     over the next ten years there's going to be twenty-five
        trillion dollars of revenue (.) that comes into our
        treasury and we anticipate spending twenty-one trillion.
        And my plan says why don't we pass one point three
        trillion of that back (.) to the people who pay the
 40     bills? Surely (.) we can afford five per cent of the
        twenty-five trillion dollars that are come into the
        treasury to the hard working people who pay the bills
        there's a difference of opinion (.) My opponent thinks
        the government erm th-the surplus is the government's
 45     money that's not what I think. I think it's the hard
        working people in America's money and I wanna share some
        of that money with you (.) So you've got more money to
        build and share and dream for your families it's a
        difference of opinion. It's a difference between
 50     government making decisions for you and you getting more
        of your money to make decisions for yourself.
```

To be sure, I have chosen this extract because it highlights the differences I want to illustrate. There are many instances in this ninety-minute debate where both candidates are arguing in a similar fashion and within the formal conventions. Here, however, it is apparent that Bush shifts the form of his address to the audience from the third-person category 'hard working people' to the second person 'you' (lines 45–7, 50) and 'your families' (line 48). In the course of this debate as a whole, Bush uses this strategy fifteen times, three times more often than Gore; and moreover when Gore does use the second person this is often in a more ritualised context (for example, 'if you entrust me with the presidency'). On one occasion Bush even refers to the audience at home as 'folks'. He is also, as he says this, looking directly at the camera.

Different degrees of formality are also apparent in the ways the two candidates make their arguments. In Aristotelian terms, we might say that Gore's rhetoric shows a strong commitment to the *logos*, that is, to reasoned propositions supported by secondary arguments and statistical evidence. The discourse marker 'I think' regularly punctuates these propositions, and Gore often refers to his supporting arguments as 'examples'. By contrast Bush produces here an argument which is more slanted towards *ethos*, or moral reasoning (indicated by the discourse marker 'surely' in line 40), with perhaps even a suggestion of *pathos* in the concept of hard-working people dreaming for their families. That some kind of emotional impact is intended here is confirmed by the fact that Bush deploys two of the rhetorical strategies designed to provoke applause, or 'claptrap' as discussed by Atkinson (1984). There is, in lines 47–8, a list of three ('to build and share and dream for your families') which is followed by a contrast (lines 49–51) where the second option ('to make decisions for yourself') is rhetorically preferred.

There is also a quite remarkable shift of footing (Goffman 1981) in Bush's statement. Clearly, in Goffman's terminology, the dominant footing throughout is that of the 'author', where both candidates are speaking for and on behalf of themselves. But in line 38 Bush shifts his footing to 'animate' his plan. Remarkably, though this is an inanimate entity, Bush's plan now speaks through him and, moreover, it asks a rhetorical question. In the previous chapter we noted the use of rhetorical questions, combined with direct verbal address, in conversational public discourse with a consumer orientation. It might be argued that 'I wanna share some of that money with you' makes a similar kind of gesture. This is quite different from Gore's 'next stage of welfare reform'. It is, to continue the metaphor, a difference of packaging, with Bush much more attuned to what has been termed the use of 'promotional discourse' in political communication (Wernick 1991).

It is probably unwise to claim any linkage between this kind of verbal performance and Bush's eventual victory. There is a mythology surrounding the importance of presidential debates, ever since the much quoted Kennedy–Nixon event of 1961. From the perspective of discourse analysis, however, we perhaps could make the more limited claim that Bush's more direct and conversational style in 2000 was perfectly consonant with the image he was trying to project – that of the provincial Texan in touch with 'ordinary folks'. His contributions to the debate frequently drew a distinction between that background and the 'Washington' identification of his opponent. In short this was old-fashioned Republican populism, where the direct sales pitch was a significant part of the package.

2. Party election broadcasts

In the UK, to date, we have yet to stage formal debates between party leaders, largely because parties in power have judged them to be too risky a venture. What we have, instead, is that very peculiar TV genre, the party election broadcast (PEB). These are allocated time slots, available to all political parties fielding a minimum number of candidates at a general election, with additional slots available to the major parties, determined by their share of the vote. Slots are generally of five minutes' duration, but in the recent past the major parties, Conservative and Labour, have opted to merge two such slots into ten-minute 'flagships'. Since 1987, when this was first introduced, a tradition seems to have developed of devoting consider-able resources to produce films featuring party leaders. Clearly, these are carefully crafted performances designed to promote the party 'brand'.

As such it is interesting to study the strategic approach to talk in the packaging of party politics. Indeed, this introduces an additional dimension to the study of broadcast talk, in so far as it is not just a matter of appealing to overhearing audiences but also of selling to them. Much as with George Bush's down-home populism, the style of talk needs to cohere with the overall image of the party, as conveyed by the appearance of its leader, by its slogans, and by the occasional policy initiative. Never before was this more apparent than in the UK general election of 1997, which secured a landslide victory for New Labour, led by Tony Blair. Indeed, with New Labour there was no longer any pretence that politics was not fundamentally involved in marketing. Here was a political party adopting a slogan as its name, just as any rebranded, 'new improved' product.

Transcripts 13 and 14 consist of extracts from the election broadcasts featuring the victorious leaders in the 1992 and 1997 UK general elections. It is perhaps helpful to supply some background details. In 1992, John Major was leading the governing Conservative Party into its first general election since the departure of Margaret Thatcher. There seems to have been an attempt to project Major as a different kind of personality, not so much in terms of ideology or class background, but more to do with a manner that was quieter and less confrontational. In a PEB entitled *The Journey* Major was filmed revisiting the Brixton (South London) of his youth, exchanging friendly greetings with market traders and reminiscing about former family dwellings.

I have no insider knowledge, but it seems possible that the 1997 Labour PEB featuring Tony Blair, was, in part, a response to *The Journey*. At least, it begins in exactly the same way, with the leader talking to an interloctor in a car, and it refers to his youthful experiences. In each case the PEB makes a point about the sporting affiliations of the young leader, where Blair's ambition to be a soccer player contrasts with Major's love of cricket. But a further contrast is provided by the way the politicians talk and we can start to investigate this by first examining the strategies used by, and on behalf of, John Major:

Transcript 13

[In car] I spent most of my youth in South London until well into my thirties at different houses. It's a very vivid area it's er it's never dull it's always changing. It has a tremendous vibrancy that very few parts of the country would
5   understand. And yet there is an innate friendliness in the area that those people who live there understand very well.

Can we turn left into Atlantic Road in a moment please? I think I'd like to go down there and have a look.

This is really the heart of Brixton. Once you come down the
10 main road, turn left into the market, it's where Brixton takes its heart from. And everybody who lives in and around the area is familiar with Brixton market and goes there and shops there.

[exchanges with market traders]

[In car] When I was in my early teens I used to occasionally erect a soapbox. I had two soapboxes one that I used to erect
15 in Brixton market and the other in Brixton Road. And I used to talk about er political matters of the day and everyone was very tolerant. Some people used to listen, some used to engage in badinage. Lots of other people smiled cheerfully and moved on. But it was very good experience.

[exchange with shopkeeper]

20 [In car] This is Coldharbour Lane. All those old houses with basements down there, and the Enterprise pub which has been there for as for as long as I can recall. And here's Eastlake Road, and that's the house we lived in for many years. Behind there in Eastlake Road we had a wicket er pitched on the wall
25 of the houses opposite and we used to play cricket up against it for hours on end.

[Interview] I think it's a fallacy for people to think er that because of my background and where I came from that I should be a socialist. Why should I be a socialist? It is people in that
30 background who have actually suffered most from the fact that we've had a society in which the free enterprise system moved ahead and then was blocked as one moved over the years from Conservative governments to socialist governments.

[In car] When I was in my mid teens we moved to Burton Road.

35   Where you see the house ahead with the two white arches
     immediately opposite there. That is where we lived. Now is it
     still there? (4 secs) It is (.) It is (.) It's still there (.)
     It's still there (.) It's hardly changed (8 secs) We lived in
     the downstairs flat (.) There was erm an area below ground, a
40   ground floor, and er I think there was a room or so on the
     first floor but not the second, the second was occupied by
     other people. And it was a <u>huge</u> improvement on Coldharbour
     Lane. It was a great step up.

The basic strategy of the opening sequence of *The Journey* is to make a
virtue of Major's relatively humble origins. Brixton is a working-class area
of ethnic diversity which is perhaps euphemistically referred to in the
phrase 'tremendous vibrancy' (line 4). However, because of its political
ideology, this strategy of associating Major with Brixton carries a certain
contradiction: he may have been born in this area, but he has now
successfully left it behind. The 'great step up' offered by the move to Burton
Road is in keeping with the Conservative ideology of self-improvement, and
it means that Major is now an outsider. This contradiction is reflected in the
style of filming, where brief walkabout shots of Major in Brixton market
alternate with longer segments of interview and of his reflective tour, in
which the streets of Brixton are glimpsed voyeuristically through the
windows of his chauffeur-driven car.

And apart from his brief conversational encounters with traders, Major's
talk for the most part remains rather formal. Generally he speaks fluently, in
grammatical sentences. He uses 'educated' vocabulary, such as the concept
of 'fallacy' (line 27), the generalised second person 'one' (line 32) and rather
anachronistic expressions such as 'erect a soapbox' and 'engage in
badinage' (lines 14, 17–18). Though this is all addressed to an unseen,
unheard interlocutor, it seems, because of its formality, to be scripted. This
is why, I think, the much commented on moment of dramatic emotion,
when Major revisits his house in Burton Road, seems staged. First of all, it is
hardly surprising, in this area of South London, that the house is still there.
But secondly the repetitions punctuated by extremely long pauses sound
like a script being animated rather than a spontaneous expression of
emotion. Contrast this with Blair's performance in 1997:

Transcript 14
     [In car] If you'd said to me at sort of eighteen nineteen are
     you going to be a politician I'd've said forget it ha anything
     else but being a politician
     V/o: Why on what grounds?
5   'Cause I thought politicians were complete pains in the
     backside

     [shots of Blair signing election poster] And there is part of

you that constantly wonders whether it is worth staying in
politics cause of all the the the rubbish that you have to <u>do</u>.
10 I mean you (.) you just have to do it. You've just got to keep
a grip on yourself and hope your humanity sees you through and
and in the end understand why you want to be in there (.) What
I keep saying to people is get behind the image it's quite
difficult to bring people to actually see the type of person
15 you are.

[In car] My ambition when I was a child was to play football
for Newcastle United, that was my greatest ambition and I kept
trying to talk my dad into using whatever meagre influence he
had with Newcastle United to get me a trial. But he never did.

20 **[Interview]** Because my dad was very active I mean he was active
in er tory politics actually locally. In fact they had him
lined up to fight to fight a seat and become a member of
parliament but then he became very ill so everything, he gave
up everything. But we (.) we discussed it and then when I
25 started being Labour there was a slight (.) problem for a time
but he never really objected to it and of course he's come over
to the Labour Party now so it's all fine.

I think my generation is trying to get to a different type of
politics which is <u>root</u>ed in strong values and convictions (.)
30 but it's not quite left and right in the way that it's been
before.

I-I just think for a whole generation of people they thought
that that if they arrived and did well then you became a tory.
You know it's like people used to say if you bought your house,
35 if you owned your own home you were a tory which is a crazy
idea.

I've always understood because of dad why some people who've
done very well come up in life and made it on their own (.)
felt the Tory party was the party for them because it was the
40 party of ambition and aspiration [v/o: right] and that the
Labour Party somehow wasn't and I think (.) to an extent (.) I
mean that's what the Labour Party be<u>came</u> it became too stuck in
the past too rooted in saying well that's where you are that's
where you stay; whereas I think today the position's changed
45 round. What I've always wanted with today's Labour Party was to
be the party of aspiration but to say you know you can you can
have a society where's there's ambition without lack of
compassion [and
V/o: [Yeh so I was going to say why aren't you a tory
50 basically?
Because I think that in the end you actually fulfil your amb- I
think your ambitions better in a society where people have some
sense of duty to other people.
[cut to shots of Blair pouring tea and talking to his children]

If this is indeed New Labour's answer to *The Journey* a key stylistic difference is established at the outset, for now we hear the interlocutor. Blair's talk is immediately established as dialogical. There is a personal identity (though still unseen) to the 'you' being addressed and she even, at one point, interrupts (line 49). Correspondingly, Blair's use of language is more conversational, as the talk is punctuated by interactive discourse markers ('I mean', 'you know') and by verbal disfluencies (such as the repetition of 'you can' on line 46 and the false start in line 51) which suggest spontaneity. Note in particular that the pauses in Blair's talk do not occur at the end but in the middle of sentences, as if to indicate their spontaneous composition as he searches for his words: 'I think (.) to an extent (.) I mean …' (lines 41–2).

It seems appropriate, then, that these conversational exchanges also contain much colloquial vocabulary ('forget it', 'keep a grip on yourself', references to father as 'dad'). There is even an expression which verges on the impolite ('pains in the backside' lines 5–6). The colloquial idiom here, allied to the dialogical features, supports an easy slippage from the second-person-singular form of address to the generalised 'you' ('you know you can have a society', lines 46–7). Blair's personal experience thus becomes his philosophy, which is now available for 'you' to share. And again, just like George Bush, this is a philosophy that speaks. There is a shift of footing as Blair first animates the philosophy of the old Labour Party (lines 43–4) and secondly articulates what New Labour has to say in response (lines 46–8).

So this is clearly dialogical and possibly indeed a 'different type of politics' (lines 28–9). It is interesting, and there could be no clearer contrast with the young Major and his soapbox, that Blair begins by casting doubts on the credibility of his own profession. No doubt this is designed to strike a chord with cynical youthful voters, but, as Norman Fairclough has demonstrated, this different political stance is perfectly in tune with the New Labour brand (Fairclough 2000). The party's rhetoric in the 1990s was founded on a so-called 'third way', beyond the old dogmas of left and right. The third way, apparently, required a new communication style, a 'big conversation' with the electorate. In Blair's style of political talk, this conversation was articulated conversationally, which is why, at least in 1997, it seemed so convincing. He did not seem to speak like a politician, but in a dialogical, colloquial and altogether 'livelier' manner.

3. Ordinary argument

We might say that Blair comes across, by comparison with Major, as more like an 'ordinary person' (and perhaps the same could be said of Bush, by comparison with Gore). Of course such appearances could be deceptive, and, as Fairclough reminds us, Blair's display of 'normalness' is just one of

several aspects of a practised rhetorical style. Nevertheless with his ability
to present political talk in conversational forms, Blair appears to be a
politician who is good at 'being himself'. Today, being 'ordinary', being
'normal', 'being yourself' seems to have become an important criterion for
successful public communication. Why this should be so, and its manifesta-
tion in various kinds of verbal performance, has become a central concern
for the analysis of broadcast talk.

To return to a key issue, it would seem to be crucial to the success of
politicians like Blair that they are not perceived merely as politicians. They
are not consumed by their role, they do not simply talk political talk, so that
as Blair puts it in the 1997 PEB 'the type of person you are' is also made
visible. This investment in 'humanity' by a professional persona does not
only apply to some politicians, but also to other public figures, such as
celebrities, as we shall see (Chapter 8). It was a widely discussed and
popular feature of the persona of Princess Diana, by contrast with other
members of the British Royal Family (Myers 2000). And this appears to be
something that broadcasting, in particular, demands. Other institutions still
demand that their personnel behave in a formal, circumscribed 'professional
manner', but something more 'ordinary' is required for contemporary radio
and TV. Indeed, for twenty years or so, TV has developed a genre of
programming which hinges precisely on this issue. This is the talk show,
which stages, often in confrontational forums, different ways of doing
political talk.

In the second part of their important discussion of transformations in
public discourse, and having outlined changes in the presentation of news,
Carpignano et al. (1990) turn their attention to talk shows. They make the
point that has been echoed many times since, that programmes such as *The
Oprah Winfrey Show* in the US, and *Kilroy* in the UK, have introduced new
political agendas and new ways of talking politics. As they put it, this is not
a politics defined 'as a form of management of the state' but rather 'as
emanating from social, personal and environmental concerns' (1990: 54). It
has been strongly influenced, they suggest, by feminism, in so far as
'women's issues' are now on the agenda, and it becomes legitimate to link
the personal and the political. Furthermore talk shows feature a diversity of
voices, not just professional politicians and commentators. Frequently they
stage confrontations between professionals and ordinary people, particularly
where the former are laying claims to specialist expertise.

These points have been further developed by Sonia Livingstone and
Peter Lunt (1994). A very useful contribution to the analysis of the talk in
talk shows is made by their argument that there are different epistem-
ologies, or definitions of knowledge, in circulation. Expert knowledge,
spoken by professionals is (or should be) objective, rational and supported
by evidence. It requires training, often involving the mastery of specialist

language. By contrast 'ordinary people' speak the language of common sense. Their knowledge is grounded in experience, or 'what everyone knows'. The validity of this knowledge is that it is personal, it has happened to them, or it can be assumed to be typical. The talk show then adds its particular ideological slant to this distinction, suggesting (and usually supported by the host's management of debate) that the voice of the ordinary person has equality with, if not greater weight than, the voice of the expert. Livingstone and Lunt point to a set of value judgements in this distinction between 'lay discourse' and expertise:

Lay	Expert
authentic	alienated
relevant	irrelevant
in depth	superficial
grounded in experience	ungrounded
concrete	*abstract*
practical	useless
real	artificial

(selectively adapted from Livingstone and Lunt 1994: 102;
my additions in italics)

On this basis, it becomes interesting to look at the ways different kinds of argument are constructed. We have already observed some general features of professional political argument in the debating style of Al Gore; that is to say, general points or proposals, supported by examples and evidence. But lay discourse doesn't work like this. As a growing body of research has shown 'common sense' is mainly articulated through two kinds of strategy. The first, and most widely studied, is storytelling, where credibility is attributed to well-formed narratives based on personal experience (Thornborrow 1997, 2001a). The second, which may or may not include the first, involves a claim to 'entitlement', where speakers account for their right to have opinions (Myers 2000). Typically this involves a display of their credentials as 'ordinary people' who therefore speak, not just for themselves, but for everyone.

We can explore some of the dynamics in this field of conflicting forms of argument in Transcript 15, which is taken from a routine edition of *Kilroy*. This programme followed what Haarman (2001) describes as the 'audience discussion format', as distinct from other, more individually focused, subgenres of talk show. It is this format which most clearly illustrates the new kinds of political agenda discussed by Carpignano et al. This edition of *Kilroy*, from October 2001, focused on the topic of juvenile delinquency, typically, for this genre, expressed in the form of a first-person statement: 'Young people are ruining my area'. This particular segment involves two

women in the audience (W1 and W2), a man (M) who has travelled a long
way to make his point, and a member of parliament (MP). Kilroy's role is to
maintain a semblance of order as several audience members try to intervene.
A further audience contribution is made from time to time in the form of
applause (xxx) and it is interesting to see when this occurs and why.
Meanwhile, while all this is going on, three teenage boys sit silent and
sullen-faced at the front of the audience, cast as the focus for the various
contributions:

```
Transcript 15
    W1: We're talking about we're talking about the problems
        we're not talking about how to solve them. Has nobody
        ever thought that when these children do damage that they
        work and they pay back for the damage they've done [MP:
 5      yeh] When they steal a car [MP: yeh] they should be made
        to work and half their wages should be made to [pay=
    MP:                                               [yeh I
        agree I agree I-
    Aud:                                              [xxxxxxxx
10  W1: =and when they go in old people's houses and they damage
        them and they damage the houses (.) they should work and
        they should work with the old people that way they will
        build up a friendship with the people that they've
        damaged and also pay out of their pocket not their
15      parent's pocket not government's pocket why should I pay
        for them (.) to be good? My children have - I've paid for
        my children to come up well and if they damage anybody's
        property I will make em pay for it and [that's what these
        lads should be doing
20  Aud:                                       [xxxxxxxxxxxxxxxxxx
        xxxxxxxxxxxxxxxxxxxxx
    MP: [aaa(.) mmm
    M:  Can I just ehm I've come a long way so I want to put my
        point through (.) Now when I was er younger when I was
25      fourteen like you know these young lads here today now I
        was doing petty crime it was literally p-petty just
        little petty things you know like having time off school
        and so on [having time
    K:            [not robbing banks
30  M:  not robbing not robbing people j-just petty crime and I
        actually got sent down to a detention centre I was sent
        down for three month (.) Now that when I w-when I walked
        through that gate believe me you won't you will not want
        to go where I went and I was scrubbing floors [literally
35      I was
    K:                                                [he's been
        five times down there five times
    Aud: (    )
    M:  yeh but after but a but after that I got sent away then
40      for another twenty one months in a care home (.) and it
        wasn't like the care homes you get[today=
```

```
      W1:                                    [that's what I'm saying
            it's so easy today=
      M:    =it was boot camp job you was out parading on the yards
45          you was [(    ) believe me that was rough
      W1:           [(    ) punishment
      Aud: xxxxxxxxxxxxxxxxxxxx
      M:    yeh but what they want
      MP:   A couple a couple of points Robert there is no one size
50          fits all (.) This lad will go in and out of detention
            centres and keep coming back it's not working for him but
            it worked for you [Aud:(    )] hold on le-let let me make
            the point but I-I I genui:nely believe that some of the
            things that we've done like reparation orders there on
55          the statute book madam like the anti-social behaviour
            orders like the restorative justice they can be made to
            work but we've got to get these kids before the courts
            we've got to give the police resources and what I don't
            buy I tell you what I don't buy is this nonsense about
60          boredom (.) There are more things to do for young people
            (.) [than ever before
      Aud:      [xxxxxxxxxxxxxxxxxxxxxxxxxxxxx (    )and why is
            boredom nonsense? Why is boredom nonsense? (    )
      M:    But if but if no let me [(    )
65    K:                            [(    ) Martin hang on Fred hang
            on Fred (.) I'll come to you in a minute
      M:    if if if when they'd been if when they'd been in a
            detention centre or wherever they might have gone borstal
            [K: yeh] once they'd come out of there if they was sent
70          into an home until they was sixteen it would make 'em
            think then
      W2:   [exactly=
      MP:   [not always not always
      W2:         =sorry I think that a lot of this [problem=
75    K:                                            [hang on please
      W2:                                               = a lot
            of the problem now is this politically correct thinking
            (.) we sort of feel so sorry for the poor underdog (.)
            and I do feel this is quite wrong (.) I'm a single mother
80          of four children my husband unfortunately died ten years
            ago (.) I have four sons I brought them up (.) They are a
            credit to me and a credit to the community [MP: Well
            done] but that is just one of those things I disciplined
            them I [smacked them and I'm sorry I don't agree
85    Aud:        [xxxxxxxxxxxxxxxxxxxxxxxxxxxxxxxxxxxxxxxxxxxxxxxxx
```

We will begin this analysis by looking at the conduct of the MP. He seizes the floor after M's narrative has been interrupted (line 49) and he initially speaks 'through the chair' ('Robert'). He then proceeds to speak as a politician. Though they are personally authored, his statements are introduced in abstract terms as 'a couple of points'. His second point (which seems to be that the government is doing something) is supported by examples and rounded off in classical rhetorical style with a list of three ('courts' … 'resources' … 'nonsense about bore<u>dom</u>', lines 57–60) which receives a round of applause. We should also note, however, that the MP is not just speaking for himself. In shifts of footing, the principal is widened to include his political party (line 54) and arguably, on line 57, society as a whole. Through a shifting use of personal pronouns he locates his personal views in a 'public sphere' of political debate.

The MP, however, does not receive the loudest or the longest round of applause – that is reserved for the contribution of W2. There may be several reasons for this. First, the content of what she is saying conforms to the general view in all these contributions, which supports tougher punishment for juvenile crime; and furthermore 'smacking' has been raised as a controversial matter earlier in the programme. Secondly, however, her contribution is delivered effectively. Again this involves the 'claptrap' of a list of three (lines 83–4), but also I think it is important to look at the way she establishes her credentials. Her entitlement to have this opinion is based on the fact that she is 'a single mother of four children'. What is the relevance of this? We should note here that his possible role as a husband or father is entirely irrelevant to the identity of the MP.

Clearly W2 is 'being ordinary' and on *Kilroy*, the most instant claim to ordinariness any woman can have is that she is a wife and mother. Note that W1 also rounds off her contribution with reference to her own children and at this point receives her largest applause. But again, in this context, being a 'single mother' might be problematic. In the populist world of *Kilroy* there are feckless single mothers who are usually considered to be part of the problem. So W2 includes the additional information that she is a widow. Her entitlement to speak as ordinary is strengthened by her claim to virtue. It might seem a bit strange that she didn't refer to her widowed status in the first place. However, the connotations of 'single mother', now given this positive inflection, would include struggle, sacrifice, perhaps poverty, thus reinforcing her moral stance.

Of all the participants it seems to be the man who makes the least impact. He receives no applause at the end of his contribution and the applause in line 47 seems to be occasioned by the interruption of the woman in the audience, not by himself. This is strange, because he has a story to tell. Moreover, his narrative of detention centres and care homes is perfectly in tune with the attitude to punishment generally taken by this audience.

My suggestion is that although this man clearly does attempt a narrative of personal experience, he does not do it very successfully. If we again refer to Labov's (1972) model for such narratives, we can observe that there is a 'story-preface', of sorts, in lines 23–4 where M takes the floor, and a segment of 'orientation' (lines 24–6: 'I was fourteen … doing petty crime') which provides background details. However, something causes first Kilroy and then the audience to interrupt the 'complicating action' on line 36, after

M 'walked through that gate'. I think it is because the action is not dramatic enough, unlike the tellings of fights and near-death experiences in Labov's data. M is too quick to move to 'evaluation' of the terrors of the boot camp without supplying the detail (somehow 'scrubbing floors' won't do). He does, however, courtesy of Kilroy's intervention, produce the coda that supplies the point of his narrative (lines 70–1: 'it would make 'em think then').

More generally it is apparent that ordinary argument looks very different from formal debate, or interviewing. This is shown by the complexity of the transcript where, in this kind of multi-party talk, participants are competing for the floor. Transition relevance places are at a premium, which is why multiple interruptions and false starts occur at particular points. Speakers also struggle to retain the floor, latching their turns across interruption (W1, lines 6–10) or relying on Kilroy to act the referee (W2, lines 72–6). These competitive transitional moments are also accompanied by general audience reaction (applause) which is a significant additional resource in the analysis of media talk. It provides the 'next-turn proof' of an effective turn or, conversely, in its absence, of a contribution which is problematic.

4. Escalation sequences

In his introduction to the Massachusetts presidential debate, Jim Lehrer refers to the presence of an audience. This is, he says, 'not here to participate', and has 'agreed to remain silent', save for introductory and concluding rounds of applause. We might expect therefore, that this debate will display little of the cut and thrust of the audience participation programme, as exemplified by *Kilroy*. Within its formal conventions, turn-taking should proceed in an orderly fashion, for there is no need to compete for the floor. The audience is expressly forbidden to demonstrate its support for either side, or for an argument effectively made. George Bush may, from time to time, push the boundaries of this formality a little, but even his promise to share the government's money with the 'hard working people of America', receives not a ripple of applause.

However, despite Lehrer's strictures, the audience is not entirely silent. On occasions, it can be heard to laugh and, what is more, this laughter has effects on the proceedings. Sometimes the candidates make jokes, as when, for instance Bush, having attacked Gore's 'phoney numbers', describes him as the inventor of the calculator. Some polite laughter ensues. But laughter is also occasioned by sequences of overlapping talk which sometimes occur as a climax to an exchange on a particular issue. Here, the laughter is not simply responsive, it is also provocative, in that it seems to prompt further developments. It contributes to what I shall call 'escalation sequences' of argument which involve some departures from the conventions of formal debate.

Here, for example, in Transcript 16, the candidates are reaching the climax of an extended argument about the provision of prescription drugs to senior citizens. As a way of rounding off this topic, Lehrer attempts to formulate their positions, with what in Heritage's terminology is a strategy of 'co-operative recycle' (Heritage 1985). That is to say, it is a formulation with which the candidates might be expected to agree:

```
Transcript 16
      JL: Let me ask you both this and we'll move on on this
          subject. As a practical matter both of you want to bring
          prescription drugs to seniors correct?
      GB: [Correct
  5   AG: [But the difference is the difference is I want to bring
          it to a hundred per [cent=
     Aud:                     [hhhh [hhh
      JL:                           [All right all right
      AG:                                 =and he brings it only to five
 10       [percent
      JL: [all right (   )
      GB: [That's just totally false that's just that's just wait a
          minute it's just totally false (.)=
      AG:                                    hhh
 15   GB:                            = for him to stand up
          here and say that. Let me let me make sure the seniors
          hear me loud and clear (.) I'm going to work with both
          Republicans and Democrats to reform the system (.) All
          seniors will be covered (.) All poor seniors will have
 20       their prescription drugs paid for (.) In the mean time
          we're going to have a plan to help poor seniors and in
          the mean time could be one year or two years [I don't
          know
      AG:                                            [Okay let me
 25       let me draw your attention to the key word there he said
          all poor seniors
      GB: No wait a minute all seniors are covered under
          prescription [drugs in my plan
      AG:              [In the first year? In the first year?
 30   GB: If we can get it done in the first year you bet. Yours is
          phased in over [eight years
      AG:               [No no (.) no no (.) It's a two faced plan
          Jim. And for the first four years >it takes a year to
          pass it< and for the first four years only (.) the poor
 35       are covered middle class seniors like George McKinney and
          his wife are not covered [for=
      JL:                          [Look=
      AG:                               =four to five years
      JL: =I've got an idea
 40   AG: Okay
      JL: If you've got any more to say about this you can say it
          in your [closing statements we'll move on okay
      AG:        [hhhh okay
```

It takes a CA style of transcript to display the dynamics of an escalation sequence fully. Here, the transcription of the audience laughter in line 7 enables us to understand the strategies of interruption immediately employed both by Lehrer and by Bush. In lines 5–6, Al Gore has scored a point. This is because only Bush makes the expected positive response to Lehrer's co-operative recycle. Gore treats this as a prompt to further argument, thus rejecting Lehrer's closing move, and it is this slight deviation from the norm that the audience finds amusing. Lehrer is then obliged to interrupt Gore to attempt to reassert his authority, whereas Bush is clearly prompted to challenge for the floor to reopen the argument with his opponent.

Thus, a sequence of interruptions and latched utterances is produced which is not unlike the competitions for the floor that occur in talk shows. In lines 12–13 Bush raises his voice and repeats himself until his co-participants give way (and Gore also acknowledges the amusement of the situation). Bush then proceeds to restate his policy in an emphatic manner punctuated by pauses. Ultimately, and this is what most clearly defines the 'escalation', following further interruptions, the candidates then engage in a direct exchange (lines 29–31) unmediated by the chair. For a moment (line 30) Bush shifts from referring to Gore in the third person, to directly addressing him in the second, but this is prompted by Gore's direct question to him. At this point it is absolutely incumbent on Lehrer to intervene (line 37); any more of this and the presidential debate is in danger, we might say, of descending into a 'slanging match'.

It is a sequence which provides a nice illustration of the process observed by David Greatbatch to occur in what he calls 'panel interviews' (Greatbatch 1992). He argues that news interviews involving two or more IEs are a useful way of staging controversy without compromising the neutrality of the IR. Indeed the latter's status is enhanced by his institutional duty to fulfil the role of moderator. Moreover, unlike ordinary conversations, IEs (or presidential candidates) can afford to argue directly with each other, in an escalating, unmitigated manner, because they know that the chair will ultimately intervene:

[N]ews IEs can pursue and escalate their disagreements secure in the knowledge that they will not have to negotiate their own way out of them. They can, in other words, maximize their disagreements because they know that sooner or later a nondisagreed-with, and formally impartial, third party will intervene and get them off the hook – since to do otherwise would involve that party failing to enact their institutional role. (1992: 298)

5. Politics as entertainment

However, though there are certain similarities in the conduct of news interviewers and chairpersons in debates, there are also some crucial differences. In particular, where debates are performed live, in front of audiences, not only is it possible that audience reaction will affect the development of the talk (as in the above example), it is also sometimes the case that escalation sequences will be used to provoke such reaction. That is to say, in some programmes, escalation sequences function like 'claptrap' in political speeches, where they are used to generate audience laughter and applause. For instance, on the long-running BBC current affairs programme *Question Time* there is a structure whereby panellists are at first allocated extended turns in which to reply to audience questions, but this is followed by sequences of unmediated, direct disagreement between panel members. Here, it is interesting that the chairperson, David Dimbleby, does not simply act the impartial referee, he also contributes to the escalation sequences. In terms of the formal procedures outlined by Greatbatch, he appears to abandon, temporarily, his neutral footing. Here are two instances of this:

```
Transcript 17
     DD: John Prescott do you accept that Kenneth Clarke didn't
         do wrong in signing the PII?
     JP: Well first about the signing Mr Heseltine approached
         these documents and expressed grave reservations that
 5       they should be withheld in the court and should be used
         in the defence. Mr Clarke saw the reservation of Mr
         Heseltine and didn't choose despite being a barrister to
         exercise the same kind of reservation. Now I know he
         didn't read the Maastricht Agreement I don't know whether
10       he read the documents pro-properly but I think there's a
         clear difference between these two ministers. Secondly
         when he refers to our exchange on 13ᵗʰ January 1994 I do
         read the documents Ken and what you said is not true and
         I could read it [here=
15   KC:                 [(   )You haven't read anything (   )
     JP:                         =but I said you were one I quote you
         were one of those as Home Secretary who signed the
         document that said that the evidence shouldn't be given
         to the court. True?
20   KC: No.
     JP: You said that the evidence would not be you signed a
         public interest certificate er committee saying this
         information shouldn't be made available to the defence
         (2 secs)
25       Yes you did.
     Aud: hhhhhhhhhhhhhhhhhh[hhhhhhhhhhhhhxxxxxxxxxxxxxxxxxxxxxxxxx
     KC:                    [no no [no no no
     JP:                    [which when which I then [asked you but=
     KC:                                             [partly true
```

```
30        and partly wrong I'm going to reply to you
     JP:  =anyway just to answer your question which wait a minute
          partly true partly wrong (    )
     KC:  [You haven't read a word of this document (   )
     DD:  He's reading he's quoting. He's quoting [what you said
35        (    ) transcript (    )
     JP:                                          [I'm quoting you.
          I'm quoting you.  You did not note it correct.
```

This exchange took place in 1995 in a debate following the publication of the Scott Report into the sales of arms by British companies to Iraq. The then Home Secretary, Kenneth Clarke, stands accused of using his powers to prevent vital evidence from reaching the court. In seeking to establish this John Prescott, in characteristically robust fashion, not only shifts from the third to second person (line 13), but also takes on the role, normally reserved for the IR/chair, of asking a direct question (line 19). A huge burst of audience laughter and applause is then occasioned by the comical effect of the exchanges in lines 19–25. Here, JP repeats his accusation, but this time fails to elicit a response from KC. There is a pregnant pause of two seconds in line 24, followed by JP himself supplying the missing response. What follows the audience reaction to this is an escalating sequence of repetition and overlapping talk, which includes DD himself briefly siding with JP's attack on KC in line 34.

In Transcript 18, the escalation sequence is provoked by DD himself. Here the then Foreign Secretary Robin Cook is dealing with a tricky question regarding the Government's possible influence on the National Lottery Commission. The issue here is that although the Commission is formally established as an independent body, the Government had expressed its own commitment to the concept of a 'not-for-profit' lottery. DD starts his line of questioning by referring to a general 'suspicion' about decisions then taken by the Lottery Commission, but (rather like Robin Day in transcript 6) pushes this to a point where he provokes a personal attack from the IE. Unlike a news interview however, the added element here is the response of the studio audience, which contributes to another escalation sequence:

```
Transcript 18
    DD:  But the confusion is that your manifesto pledged a not
         for profit lottery (.) Your government then appointed the
         Commission [RC: yes] and the of course suspicion is that
         they were appointed in order to appoint er the the
 5       Peoples Lottery Rich-er Richard Bra-Branson's one er and
         not Camelot and that's the start of the whole confusion.
    RC:  Yeh there was no fix of the Commission so that it should
         not be Camelot and not be any other company
    DD:  But if that was your [policy (   ) official policy
10  RC:                       [yes yes and of course of course it
         was our it is it is our policy not was our policy
```

```
      DD:  So you don't want Camelot because they're not a not for
           profit organisation.
      RC:  We decided we would not take this decision the decision
15         would be taken by the Commission. The Commission will
           take the decision. We will obviously be very happy if it
           is a not for profit lottery that maximises the money for
           good causes and I frankly think the majority of the
           people in Britain would be too.
20    DD:  So you're leaning on them
      RC:  No we're not leaning [on them=
      Aud:                      [hhhhhhhhhhhhhhhhhhhhhhhhhhhhhhh
      RC:                              =it is their decision
           David. No th-the the yes you've absolutely no evidence
25         whatsoever to suggest we're leaning on them we are not
           leaning on them but I do find it bi[zarre=
      Aud:                                    [hhhhhhhhhhhhhhhhhhhh
      RC:                                      = I do find it
           bizarre well you don't do you well if you've got evidence
30         let's hear it, share it, share it with the audience
           [share it with the audience
      DD:  [I'm just asking questions (   ) I'm just asking
           questions
      RC:  Oh yeh yeh yeh you're not answering them are you David
35         you're not answering the questions [but you ask (...)
      DD:                                     [No no I'm not allowed
           to I'm not allowed to. I wish I were allowed to but I'm
           not allowed to
      Aud: [xxxxxxxxxxxxxxxxxxxxxxxxxxxxxxxxxx
40    RC:  [what is preposterous [what is=
      DD:                        [it's against the rules
      RC:                               =preposterous about
           your line of inquiry David [DD: ah] is that you are
           turning what is actually a popular concept into as if it
           was a government prejudice ...
```

This transcript presents a highly condensed illustration of several key
features of political talk, found both in news interviews and in political
debates. First, we see the chairperson acting like a news IR, producing two
'inferential elaborative probes' (lines 12–13 and 20) which carry hostile
implicatures for the IE. RC retaliates to the second of these by invoking
Grice's maxim of Quality, questioning DD's evidence (line 24), and holding
him publicly accountable. Characteristically on such occasions, DD then
takes refuge in a metastatement of his role, insisting on his neutral footing
('I'm just asking questions', lines 32–3). But in this context the exchange is
played out before an audience who laugh and applaud as the sequence
escalates. As with the discourse of talk shows, this audience response
provides an added level of data by which to judge the effects of argumentative interventions.

However, it is difficult to reach a definitive conclusion, for there are two
possibilities. First, looking at the fact that it applauds immediately after DD

completes his metastatement (line 39), it might be suggested that the audience is 'on his side', and that its previous laughter is at RC's expense. It could be argued that the amusement here is that DD, within the confines of his role, has successfully revealed the inconsistencies of a prominent politician. However, I think it is equally plausible to argue that the audience is not laughing at a particular participant, but rather at the exchange as it develops. The two bursts of laughter punctuate precise points of escalation as RC shifts from defence to attack, and it is equally possible that the applause is for the escalation sequence as a whole. This interpretation is supported by the body language: both participants are smiling and gesturing towards the audience as they speak, and seem to be treating this as a piece of good-humoured 'knock-about'.

In short, to employ another of Goffman's concepts, there are different 'frames' in political talk. There is, as we have seen, serious argument, which is rhetorically packaged in different ways, depending on the strategies and the status of the speaker. However, in contemporary political talk, there is a clear tendency for some politicians to want to break the frame of conventional debate, and to experiment with ways of being 'ordinary'. This would seem to mirror the 'conversationalisation' of news, as part of a general shift towards less formal, more colloquial ways of presenting public talk. This tendency also represents a convergence of professional political talk with the language of talk shows, in which ordinary people have their say.

But a third frame for political talk is apparent in escalation sequences, particularly where live audiences are involved. For all its seriousness, whether formal or informal, there are also instances where political talk is entertaining. Sometimes, as in the presidential debates, humorous moments provide a little light relief, as asides to the main event. Politicians like Bush and Blair also use humour as a way of supplementing their public image, revealing their more 'human' side in chat shows, for example. But in programmes like *Question Time*, humour is not just a momentary break in an otherwise formal frame – rather it is a key part of the overall format. It is what makes this kind of political debate lively and entertaining. It illustrates once again that, even in news and current affairs, successful media talk does not just seek to inform and educate, but to construct a broader strategy of appealing to the overhearing audience. This is surely why David Dimbleby does not rigidly adhere to the formal confines of his role as interviewer or as chair. He does not simply occupy the neutral footing, even when he insists that he does! For it is part of his job to make politics entertaining, which escalation sequences help to achieve.

Sports Talk

1. Radio Five Live

One of the success stories in the recent history of British broadcasting has been the performance of the BBC's fifth national radio channel, Radio Five Live. Introduced in 1990 in response to government demands that the BBC should offer more choice, the channel only established its current distinctive identity following a relaunch in 1994. In this, it was transformed from a 'dumping ground' of mixed programming (Crisell 1994) to the dedicated news and sports channel of today. It celebrated its tenth anniversary in 2004 by achieving, for the first time, over 5 per cent of the national audience share, with a weekly reach of 6 million listeners, rapidly gaining on the more established BBC stations, Radios 1 and 4. Five Live has also become a pioneer of technological convergence, as its sports phone-in programme, *6.06*, has been made simultaneously available as a web-site, and through interactive digital TV.

For the analysis of media talk, Five Live offers a particularly rich source of data. Impressionistically, there seems to be a wider range and diversity of voices heard on this, as compared most of the other BBC radio channels. This is despite its concentration on news and sport which has prompted the nickname 'radio bloke'. For whereas Radios 3 and 4, with their Reithian roots, remain hearably middle class, and Radio 1 specialises in the 'youth talk' to be discussed in the next chapter, Radio Five presents a rich mixture of class and regional accents, from its presenters as well as its accessed voices. It is, we might say, the BBC's national radio talk show, and perhaps indicates a belated recognition, by the corporation, of the vitality of the talk radio format (Higgins and Moss 1982; Munson 1993; Hutchby 1996).

This chapter offers some observations on the forms of talk associated with sports, mainly on Radio Five Live. It is in sports talk that its social class and regional diversity is most evident, in interviews with players and managers, in commentary where former players are employed as pundits, and in phone-in programmes. The focus will be specifically on talk about football (soccer), partly because this sport is massively in dominance, but also because it can be no coincidence that the success of the rebranded Radio Five is related to its saturation coverage of the English premier league. This radio channel is part of the 'sports-media complex' which has transformed the global economics of sport and acted as a market leader in the development of digital broadcasting (Boyle and Haynes 2000).

2. The football phone-in

We will begin with *6.06*, the newly digitalised football phone-in. There are some links here with the analysis of political talk presented in the previous chapter, for not only does the football phone-in offer further interesting illustrations of the ways lay speakers construct arguments, it is also another example of argument as entertainment. In *6.06* arguments are packaged in lively ways designed to appeal to their particular target audience. Most callers, it seems, appreciate this expectation and they understand what, in the discourse of this programme, is an acceptable way to make an argument.

It is important to be clear about this, because different types of talk radio involve different expectations. If argument can be defined as a 'speech genre' (Bakhtin) then we have to recognise that there are subsets of this category, subgenres, which are appropriate for different social contexts. In fact the social context most obviously suggested by *6.06* is that which Bakhtin/Volosinov (1973) himself rather quaintly described as the 'urban carouse' (more on this later).[1] This approach to argument is rather different from that which has dominated the previous literature on phone-ins, where a focus on political talk, or topical debate, has been most in evidence (Moss and Higgins 1984; Hutchby 1996; Thornborrow 2001b; Thornborrow and Fitzgerald 2002). Radio Five also features topical debate, particularly in its 9 a.m. phone-in 'the nation's conversation', but with *6.06* we are about to enter somewhat different territory.

To clarify this point, let us return to the work of Ian Hutchby. In Chapter 2, his analysis of 'confrontation talk' was discussed as an illustration of the CA interest in 'sequencing'. In the topical phone-in programme analysed by Hutchby, sequences of argument develop after the caller makes a point which is treated as arguable by the host. The host's turn, in the 'second position', is sequentially positioned to enable this, and certain formulae ('you say X but what about Y?') are available to develop the confrontation. This can be pursued, as Hutchby demonstrates, through escalation sequences, often involving interruption; but, crucially, the 'what about Y?' formula does not commit the host to making his own counter-argument. Rather his function is to act as a kind of irritant, from a position of 'professional scepticism', which is adopted consistently, and to which callers, familiar with the show's format, must necessarily be oriented:

A fundamental feature of interaction on talk radio is that callers are oriented to the task of presenting their opinion and, if necessary defending it against the host's attacks. Hosts on the other hand, may typically be oriented to the task of pursuing controversy, finding something to argue with in what the caller is saying. In this sense, hosts adopt a stance of 'professional scepticism' as regards callers claims, hearing anything the caller says in terms of its potential arguability. (Hutchby 1996: 74–5)

The problem here is that this kind of 'confrontation talk' is only characteristic of some formats and not talk radio in general. To be more precise, the general structure of the radio phone-in which Hutchby describes may be universal, in that callers firstly make a point to which the host then responds, but in *6.06* there are additional features which take the talk beyond confrontation. For example, in Transcript 19, the host Alan Green, clearly begins by treating the caller's initial proposition as arguable. He explicitly disagrees with Patrick's general view that British soccer is 'in the doldrums'. However, as the call develops, through various twists and turns, a level of mutual consensus is reached. This is rounded off with the host offering a term of endearment to the caller ('Thanks for your call mate') and laughing at a witticism he produces at the expense of David James, the England goalkeeper. What then is the distinctive purpose of this form of talk?

```
Transcript 19
    AG:  Patrick from Newport on line one.
    P:   Hello Alan
    AG:  Hi good evening
    P:   Er I'd just like to talk about the midweek games we saw
5        Man United against Dortmund [AG: go ahead] Liverpool at
         Paris St Germain. Erm let's face it British soccer is
         well it's in the doldrums innit?
    AG:  Well hold on a sec, hold on a sec, if we were talking
         last Saturday, I would have said I really felt very
10       strongly that both Manchester United and Liverpool would
         reach their respective finals. I agree completely about
         the results, erm I mean Liverpool Liverpool were feeble
         in Paris, disappointingly feeble in Paris and even though
         it was a narrow defeat for Manchester United in Dortmund
15       I-I think the Germans will have enough. I really do. So
         I'm disappointed but I don't say that means that our
         football's in the doldrums. I disagree.
    P:   Well well let me say this then. I wouldn't say that er
         Man United are out of it but I mean look at the soccer,
20       the play, we're not comfortable passing the ball when we
         play against continental sides are we? You know we go
         across the park and invariably, I was pointing out to my
         son the other night we watched the two games, I said the
```

25	ball goes back to the goalkeeper and what happens? The long punt up the pitch and it's anybody's ball.

[sounds of electronic alarm]

AG: Er, have you got a burglar alarm just gone off?
P: Oh it's a fire alarm. It's all right the fire engine's outside we're OK.
AG: Eh eh eh eh well let it burn down, don't worry about it
30 Patrick.
P: Soccer is more important.

But er, you know, it goes back to the goalkeeper. He kicks the ball up then it's anybody's ball. And then we start off again, you know and now Alan this is a fact you
35 if you watch the games I listen to you a lot on Radio Five it's a marvellous show and y-week after week after week it's the same old thing innit? Across the park, Ray Wilkins syndrome I call it. Across the park, back to the 'keeper, straight up. What have you, come on now, what
40 have you got to say?
AG: Well I-I tell you what I've got to say about this. I think that the Premiership, the English Premiership is very over-rated. It thinks far too highly of itself. I don't think it's remotely as good a league as it thinks
45 it is [P: I reckon you're right]. And I get letters all the time saying you know 'Oh lay off it' you know 'the football's great'. The football may be dramatic and it may be exciting but it doesn't necessarily mean that it's good. And I-sadly I-I have to say I think the Italian
50 Serie A is still well ahead of us.
P: Well that's right. I mean when do we shoot from outside the eighteen yard box? We don't. Our game is get to the by-line, cross it, but when you cross it Alan it's anybody's ball again going into the middle isn't it? [AG:
55 true] it's a fifty fifty [ball.
AG: [True Patrick thanks for your call mate.
P: And if you've got James playing for you it's probably a sixty forty ball.
60 AG: Eh eh eh all right Patrick. Paul from Gwent on line three ...

Of all the various twists and turns, a key moment in this call is the temporary break of frame in lines 26–31. An electronic alarm can be heard in the background which becomes the pretext for an exchange which is of course entirely unpredictable and spontaneous, but where the caller injects a moment of humour to which the host responds. Even more wittily Patrick then (on line 31) produces a metastatement which articulates the philosophy of the show. Thus, whatever disagreements the participants might have, these only serve to articulate a shared common interest in football. That interest is also confirmed by personal asides in which, first, the caller grounds his entitlement to an opinion in his consumption of sports programmes and, secondly, the host buttresses his opinion by animating the views of his wider audience. Such statements of opinion by the host are entirely untypical of the material Hutchby has analysed, as, in response to the caller's prompting and questioning, the stance of 'professional scepticism' is abandoned. But clearly the whole call is founded on an assumption of mutual solidarity, displayed in repetition of first names, the tokens of sympathetic circularity and affiliative responses ('I reckon you're right').

Hutchby argues that there is an imbalance of power in the topical issues phone-in, where the host's scepticism continually threatens to undermine the position of the caller (one wonders why they call). On *6.06*, however, the power situation is less clear cut. Of course the host retains the power to initiate and to terminate the call, and Hutchby's 'action–opposition' sequences are evident. However, there is also a more fluid negotiation of roles, as all participants, by virtue of their common interest, have the right to 'have their say'. Moreover this right is explicitly articulated through a very interesting use of discourse markers. 'Well well let me say this' (line 18) and 'I tell you what I've got to say about this' (line 41) seem to function as prefaces which cast the subsequent argument in a particular light. These are statements of opinion, not personal disagreements, to which everyone is entitled who has this commitment to football. The personal references, sympathetic circularity and interpersonal banter establish a common ground on which the right to state an opinion is founded.

3. Sociable argument

We will explore some further dimensions to these entitlements, and to the forms of argument they produce, in two further transcripts. For the moment, however, a theoretical side-step is necessary, to observe that the discourse of the football phone-in has much in common with what some sociolinguists have discussed as 'sociable argument'. Building on Georg Simmel's socio-logical concept of 'sociability', Deborah Schiffrin argued that 'argument as sociability' was a feature of the Jewish subculture in Philadelphia where she conducted some fieldwork (Schiffrin 1984). Some of her arguments have been questioned and her findings disputed in subsequent work, but interestingly this also engages with mediated argument, as displayed in the Australian docu-soap *Sylvania Waters* (Lee and Peck 1995).

Sociability is defined by Simmel as social interaction with 'no ulterior end, no content and no result outside itself'; it is simply the enjoyment of social intercourse for its own sake (Schiffrin 1984: 315). In this definition, argument can be sociable so long as it 'does not permit the seriousness of the momentary content to become its substance' (316). Schiffrin glosses this as argumentative talk which is 'free of substance' (317), and as 'exchanges that have the form of argument but not the serious substance of argument' (331). For this she is criticised by Lee and Peck, who argue that to build a definition of sociable argument around a distinction between serious and non-serious forms, and further to hope to demonstrate that these are realised in distinctive features of discourse, is misconceived. In their data from *Sylvania Waters*, serious and sociable aspects of argument occur together and the arguments always have substance in the cut-and-thrust of family relationships.

Returning to the discourse of the football phone-in, I think we would also have to agree that there is some substance to the argument about the quality of British soccer. This is not an argument which is devoid of content, and for the participants in this programme it is a serious matter. But it may be, as the original quote from Simmel puts it, that the 'seriousness of the momentary content' has not 'become its substance'. We might take this view if we accept that the seriousness of the argument works as a device for demonstrating the more fundamental commitment to a community of interest in football. The sociolinguistic debate about argument as sociability seems to have become mired in a set of unhelpful dichotomies – serious/with substance vs non-serious/free of substance – but the radio football phone-in is a bit of both. The main point of going on the show as a caller is to participate in a lively, sociable exchange with Alan Green, and this is effectively realised through forceful statements of opinion.

Schiffrin introduces three criteria for recognising argument as sociability, including the vulnerability of frames, and displays of co-operativeness, both of which are evident in Transcript 19. Her third criterion, however, is not so much a feature of the discourse but rather its subsequent evaluation, where participants display a positive orientation to their arguments and 'fights'. In their discussion of this point, Lee and Peck raise the possibility that this might be a particularly masculine trait, but a further indication of enjoyable argument is when 'participants refuel the argument when it shows signs of dying' (1995: 43). Both these observations would seems to apply to Transcript 20, where Alan Green prolongs an argument even when he is in 'complete agreement' with the caller. The point raised by the caller is that, because of their success in all competitions, Manchester United are having to play too many games in too short a time at the end of the season (1997). At the point where this extract begins, agreement on this has already been reached, but, rather than terminate the call, first AG and then the caller C seek to broaden the range of examples and issues for debate:

Transcript 20

```
     AG:  Yeh I let me say let me tell you some-I completely agree
          with you I do not understand (.) why Manchester United
          have not been offered an extension to the season[C:(    )]
  5       I had a letter this week from a guy called Stuart Taylor
          from er South Oxhey in Herts, and he's clearly an Arsenal
          fan and he says er (.) he points out that in seventy nine
          eighty Arsenal had to play two cup finals in five days(.)
          that er of their seventy first class games that season
          seven of those matches came in the last nineteen days of
 10       May. Well I say so what? Okay that was a terrible
          situation for Arsenal but because it happened before
          doesn't make it [right=
     C:                   [absolutely (.) sure
     AG:                              =and it's completely wrong,
 15       completely wrong that Manchester United have to play four
          games in eight days it's a nonsense and it should be .
          changed
     C:   Absolutely I mean the thing is the most important thing
          I'm phoning about is that is that it should never be
 20       allowed to happen again. I mean Man United actually won a
          cup final against Everton when Everton were an extremely
          good side weren't allowed to go into Europe because of
          the erm because of the er Heysel ban (.) but they lost
          the cup final Everton because exactly they were very very
 25       tired and it sh-it shouldn't happen b-it's just self
          interested nonsense the statements that people like
          Wenger I think and it really has annoyed me. Either
          you've got to extend the season you've got to allow the
          big clubs that are in Europe not to go into into the Coca
 30       Cola cup or you have to start the season earlier or
          finish it later or reduce the number of teams in the
          premier league which of course the chairmen will [never
          vote for (   )
     AG:                                                   [uhuh
 35       there are any number any number of issues here I-I
          personally I'd scrap the Coca Cola cup [C: absolutely]
          and I'm doing the commentary on Wednesday [C: all right]
          for the replay I'd scrap the [competition (.) Secondly
          I'd reduce the size of the premiership
 40  C:                                [I agree with that well it
          could be a competition for fourth and second division
          teams second and fourth division teams second and third
          [division teams
     AG:  [Well they can [do that=
 45  C:                  [Sorry
     AG:                         =they can do that if they want
          to [C: yeh] I'd reduce the size of the premiership but
          there's too much self interest there [C: right] they
          don't want to they don't want to lose it do they? [C: No
 50       they don't] They don't want to jump off the gravy train.
          But the key thing I'd like to say, from a personal point
          of view is I- frankly it doesn't matter a stuff to me
```

```
        that we're talking about Manchester United [C: correct] I
        would argue this forcibly whoever was involved I think er
55      I think I look at the situation that United have got
        themselves in which in my view is not their fault (.) and
        the prime example of that is the Middlesborough fixture
        which has been cancelled three times now [C: that's
        right] so w-what are people going on about? [C: yes] I
60      mean why can't you change the rules mid-mid stream (.)
        Why [can't you?
   C:      [a-absolutely I completely I completely and utterly
        agree with you.
```

It is difficult, in a written transcript, to convey adequately the atmosphere of this exchange. Compared to Transcript 19 there is a heightened sense of urgency and emphasis – a shift 'up-key' in Goffman's terminology. Both participants are speaking very quickly, to the obvious detriment of C's turn in line 40 which becomes very confused. They are also at this point speaking over each other, seeming to compete for the floor, in an extended piece of overlapping talk which only ends with C's repair in line 45. There are many disfluencies, false starts and repetitions, which heighten a sense of emotional commitment to the views being expressed (lines 25, 52, 62). We might say that this is the radio phone-in equivalent of an escalation sequence, which clearly has many of the formal features of committed, serious argument.

Except, of course, that it is predicated on 'complete agreement'. The paradox of this type of sociability is that serious argument can be fun. Solidarity between the participants is clearly evident in C's back channel behaviour, regularly offering supportive minimal responses to AG's rhetorical and tag questions (lines 49, 59–61). For his part, AG produces an interesting variant of 'you say X but what about y', here recycling the views of another correspondent to confirm his solidarity with the caller: 'he says X but I say, so what?' (line 10). It is also very clear in this context that 'opinion prefaces' are part of a general strategy whereby arguments are modalised in a hypothetical-conditional form: 'personally I'd scrap the Coca Cola cup', 'the key thing I'd like to say', 'I would argue this forcibly'. Here the legitimacy of an opinion is founded on an interpersonal recognition of the right to state it, and arguments are recycled back and forth in a kind of 'language game'.

To return to Volosinov's 'urban carouse', an immediate reaction of many people who have heard this tape is that it sounds like an argument about football over a pint in a pub. Indeed the scheduling of 6.06 reinforces this impression: at six minutes past 6 p.m. it follows the afternoon's match commentary and reporting of games and results. It is as though we have returned from the game and are now reaffirming solidarity with our 'mates'. The opinions are tokens in a communal social ritual, however, because as this is BBC radio the 'imagined community' is national. An imagined

national geography is reproduced, just in the routine way that callers are
introduced with reference to their locations. But this is not the only identity
assumed by callers, as the following example illustrates:

```
Transcript 21
      DM:  And Kath is on line one from County Durham Kath good
           evening
      K:   Good evening
      DM:  So what do you make of all that?
  5   K:   I think it's er I think you've been unfair to Kevin
           Keegan to be honest, ever since he left you've been
           saying he's achieved nothing and I think this proves
           what he has achieved.
      DM:  No I didn't say he'd achieved nothing what I said was
 10        what indeed it's not what I think it's what other people
           who've been on the show think, that he walked out at a
           crucial time in the team's season and had he not been
           Kevin Keegan he'd have been slagged off for it (.) as it
           was because he was Kevin Keegan it was as if he'd died.
 15        But in fact, had he chosen he could have been there,
           guiding them to this slot, assuming that er he would have
           done and none of this is down to er down to what's been
           achieved by er Kenny Dalglish.
      K:   Well I think that er the way that it's looked at up here
 20        is to look at what Keegan did for us, for a start erm,
           and that's why it was received in such a way when he
           went.
      DM:  Why do you think he left Kath?
      K:   I think well the general feeling up here is that he
 25        wanted to stay 'til the end of the season and that it's
           the board who have er have made him go.
      DM:  I think you're wonderfully broadminded people not feeling
           any resentment that a man who'd been given all that money
           in whom you reposed all those hopes wanted to walk out on
 30        you.
      K:   I think you've got to be a Newcastle fan to understand it
           because er if you look back say 1990-91 when I went to
           the games regularly when I was actually living in
           Newcastle erm we were playing against the likes of Hull
 35        City and avoiding relegation [DM: mm]. Erm we were a
           laughing stock basically.
      DM:  But with fifteen million to spend most people could have
           got you into the Premiership the question is what then
           happens isn't it?
 40   K:   I don't know I think it's Keegan's erm, the way that he
           changed the team the way that he made us attractive
           [DM:mm] to watch.
      DM:  Well there you are I'm obviously not going to shake your
           faith [K: certainly not] nor should I nor should I nor
 45        should I even try but er it's a funny way to run a
           railroad Kath that's for sure ...
```

As an occasional exception to the 'radio bloke' characterisation it should be recognised that some callers to *6.06* are women. In this transcript, the host is David Mellor, the former MP who hosted the show before Alan Green took over. In characteristic fashion he exploits his second position to argue with Kath over the question of whether Kevin Keegan had let Newcastle United down by resigning in mid-season as their manager. Equally professionally, DM simultaneously protects his position by making a shift of footing from a personal to a collective opinion. The 'principal' on behalf of which he speaks is not himself, but other contributors to the programme.

Kath's response to this is to speak as a Newcastle United fan. In this, she too claims a collective entitlement which is absolutely central to the programme's communicative appeal. For the 'fan footing' does three things at once: it establishes the identity of the caller, it bestows a credible entitlement to an opinion which is not simply personal, and of course it refers to a geographical location within the imagined national community. Note that this is a relational geography – Kath characterises it as 'up here' in relation to DM's avowedly London location. So, through calls like this, the phone-in talks into being an imagined community of fans of the English national league. Everyone has his or her own affiliation (apart from Alan Green who, because he also commentates, has to be neutral) just as everyone has the right to have an opinion, but all are mutually dependent in the wider entity which is the fan community. Thus, the arguments on *6.06* are sociable because, just like the Jewish families studied by Schiffrin, their primary function is to 'ratify' social relationships.

4. Radio commentary

In so far as it serves as a forum for the circulation of opinions, the football phone-in acts as a kind of public sphere. In fact, it probably has more credentials in this respect than other genres of broadcasting, since over time, and orchestrated by the host, general 'public opinion' begins to crystallise from the serial points made by callers. Recurring issues include the changing economic infrastructure and exploitation of ordinary fans, declining standards of player behaviour on and off the field, standards of refereeing, and a continued anxiety about the so-called 'English disease', football hooliganism. This last issue is particularly prevalent whenever the England team plays abroad, especially in tournaments such as the European Championship. The debate tries to draw a line between the behaviour of 'genuine fans' and the hooligan element, with callers protesting their innocence in the face of heavy handed policing. But callers themselves are not the only contributors to this debate; here's how Alan Green began his commentary on the game between England and Germany in Euro 2000:

Transcript 22
Well I'm sorry to start on a sour note er but that's the first
time I've heard a national anthem being <u>boo</u>ed during the
European Championship when the England fans er booed the German
anthem erm **when will we ever get it right.**

[..]

Er fearful verbals for Oliver Kahn the German goalkeeper as he
makes his way to the penalty area to our left behind which are
the <u>Eng</u>land fans. Seaman has the <u>Ger</u>man supporters behind him
so a little bit of needle for the two goalkeepers.

Still bright sunshine in this er (.) rather (.) well not
exactly pretty Belgian city of Charlerois (.) It's a very odd
setting for a match of this magnitude **this game should have been
played in Brussels (.) And if anything goes wrong tonight
in the streets or in this inside this stadium then UEFA have
only themselves to blame.**

Let's concentrate on the football. England wait as does the
referee for television to say it's okay to kick off this game
(.) **It's happened more than once and it's er really something
these players could do without.** They're anxious to get under
way.

The referee Pierluigi Collina **the best in the tournament
without a question in my book** (.) and if Italy don't reach the
final then he's bound to make it just checking 'oh yes thanks
you very much television says it's all right' we're under way.

In the space of a few seconds Green sets an agenda here which includes a
comment on the quality of the referee, another instance of exploitation of
football by the demands of television, and of course the bad behaviour of
England fans and possibility of crowd trouble exacerbated by incompetent
officialdom. In this section, I want to explore the way radio commentary
functions to generate controversy, not only in general observations like
these, but also in the way particular events or incidents in the games are
literally 'talked-up' to become emblematic of on-going issues. Indeed
because of the routine scheduling of the football phone-in so that it follows
the match commentary and because, in the current arrangements, Alan
Green both commentates on matches and hosts the phone-in, callers
frequently discuss the controversial incidents that have arisen in his
commentary. Close analysis of the discourse of commentary can illuminate
how such controversies are talked into being.

   This will entail some reflection on the 'art' of commentary in general, and
on the differences between radio and TV in particular. Commentary is a
distinctive genre of media talk, and has long been regarded as such by
professional broadcasters. No outside broadcast can function without

commentary – at least not since the BBC's disastrous experiment in broadcasting only the sounds of The Derby horserace in 1926.[2] Manuals have been written on the art of commentary, and then rewritten as radio commentators were obliged to adapt their styles for TV (Whannel 1992: 26–32). The distinctiveness of live commentary has also been recognised in the few stylistic studies of the genre. In Crystal and Davy's detailed account of prosodic features, intonation patterns and variations of sentence structure, live radio commentary is described as having 'a fluency far in excess of that found in most other forms of unscripted speech' (1969: 130). For Kuiper (1996) the art of live commentary is akin to the use of the repetitive formulae employed by the 'singers' of poetry in oral tradition.

However, such accounts are concerned more with the production of commentary than with its reception. They do not discuss the experience of listening to commentary or the ways in which it produces particular versions of events. From this point of view, the most significant previous work has focused on TV, particularly in its use of the action replay (Morse 1983; Marriott 1995, 1996). With one significant exception (Crisell 1994) there has been very little detailed analysis of the listener appeal of radio commentary. This lack of attention to radio confirms, again, its status as the poor relation of media studies, and because of this, even in the standard text books, all sorts of half-truths and myths have been allowed to develop.

To mention, briefly, three of these. It is problematic to argue, as do Boyle and Haynes, that there is a 'congruence between radio and television commentary' and that many techniques of television commentary have 'carried over from radio' (2000: 86–7). Some have, and some personnel have worked in both media, but actually the founding fathers of BBC sport recognised that the two media require differences of technique which have evolved into distinct modes of address, as we shall see. In this context, it becomes equally difficult to support the assumption that the dictum applied to early radio commentary, that the commentator 'should behave as if the audience is one person, and just address that person' (Whannel 1992: 26) still applies today – in fact it is not, in any straightforward way, a feature of modern radio commentary. And in the light of what we have just seen from Alan Green, what are we to make of Rowe's remark that 'few live commentators ... are permitted to be provocative, unlike their broadcast and print colleagues, who provide the necessarily opinionated editorial' (Rowe 1999: 105)? In fact editorialising is standard practice, especially in radio sports commentary.

We can go some way to understanding why this is so, if we reprise the one discussion which actually analyses some commentary. In *Understanding Radio*, Crisell devotes a chapter to the radio cricket commentary of John Arlott. He emphasises the distinction between the demands of TV and radio, pointing out that because radio is a 'blind' medium, the event it recreates is, in a sense, imaginary — it exists in the listener's imagination. Unlike TV, where the commentary supplements a picture which the viewer can see, on radio the commentator is central to the creation of the imaginary scene. As such, Arlott did much more than simply describe, or narrate, the events of the game; he also interpreted them and embellished them with his own distinctive style of 'poetic' flourish. Thus, argues Crisell, a link is forged between the listener and the commentator such that: 'we might say that our interest in the test match is much the same as an enjoyment of John Arlott's company ... the commentator as "personality" and the listener as his companion' (1994: 137).

In short, on radio, we are not simply listening to a game, we are listening to a commentator's experience of a game, as displayed in various forms of talk. With this in mind, let us now return to football. Here are a few seconds of commentary from the 1997 Coca Cola Cup final between Middlesborough and Leicester City. The commentator, Alan Green, is accompanied by a 'summariser', the former Liverpool player, Jim Beglin. This immediately introduces a variation from Crisell's account, for here we are in the company not of a single individual but two colleagues (and in contemporary cricket commentary there are three people with microphones in the commentary box), who talk to each other as much as they address listeners directly:

```
Transcript 23a
     AG: Juninho. Juninho's return pass to the Italian not a good
         one and it's easily out of play by Heskey for a
         Middlesborough thrown in close to the corner flag down
         the Middlesborough right, Ravanelli took it quickly and
  5      Juninho wasted possession and it's hooked high and away
         towards the halfway line by Leicester's defence. Back it
         goes towards that penalty area. Cox heads it infield.
         Emerson er lashes it towards the near side it's not a
         good ball but Beck has to er chase back to win it back.
 10      Has he won a throw in? The linesman at first - I'm sure
         the linesman at first gave it to Middlesborough then he
         looked at the referee saw that the referee was giving it
         to Leicester then suddenly the flag swapped hands.
         There's a surprise.
 15  JB: Yea I think they got it right between them because you
         can always tell from the players' reactions who it's gone
         against and er Beck didn't complain about it, he got on
         with it.
     AG: If in doubt stick up both your hands linesman and then
 20      you can always transfer it. Don't worry about it.
         Thirteen minutes to half time Leicester nil
         Middlesborough nil and it's er well it's closing in on
         woeful now it really is but at the moment it's still just
         very poor.
                              [..]
 25      Fleming to Beck. There over the halfway line now
```

> Middlesborough. Emerson and Mustoe. Juninho desperate to
> find some room but Kaamark's almost ignoring what's going
> on around the game just watching the Brazilian. *L-look at*
> *Kaamark! He's just running after Juninho doesn't matter*
> 30 *where the ball is.* Cox on the far side. It's down the right
> flank and now Juninho has it and Kaamark's a couple of
> yards away. And then a second challenge comes in.
> This from Gary Parker. Parker's tackled by Hignett. Hignett
> to Juninho. Kaamark brings him down that's a
> 35 foul. And the Middlesborough fans' frustration is
> evident. *Oh well!* Erm **I don't think Martin Bodenham had**
> **any intention initially of booking Kaamark but maybe the**
> **reaction from the fans was so hostile he suddenly looks**
> **and he thinks it's a yellow card.**
> 40 JB: Well what makes it even stranger is there was an almost
> identical tackle earlier in the game and Martin Bodenham
> let it go completely. That time we saw it again and he's
> given Kaamark a yellow card.
> AG: **And I'm sure that wasn't his original intention when he**
> 45 **blew for the free kick. Anyway, what do I know about it?**
> Free kick to Middlesborough. Forty yards out. Taken
> quickly. Juninho ...

Again, it is clear from this that radio sports commentary does much more than simply describe, or narrate, the game. We might say that narration is a 'default' activity, a baseline, on which various other practices are built. I want to suggest that these other practices are best understood, in Goffman's terminology, as shifts of 'key', which, as it were, take the commentary to a higher (and sometimes louder) level. Two sorts of key shift are illustrated here. First, AG produces statements of opinion (in bold face) where he doesn't simply commentate, but rather comments on the action (and frequently these comments spark an exchange with the summariser). In this extract two statements of opinion have to do with the quality of decisions made by the officials and so they feed into the ongoing debate about standards of refereeing. This is a routine way in which the commentary produces moments of controversy for further debate, as previously noted.

Secondly, however, another kind of key-shift is also evident here, and this connects with the points made by Crisell. From time to time AG produces an exclamation, a sort of direct reaction to what he sees on the pitch (here in italics): 'L-look at Kaamark!' (lines 28–9). On radio this is a most interesting device because we cannot, of course, see Kaamark for ourselves. So who is AG addressing at this point? He could be talking to JB who is sitting beside him or he could be talking to himself in a spontaneous expression of emotion. Either way, this key-shift momentarily confirms the 'blindness' of the listeners, and so insists on their distance from the event. Listeners can only consume the event at this level through the experience of the commentators. As Crisell puts it, we are their 'companions', but more precisely we are cast, via radio, as eavesdroppers on their responses and reactions.

At other times some of AG's reactions characterise him as a member of the crowd. He calls out directly at the game, as a spectator might: 'stick up both your hands linesman' etc. (lines 19–20). Again the listener can only experience vicariously this level of direct involvement in the game. This begins to suggest that Crisell's notion of companionship is actually a rather complex construction in which our imaginative participation is somehow predicated on our absence from the scene. In her discussion of TV commentary Marriott (1996) argues that 'making viewers conscious of their absence from the scene' is problematic for television and we will return to her discussion of how this is resolved in the next section. On radio, however, the listener's absence is routinely confirmed as a necessary part of the experience. And, paradoxically, utterances which would normally confirm co-presence here serve to reinforce the listener's experiential distance. This is particularly apparent where the summariser joins the commentator in an exchange of direct reactions to something they can see, but we cannot:

```
Transcript 23b
    AG:  On to Hignett. Ravanelli's unmarked, edge of the penalty
         area. So too is Beck. Left foot volley. Fabulous
         challenge by Prior to block it. Beck again. Inside the
         penalty area. Izzet's there and diverts it behind for a
 5       corner.
    JB:  Well Leicester again getting so many [blue shirts=
    AG:                                        [Oh!=
    JB:                                                  =[behind
         the ball
10  AG:                                                  =[hold
         on it can't be a goal[kick!
    JB:                        [I can't believe that
    AG:  It can't it can't be a goal kick! No wonder they're booing
         the decision. It can't it can't. And Juninho is
15       going to get booked for dissent. And now we've got a
         foolish streaker on the field ...
```

Here AG's key-shift is supported by JB's deictic reference (use of 'that', line 12) to an event in their experiential space which we, by definition, cannot share. But this is a common feature of radio talk and it suggests that the appeal of this medium, at least in the modern era, is much more complex than the dictum that direct address should be used to speak to listeners as individuals. It is true that listeners are directly addressed, though in Alan Green's football commentary this is usually in a collective form, but the audience is also invited to listen in to scenes they can only imagine. The imaginative element emphasised by Crisell seems to be reinforced, and is perhaps dependent, on the inclusion forms of talk in the commentary which *do not* speak directly to the listener. And in football commentary it is interesting that these especially seem to occur precisely at the most intense moments, where the controversial incidents are described.

5. Football commentary on TV and radio

At Euro 2000, England did in fact manage to beat Germany, by one goal to nil. That goal was scored by Alan Shearer, through a header from a David Beckham free kick. During the tournament there had been some debate about Shearer's form, as he was now approaching veteran status, and this was reflected in the commentaries both on radio and TV. However, in the light of the previous analysis we can also examine the ways these commentaries offer different experiences for the consumers of each medium. From this point of view, the 'congruences' between TV and radio are more than counterbalanced by their differences. In this transcript, Alan Green on BBC radio is joined by Terry Butcher as summariser; the BBC TV commentator is John Motson with summariser Trevor Brooking. The commentaries are presented side by side for ease of comparison:

Transcript 24: TV	Transcript 24: Radio
JM: Free kick to England (8 seconds)	AG: Free kick to England. Beckham To take it. Five yards in from the right touch line
Owen and Shearer being 5 supported over on the edge of the penalty area by Scholes. Now. Ince goes to join them. Phil Neville trots up from left back.	Gary Neville's there too(.) er has a word with Beckham. Ince has moved forward so too has Phil Neville on the far side. So five players in attacking positions for
10 Owen coming in near post. SHEARER GOAL FOR ENGLAND OH AND ONE FROM ALAN SHEARER THE MAN FOR THE 15 BIG OCCASION (4 seconds)	England. Beckham swerves it in. Owen goes to meet it chance for SHEARER SHEARER SCORES ALAN SHEARER SCORES FOR THE FIRST TIME IN EIGHT GAMES A CROSS DELIVERED BY BECKHAM BEAT ALL THE
They're cheering here and you'll be up on your feet 20 at home I should imagine (.) Alan Shearer for England his first goal in eight internationals.	ATTACKERS APART FROM ALAN SHEARER ONE THAT JUST SHOWS CRITICS LIKE ME SHEARER SCORES FOR ENGLAND SEVEN MINUTES INTO THE SECOND HALF IT'S ENGLAND ONE GERMANY NIL.
What a moment to get it. 25 Owen came in first, it went on to Shearer and he guided the header away from Kahn.	TB: Well once again Beckham supplied the cross for the goal it was a free kick it wasn't the best of Beckham free kicks but he angled it

30 TB: That is a fantastic free
        kick such a long way out
        but the pace of that and
        the distance (.) so
        difficult to deal with
35   goes right across the face
        of goal you could not have
        hit a more perfect free
        kick across the six yard
        box Alan Shearer waiting
40   keeping his fingers
        crossed 'everyone miss it
        please' it sat up there
        waiting to be tucked away
        he used all of his
45   experience and England are
        in front.

    JM: Oh look at the reaction
50   there from Kevin Keegan
        and Arthur Cox and company
        but Germany are on the
        attack on the pitch (.)

55   Alan Shearer's twenty
        ninth goal in his sixty
        second international but
        Germany are coming back
        straight away that's
60   Karsten Jancker

        It's his first, Shearer,
        since he scored against
        Belgium at Sunderland in
65   the autumn.

    TB: I can't emphasise how what
        a wonderful free kick that
        was the <u>dist</u>ance it went
70   at the pace it went I mean
        they just didn't cope with
        it and didn't deal with it
        and there Shearer waited
        at the back post tucked it
75   away.

    JM: A moment to lift all
        English hearts.

towards to the near post it
was missed by everybody
Michael Owen had made a run
towards the near post missed
by everybody Alan Shearer
right on the six yard line
the ball sat up nicely and
who better than Alan Shearer
when a chance like that comes
into the box because all he
had to do was head it back
across goal Kahn had no
chance.

He should be listening to
Radio Five he probably was
listening to Radio Five with
all the criticism [he was
getting=
AG: [eh eh get
    out (   )
TB: [=but at
    the end of the day I said
    before the game one chance
    for Shearer it's going to be
    in the back of the net.

AG: Well it is. It's the only
    chance he's had and to his
    great credit as skipper he
    delivers it. Delivers it into
    Kahn's net. Germany a goal
    down. England a goal in
    front. Hey this is a bit
    better. Outplayed for this
    first thirty minutes England
    outplayed. Much better
    towards half time and now in
    front.

    And the stadium is pulsating
    (.) with England supporters
    singing and dancing up and
    down.

    It's not quite like Rotterdam
    That stadium actually moves
    but er Charlerois might be
    moving. England one Germany
    nil.

Marriott's basic point about TV commentary is that television constructs its own version of the event, so that the 'commentary takes as its subject matter not the original event but the televised reconstruction of that event as viewed on the television monitor' (Marriott 1995). This is most evident here when first the summariser and then the commentator talk over action replays. Brooking reproduces what Marriott argues is a characteristic pattern of alternation between present and past tenses ('that is a fantastic free kick ... it sat up there', lines 30–1, 42) as the replay talk, in presenting a rerun (now) of a past incident (then) occupies two simultaneous time zones. A 'shared perceptual space' is created for both commentator and viewer (Marriott 1996: 84); and within this space, as we see a close-up shot of Shearer, Brooking actually begins to animate his thoughts, as if to encourage our identification (lines 41–2). Similarly Motson directly exhorts the viewer to observe the reactions of England's management team (lines 49–1). On TV then, the commentary forges a link between the viewer and the jointly witnessed live action, where deictic markers of co-presence ('*that* free kick', 'it sat up *there*') function in the conventional way.

With the absence of a visual image, radio commentary talks all the time. It is obviously the case that radio cannot afford the seconds of silence which occur on TV as the free kick is being set up. Equally, it is apparent that it is only through talk that the excitement of the event can be conveyed. After the goal is scored, Motson pauses for four seconds to allow the visuals to speak for themselves, whereas Green repeats, at the top of his voice, 'Shearer scores ... for England'. The function of the radio summariser then seems to be to renarrate the incident in a more measured style, using the past tense alone. Clearly this is designed for the listener, perhaps to give a more fully rounded account, and it does function a bit like a replay, but it does not assume the listener's co-presence, nor is the listener directly addressed. Instead, another discursive shift occurs.

The defining feature of the radio commentary is the interactive exchange between summariser and commentator. Picking up on the fact that Green has been critical of Shearer, Butcher ends his summary with a moment of interpersonal banter to which Green responds (lines 43–9). With the additional reference to the radio station, both parties are confirmed here as media 'personalities'. Or, better still, they are constructed as characters at the game, engaged in friendly asides and exchanging opinions, not directly with the listener, but with each other. There is a distinctive alignment to the recipient here, which again confirms the difference between technological co-presence and absence. Marriott's argument is that TV compensates for the viewer's absence by offering the co-presence of the replay. So how does radio tackle this issue?

I want to suggest that the listener is positioned by the commentary as a virtual member of the crowd. This may be a controversial suggestion, for

Marriott (1996) has taken Morse (1983) to task for her suggestion that TV coverage brings us a 'crowd-event'. However, Morse's discussion of an 'aural realism' of commentary which emanates from 'ideal spectators' at sports events does seem to be applicable to radio (1983: 53). Whereas TV offers its viewer a position of ideal spectatorship, radio offers its listeners an imaginary identification with ideal spectators. The problem that we can only experience the event through the commentary is resolved by characterising the commentators as members of the crowd with whom listeners are encourage to identify.

This is why radio commentators draw our attention to their own location in the stadium, to their personal experiences of getting to the ground, to their discomfort in inclement weather and the very welcome half-time cup of tea. It is why they display their personal reactions, call out, and exchange extensive banter with colleagues. All this establishes the commentators too as fans of the game. It also makes sport on the radio a more excited, collective experience by comparison with the more cerebral, analytical approach of TV. It is TV which directly addresses its audience as individuals, not radio. In Transcript 24 the basic difference between the two media is summed up in the commentators' metastatements: 'Hey this is a bit better' as opposed to 'moment to lift all English hearts' – Green is personally committed, whereas Motson is neutral and cool. Perhaps I might be permitted to close this chapter on a personal note by saying that on these occasions I always prefer to turn down the TV sound and have the radio on. The TV commentary sounds comparatively boring to me.

Notes

1. There are suggestions that 'V. N. Volosinov' was a nom-de-plume adopted by Bakhtin for the publication of *Marxism and the Philosophy of Language* in Soviet Russia in 1929. At any rate the two authors were closely connected and this early text clearly prefigures Bakhtin's later work on speech genres:

    'In the case where a random assortment of people gathers – while waiting in line or conducting some business – statements and exchanges of words will ... be constructed in ... completely different ways. Village sewing circles, urban carouses, workers' lunchtime chats etc ... will all have their own types. Each situation, fixed and sustained by social custom commands a particular organization of audience and, hence, a particular repertoire of little behavioral genres' (Volosinov 1929/1973: 97).

2. 'The transmission of The Derby from Epsom was allowed on condition that only the sounds of the race itself should be heard. There could be no mention of the results. Under these conditions the BBC's first coverage of the race, in 1926, was a fiasco. It rained solidly all day, "and during the race, not only were there no sounds from the hoofs in the soft going, but even the bookies, tipsters and onlookers were more occupied in taking shelter under their umbrellas than in speeding home the winner"' (Scannell and Cardiff 1991: 25–6).

6 Youth Talk

1. The revolution at Radio 1

The structure of radio sports commentary discussed in the previous chapter can best be understood in the light of Paddy Scannell's concept of 'double articulation' (Scannell 1991). He introduced this concept to define the very basic point that broadcast talk is always in two places at once, the places of its production and reception, a 'there' and a 'here'. This effect is accentuated by liveness, where the production is transmitted from an institutional space, such as a studio, as opposed say to a recorded drama or film. Much previous work on broadcast talk has focused on ways in which this double articulation is bridged, for example, by news interviewers asking questions and formulating answers on the audience's behalf. There is also of course the very mundane fact that hosts invariably introduce their studio guests to the overhearing audience before the studio business can begin. It is thus a fundamental feature of broadcast talk that, as viewers and listeners, we know that whatever is happening 'there' is being produced for 'us', which these bridging devices work to achieve.

However, in contemporary radio talk, the double articulation doesn't always work quite like this. On occasions, listeners appear to be able to tolerate a different structure of alternation between talk which is addressed to them and talk which is not. This is the structure that is momentarily produced when AG responds to TB's banter in transcript 24; it may indeed by intended to be overheard by the listener, but it does not betray this in the design of the utterance: 'eh eh go on'. Modern listeners thus seem to be comfortable with a shifting participation framework in which, on the one hand, they are acknowledged as 'ratified' listeners and, on the other, they are cast as eavesdroppers on distant conversations. As we have seen, sports commentary contains moments of this, but these are embedded within a format which is otherwise entirely listener friendly. This alternating structure of double articulation is taken much further, however, with interesting consequences, in the radio talk that is the focus for this chapter.

Specifically this chapter considers a genre of DJ talk which is found in some forms of popular music radio. Popularly known as 'zoo' radio, this first became available to a UK national audience in the early 1990s, on BBC Radio 1, where it remains the dominant style. It was pioneered by DJs Steve Wright and Chris Evans, reaching new heights of artistry when Evans was recruited, in 1995, to present the Radio 1 Breakfast Show. It should be noted that this style of zoo radio was constructed from a mix of influences, ranging from the 'shock-jock' style of radio presentation in the USA, most famously associated with Howard Stern, to new experiments with 'youth TV', particularly at Channel 4, where Evans had previously presented *The Big Breakfast* and a game show *Don't Forget Your Toothbrush*. In all contexts, this was a style that was very much to do with the testing and breaking of boundaries, sometimes of 'taste and decency' but more generally of conventions of production and reception.

Why BBC Radio 1, in particular, should have been interested in securing Evans's services at this time is a point worth some consideration. There were institutional imperatives here which underpinned the willingness to experiment. In the field of popular music radio, commercial competition had cut into Radio 1's earlier monopoly and, over three years, from 1992 to 1995, the station lost around one-third of its audience (from 17 million to 12 million, the current figure stands at nearly 10 million). In 1994, for the first time, the total audience for commercial radio outstripped that of the BBC. In this context Radio 1 was facing something of an identity crisis, which was addressed partly in a review of its public service commitments (in the document *Extending Choice*, 1992) and partly by the appointment in 1993 of the chief author of that document, Matthew Bannister, as controller of Radio 1. Bannister immediately sacked some long-serving DJs and started to affirm a distinctive commitment to inventive 'new music'. David Hendy shows how this music policy began to transform play-lists and ultimately, partly through Evans's collaboration, established Radio 1 as a prime mover in the so-called 'Britpop' phenomenon (Hendy 2000b).

What has not been previously discussed is the style of talk that accompanied these developments. This is despite the fact that 'speech content' was one of the key public service commitments identified in *Extending Choice*. Simultaneously with the introduction of the revised music policy, there occurred something of a revolution in the approach to DJ talk. Not only was the 'new music' being played more often, but also it was punctuated by the lively sounds of zoo radio, or, more typically with Evans, it was the music that occasionally interrupted the speech. Nevertheless, at first it seemed a successful gamble, for three months after his appointment it was reported that 600,000 listeners had returned to the station. And despite the subsequent controversies and contractual disputes which dogged Evans's own career (he left Radio 1 for Virgin Radio in 1997) his stylistic legacy has remains (for example, in the style of the current presenter of the *Breakfast Show*, at the time of writing, Chris Moyles).

2. Traditional DJ talk

To begin to appreciate the novelty of zoo radio, it will be helpful, first of all, to return to previous studies of 'DJ talk'. In fact Montgomery's (1986b) analysis relates precisely to the style of the DJs sacked by Bannister, and the other major study in this field is of Radio 1's first ever DJ, Tony Blackburn (Brand and Scannell 1991). As noted in Chapter 1, Montgomery's article was innovative at the time it was published because it argued that media talk could be analysed for more than its ideological content. Indeed, part of the interest in DJ talk is that it is of marginal 'ideational' interest; its main purpose is to foster and maintain an ongoing relationship with listeners. In Montgomery's terms it 'foregrounds the interpersonal' and it does this, primarily, in a sophisticated use of direct address.

Montgomery identifies three main strategies used by DJs to develop interaction with their listeners. The first strategy is to maximise co-presence, or, to adopt a phrase often used to characterise modern mediated relationships, a sense of 'intimacy at a distance' (Moores 2000). This is achieved by 'response demanding utterances' consisting of direct requests and imperatives to listeners, and through extensive use of markers of temporal and spatial deixis (now, here, this, that). In the light of our previous discussion of football commentary, it is worth giving some particular attention to these. Temporal deixis is, of course, no problem on radio and in DJ talk it serves to confirm the liveness of the show. But spatial deixis, as we have seen, runs the risk of highlighting the absence of the listener. In this respect I think it is interesting that in the data presented by Montgomery, markers of spatial deixis are embedded in forms of direct address: 'can you see that?', 'I wish you could see this place'. They do not have the unequivocal force of Beglin's 'I don't believe that'. So in this kind of listener-friendly DJ talk it is as if the 'blindness' of the listener is treated as a matter of regret.

Secondly, DJ talk personalises the DJ, particularly through the use of what Montgomery calls 'interpolations'. These are asides and metastatements which express the personal alignment of the DJ to the topic of the talk. There is thus a high level of self-reflexivity in DJ talk, and it is this that is highlighted in Brand and Scannell's discussion of *The Tony Blackburn Show*. As a veteran DJ, Blackburn knows that aspects of his past and personal life are in the public domain; he has been known to express controversial opinions but, more routinely, his programme is built around the performance of a 'playful self'. This is a media persona which regular listeners recognise and with which some of them interact. The programme as a whole works as a 'discursive kingdom', for Blackburn to perform this identity, supported by the usual array of recorded jingles, station identifiers and trailers.

But thirdly, Montgomery recognises that the audience too is person-alised. This is constructed in what he calls 'social deixis', where the DJ talk addresses individuals, or social categories in the audience. Individuals are addressed by name and location, as in the conventional introductions to calls to phone-in programmes. But categories of listeners are also identified by place of origin, occupation and even (in the old DJ talk) by star sign. The key point here is that listeners are not addressed as if they were a general mass audience. The audience is diversified and fragmented by the use of identifiers, and then it is reconstructed, in all its diversity, as a community. In this reconstruction, the listener's participation framework is continually shifting:

> But its very instability lends to it a special kind of dynamic. On the one hand, it is continuously inclusive with respect to diverse constitu-encies within the audience in a personalizing, familiar, even intimate, manner ... On the other hand, although the discourse may constitute the audience in fragmentary terms, it also manages simultaneously to dramatize the relation of the audience to itself: as listeners we are made constantly aware of other (invisible) elements in the audience of which we form a part. (Montgomery 1986b: 438)

Thus the old style of DJ talk engages listeners in an ongoing process of identification which is built around shifts of alignment. One moment we are being addressed directly as ratified listeners; the next moment we are listening to other individuals or categories of listeners being addressed, or callers phoning into the programme. We thereby imagine ourselves to be members of a large, diverse community, linked to each other by virtue of being listeners to this show. And it is the personality of the DJ that orchestrates this, in the live time that is the 'here and now' of his show. In his 'discursive kingdom' absences are regretted, and distance or difference is only admitted on the basis that it contributes to a higher level unity. In short, this is all about our inclusion; and on national radio we are all cast as members of a national 'imagined community'.

3. Frontstage/backstage

The traditional strategies of DJ talk analysed by Montgomery are not simply superceded by zoo radio, rather they are embedded in a more complex participation framework. Just a hint of this is contained in the following transcript where, at breakneck speed, Evans demonstrates his competence at producing conventional DJ talk:

```
Transcript 25
    It's five minutes past eight that's the time eight oh five on
    Friday morning April 26ᵗʰ 1996 the last day that we're here for
    four weeks [studio cheers] we're out for four weeks [studio:
    bye] okay there's just one day to go until we see Oasis at
  5 Maine Road tomorrow joining us will be you the listeners if
    you're not going to be at Maine Road you ain't going nowhere
    you're losing out on a weekend of your life you should have
    bought tickets you should go to the gig of the century Oasis on
    Sunday and Saturday (.) Coming with us Bud, Neil Hawes, Adam
 10 Whitely and Lindsay Brown from Chandler's sixth form in
    Ipswich, Jim and Nick in Buckinghamshire, Katie Lesson and Lucy
    Ellery from Kendal they're up to Manchester >down to Manchester
    from Kendal I suppose< they're going on Saturday (.) On Sunday
    Adam and Sam in Blackburn and six luscious girls Gina Louise
 15 Katie Lindsay Angela and Ruth from Formby in Merseyside they're
    just getting the train. The weather's expected to be dry but
    cloudy with some chance of rain and a maximum temperature of
    thirteen degrees (.) Retrograde (.) It's six minutes past
    eight. We're going to be there give us a wave, Holly's going to
 20 be there, Justin's going to be there, Jamie's going to be
    there, Danny boy, myself, the whole team.
```

This is, of course a piece of promotion for Britpop, and thus entirely consistent with the 'new music' policy of Bannister's Radio 1. It is also, however, a piece of classic DJ talk, directly addressed to the listeners. Note again, that listeners are addressed in the plural not as individuals (line 5), but this plurality is immediately broken down in third-person references to a series of individuals, groups and locations. Once again, this constructs an imaginative national geography, in relational terms as Evans reminds himself (lines 12–13) that Kendal is north of Manchester. As Montgomery puts it, this 'dramatizes the relation of the audience to itself'; an effect which is further reinforced by the imaginary interactive possibilities offered by Evans, and the response-demanding utterance (line 19). Evans also dramatises his own persona in the interpolation following his announcement of the weather (line 18): I take 'retrograde', in this context, to be a 'hip' expression consistent with the production of youth talk. And all this of course is live, as the time-checks insist, and as the distance of the listeners from this studio is transformed into an imaginary co-presence by the deictic marker 'here' (line 2).

So far then, so conventional. But the hint of another level to the participation framework is produced where Evans refers (lines 2–3) to the fact that he and his team are going on holiday. Members of the production team are heard to cheer and, as it were, playfully take their leave. In what sense are these cheers (line 3), which emanate from the studio, addressed to us? Rather, they might seem to be a spontaneous outburst from the crew which we happen, perhaps accidently, to overhear. This is a 'backstage' utterance which may or may not be intended for the listener, and which would normally be off-air in conventional forms of radio. In fact the subsequent leave token 'bye' (line 4), which *is* addressed to us, acts as a kind of acknowledgement that some kind of transgressive behaviour might have just occurred.

In exploring the dynamics of zoo radio it is this kind of backstage utterance, and the questions it raises about this type of media talk, which is of particular interest. For we do not, in this context, assume that this is accidental or the result of a technical fault; rather it is intended that we are able to listen to talk and other kinds of sound effect from the backstage production areas of the show. Furthermore, though Evans mediates between these backstage areas and the listening audience (cf. 'the last day that we're here', 'we're out for four weeks' etc.), the 'we' that is his collective subject is as much exclusive as it is inclusive, if not more so. There is thus an alternation in this discourse between inclusivity and exclusivity which insists on a gap between the production team and listeners, at the same time as it constructs co-presence. At times, the team is hearably engaged in its own business which is not always clearly directed towards us, even though it is intended that we overhear it. How do we understand the communicative rationality of this situation?

We can begin to appreciate something of what might be at stake in these developments, if we return to the work of Goffman. In his (1981) essay on radio talk, Goffman discusses radio announcing in general, but he does prefigure the work on DJ talk in particular, with his comments about the maintenance of an attractive 'air personality' and the preference of some popular DJs for unscripted 'free association' (1981: 280). However, basing his work on a collection of 'bloopers' in American radio talk from the 1950s, Goffman assumes throughout that it is normal practice that the voices of support personnel will not be heard (235). At most what can occur is a form of 'ratified by-play' where announcers temporarily and rarely make comments to the off-mike crew and then may 'bring the audience in' by explaining to them what has happened (236). This practice typically occurs where mistakes have been made and some kind of 'metacommunication' is necessary.

Several different forms of metacommunication are identified by Goffman, some of which prefigure the work on DJ talk. For instance, Montgomery's concept of 'interpolation' certainly includes changes in the speaker's alignment to the utterance evident in 'a repertoire of ironic, self-dissociating phrases' (286), and 'the pat metalinguistic device of referring to self in the third person' (290) etc. Alternatively:

> One way an announcer can face a production hitch *and* comply with
> the norm that there should be no dead time, is to constitute his [*sic*]
> own situation ... as the subject matter to describe ... If he is willing to

change footing and introduce references to his own circumstances at the moment, then he need never be at a loss for something to say ... he may introduce a running report on his own remedial actions and his own predicament as someone trying to assemble a proper production, these being backstage matters ordinarily concealed from listeners. (1981: 291, 293)

In other words one strategy for referring to 'backstage matters normally concealed from the audience' is unremarkable, since it explicitly takes the listener behind the scenes of the show. We shall see that this strategy is routinely displayed in zoo radio.

However, Goffman also raises the possibility of a much more radical intrusion of backstage material, in what he calls the practice of 'subversion'. Here what is normally backstage becomes frontstage, either through technical confusion, or sometimes deliberately. If the intention is deliberate, and not mitigated in some way, the 'rough' voice presents a direct challenge to the listener:

there will be occasions when an announcer *thinks* that his staff directed remarks are not being broadcast when indeed they are. At point here, however, is a further possibility: under no misapprehension that the microphone is closed, the announcer can blurt out a behind-the-scenes comment to the technicians present, using a 'rough' informal voice, as if momentarily blind to − or uncaring about − its wide reception. (1981: 302−3)

The point that Goffman is making here touches on the very essence of the 'communicative ethos' of broadcasting (Scannell 1989). For if this 'blurting out' is not simply a mistake, and if indeed the announcer does not care about its reception, then this would pose a threat to the 'care-structures' which Scannell argues are fundamental to broadcast talk. As audiences we have to assume that a communicative rationality is in place and what we hear is intended to be heard, or else a mistake has occurred. But if we overhear something which is not intended for us, with no further explanation offered, the question of what the 'care-structure' might be is left open. That, in Goffman's terms, is what constitutes 'subversion'. But we will see that zoo radio, for all its willingness to open up these backstage areas, is never quite as subversive as this.

4. The zoo aesthetic

We can explore the dimensions of zoo radio in three extracts taken from the *Breakfast Show* in 1998, after it had moved to Virgin Radio (though with its format and key personnel still intact). These extracts have been chosen to illustrate the defining features of the 'zoo aesthetic', namely: (1) that backstage areas of the show are routinely foregrounded, particularly where there is no attempt to disguise technological problems; (2) that participants routinely engage in talk which appears to be unscripted, ad-libbed on the spur of the moment and often involves playing with the conventions of the medium; but (3) this is indeed made intelligible within a new kind of 'care-structure' which revolves around the personality of the DJ, as its chief presenter. What 'blurting out' occurs here is not produced by the DJ himself, for it becomes his job to contain it and to re-present it in an intelligible form for the listener.

4.1 The technical hitch

First of all, let us consider a scenario which is not unlike Goffman's example of metacommunication. Here a technical hitch has almost occurred, but this is dramatically exploited, not minimised as it might be in more conventional forms of radio. We are then taken backstage to discover how it happened and in this move a double articulation occurs. First, we overhear studio personnel talking to each other, but almost immediately we are included in the imaginary scenario as ratified listeners:

```
Transcript 26
   TR:     Radio 1 newsbeat (.) I'm Tina Ritchie.
   CE:     Two things [Tina
   TR:                [Oh
   CE:     I'm sorry about that
 5 TR:     Heart attack or what?
   Studio: heh heh heh
   TR:     I'm sitting here and he goes 'right time for the news'
           and I'm in completely the wrong [room=
   Studio:                                 [eh eh eh
10 TR:                                      =completely the
           wrong microphone completely the wrong everything and
           there are five people in front of me going OH MY GOD
           what's going to happen?
   CE:     Now listen, listen eh y-eh-you're in the travel booth
15 TR:     I'm in the travel pod now
   CE:     You're in the travel pod now are you?
   TR:     Yes
   CE:     Okay, so so somebody sorted it out for us technologically
   TR:     Yes we have er er er
20 CE:                        a brilliant person
   TR:                                           called Richard who
           coped with the situation admirably
   CE:     Richard thank you (.) So he flicked from the news booth
           fader to the travel booth fader 'cause you were in the
25         travel booth from twenty past eight waiting to do a
           travel bulletin that was never going to happen.
```

```
       TR:     Well I just thought you might do a quick travel sometimes
               like you do you know [I go an-
       CE:                         [but when it got to twenty nine and
30             a half minutes past eight[did you=
       Studio:                          [eh eh eh
       CE:                                      =think maybe oh er let's
               wind this one up a little?
       TR:     Listen experience has taught me never to think in a sort
35             of sensible[way
       Studio:            [too logical eh eh eh
       TR:                     in a logical way
       CE:     okay
       TR:     Experience has taught me never to think logically when it
               comes to you and me.
```

What establishes our position of intelligibility here is, of course, TR's shift into the third person in line 7. Up to the point she and CE have been engaged in an exclusive exchange, to which they return in line 27. These exchanges do not directly acknowledge the listener, who is therefore obliged to eavesdrop in a similar way to the exchange of banter between sports commentators. However, between lines 7 and 26 there is a shift in alignment towards the listener, effected through two discursive strategies. First, TR's third-person reference to Chris begins to provide a narrative of the causes of the drama we have just overheard. Secondly, in lines 14–26 CE and TR engage in an interesting hybrid form of double articulation where they are both talking to each other and, at the same time retelling the incident for the listener. This is similar to Goffman's account of a 'running report on remedial actions' in which the backstage business is re-presented for the listener's benefit.

We might also note the high levels of co-operativeness on display here. In fact the incident's retelling is co-produced by CE and TR at the point where Richard is introduced (TR seems to be seeking CE's sanction here possibly because Richard is an inaudible backstage technician). More generally other studio personnel provide the usual supportive laughter and contribute to sentence completion (line 36). What might have been a moment of chaos is thus re-presented, in its re-enactment and retelling, as orderly. The backstage drama is only allowed to intervene on the condition that it is repackaged for the listener's benefit.

4.2 The ad-libbed exchange

At first sight, Transcript 27 might seem to contain a more 'subversive' possibility, where the intelligibility of what we are invited to overhear is problematic. Having previously engaged Dan, a production assistant, in a conversation about the business activities of Lisa, his girlfriend, Evans abruptly switches to a much more personal topic. This again revolves around the issue of the frontstage transmission of what would normally be off-air, but here this is not retold as a narrative:

```
Transcript 27
   CE:     I know about your situation
   D:      what?
   CE:     your contraceptive situation 'cos you told me
   Studio: oh eh eh eh
 5 D:      what?
   Studio: eh eh
   D:      can you enlighten me?
   CE:     Well I can if you want me to. We'll talk about it
           afterwards. I don't mind not talking about it on the air
10         if you don't want me to
                     [30 secs omitted]
   D:      Are you talking about if I want to have kids? It does
           does it not?
   CE:     but it isn't true
   D:      no
15 CE:     Can I write it down?
   D:      No you got it all wrong (.) [I think you've got it all
           wrong=
   Studio:                            [write it down
   D:            =end of the stick
20 CE:     Hang on we'll write it down 'cos I don't want to
           embarrass Dan on the air
   D:      no okay [sound of rustling paper] Oh yeh yeh that's
           [right
   CE:     [that's true right?
25 D:      yes yes
   CE:     but she's not become (.)
   D:      right
   CE:     So what makes you think then [inaudible whispers]
   D:      Because no
30 Studio: eh eh eh
   CE:     other form of (.)
   D:      yes
   CE:     ah right okay, been used
   D:      yes
35 CE:     regularly
   D:      yes
   CE:     cool
   D:      yes
   CE:     I got to tell you that's not what Lisa told Suzy
40 D:      no
   CE:     a-ha-[ha
   Studio:      [he heh heh
   D:      When we play a record I'll tell you
   CE:     Okay I got to tell you I can't feel a record coming on
           today a-ha-hah.
```

It was a feature of the *Breakfast Show* that it regularly flirted with the possibility of transgressing boundaries of taste. No doubt this can be attributed to the production team's sense of the youth market for the show, with an inexhaustible interest in all matters sexual. Here, however, as soon as it is established that the backstage, off-air, option will not be taken up we are treated to what at first sight threatens to become a private conversation, on-air. Very few discursive concessions of the traditional sort are made to the listener – only CE's third-person reference to Dan (line 21) works like this. Otherwise the entire exchange seems to revolve around not explaining things, and exploiting, not minimising, the listener's 'blindness' (line 22). To this extent, the listener seems to be excluded, and indeed after all this discussion we are still non the wiser about Dan's 'contraceptive situation'.

But of course there is a double articulation here, working at another level. The dialogue is presented as a 'tease' to the listener, which is to say that it has a different kind of communicative rationality. Quite clearly, the possibility of listening to something we shouldn't, or eavesdropping on a private conversation, is not at all 'blurted out' here, but rather is carefully performed, in a double-act. In fact this seems to me to be reminiscent of the style of the 'mass middlebrow' tradition of radio comedy, as discussed by David Cardiff (1988): write this down so the listeners won't hear/noise of rustling paper – seems like ad-libbed attempt at a comedy sketch. Clearly the distinction between public and private is aligned here with a play on the sayable/unsayable, and this is predicated on the fact that the boundary between backstage and frontstage has all but disappeared. If there is no longer any off-mike backstage space where such matters might be discussed, one is faced with the problem of not talking about them on-air, which is what this performance attempts to dramatise.

In some forms of zoo radio, Goffman's 'further possibility' that behind-the-scenes business might be intentionally communicated is transformed into a kind of drama. Alternately, listeners are addressed directly and invited to listen to the fun in the studio in which they are teasingly included and excluded at the same time. There is, however, a greater sense of inclusion for the regular listener: for example, a key assumption is made in Evans's punchline on line 39 that we not only know the identity of Lisa, but also that 'Suzy' was at that time his own (intermittent, long-suffering) girlfriend. In other words we are here being treated as if privy to a piece of gossip, rather as if these are all characters in a soap opera. Indeed I want to suggest that this is very much how the *Breakfast Show* worked. It provided a daily visit to the on-going drama of the production of a radio show, in which 'backstage' gossip was a necessary element, and where the production personnel didn't just do their jobs, but became, together with their wider entourage, a cast of characters.

4.3 The discursive kingdom

All this was presided over by Evans himself, acting as narrator-in-chief. In this structure retold incidents and dramatic dialogue were contained in a new kind of 'discursive kingdom' which Evans presented for us:

```
Transcript 28
    CE:    See listeners what happens is in between every record and
           during every ad break I'm thinking about the next link
    Studio: eh eh eh eh
    CE:    How to entertain the country
 5  Studio: eh eh
    CE:    and you lot are just having a chat
    Studio: eh eh
    CE:    sorting out your life
    Studio: eh eh
10  CE:    on the phone to your accountant and things
    Studio: eh eh
    CE:    getting the biccies 'biccy John?' 'Thanks Hol' (.) You
           lot just come in here for a relax don't you?
    H:     We have a nice time
15  CE:    I know you do actually (.) Actually Dan (.) Holly and
           John do have a [great time=
    Studio:                [yes they do
    CE:                                 ='cos Dan never stops putting
           CDs on and all this kind of stuff he's bringing stuff out
20         on the table beside (.) Dan stands behind me er which is
           fine 'cos it's day [thirteen=
    Studio:                    [eh eh
    CE:                                  =er stands behind me and does
           loads of stuff all the time busy busy boy
25  Studio: yeh yeh
    CE:    and Holly and John just sit there having a [chat
    Studio:                                           [chat
    CE:    and now and again they'll talk to me
    Studio: eh eh
30  CE:    but they do save their best stories for when the
           microphones aren't on and I had to tell them at quarter
           past seven I said 'look can we stop all this fun and
           banter can you do it on the radio please' and then I
           turned the microphones on, the song had finished and they
35         both went (.) they both shut up and I guarantee that when
           I turn the microphones off now play the next record
           they'll start chatting again (.) and it'll be dead funny
           [dead interesting
    Studio: [keep quiet keep quiet
40  CE:    You're mad in the heed you lot (.) now listen do you
           remember when we did that phone in erm about erm all the
           fact that women are mad ...
```

At this level, Evans's discourse is heavily oriented towards the listeners, again addressed in the plural. Thus the fragment of second-person exchange with production personnel (lines 6–15) is more than counterbalanced by third-person reference to them, as individuals. Again this teases the listener to imagine what they might be saying ('dead funny, dead interesting') off-air, but it also animates them as characters in a very mundane narrative scenario ('biccy John?' etc.). In this, Evans himself is 'doubly articulated' for he is both a character in his show, and he is the gatekeeper between its narrative world and the audience. Herein lies the key difference between traditional DJ talk and zoo radio. In the former, the DJ's discursive kingdom was constituted as an inclusive community of listeners. In zoo radio, it is an imagined scenario, the soap opera of a radio show, which both excludes and includes the listener in a teasing double articulation, but which is never reduced to the subversive 'blurting out' as envisaged by Goffman.

5. Youth talk

As previously mentioned, the zoo format on radio and TV in the 1990s was designed to appeal to a specific target audience, the so-called 'youth' market of 15–25 year olds. This raises an interesting issue for the study of broadcast talk, which will need to be investigated further in future research, namely, that the 'overhearing audience' is increasingly defined demographically, in a competitively differentiated market. Different styles of talk may be appropriate for different markets, and it will also be necessary to look at the ways these styles develop, as their markets change. It would seem that the revolution in DJ talk at the BBC in the 1990s was one example of precisely this kind of development, but we have yet to account for the popularity of zoo radio, and particularly the Chris Evans *Breakfast Show*, with the target audience for which it was intended.

As indicated, I think the topical content of much of this radio talk needs to be taken into account. The preoccupation with sexuality was just one aspect of a general focus on the lifestyles of Evans and his crew. This lifestyle was known at the time as the 'new lad' phenomenon, a sexist and hedonistic masculinity, associated with transgressive humour and binge drinking. Evans and co. were regularly featured in the tabloid press, associated with other minor celebrities and footballers such as Paul Gascoigne. The barriers of taste and decency were regularly pushed on the show, with Evans taken to task by despairing BBC bosses on more than one occasion. To some, in his target market, this must have seemed like fun at the time.

However, as far as the media talk is concerned, it is more interesting to consider the appeal of the mode of address in zoo radio. And in this light, the fascination with a tabloid celebrity lifestyle can be seen to be supported by the talk's 'double articulation'. Specifically, the alternation between exclusion and inclusion places constant demands on the listener. It consistently poses the question, do we know what is going on? Do we understand what we are hearing? This effect is intensified when insider knowledge is assumed, and fans of the show might be expected to understand references and get the jokes that casual listeners might miss. If there was a general audience, and the BBC's aim was certainly to maximise audience figures, this was nevertheless, and somewhat paradoxically, built on a structure of differentiation, a structure which created a cohort of loyal fans who could feel themselves to be 'in the know'.

We can observe that this strategy was perfectly consistent with the 'new music' policy at Radio 1. Quite explicitly at the time, Bannister's management team was concerned to differentiate Radio 1 from other commercial forms of music radio. These could be represented as playing more mainstream types of music to less-discerning listeners. Radio 1, however, not only had the public service commitment to a greater proportion of speech; but, in the style of Evans, that speech was now demanding more attention from 'knowing' listeners. Of course this was a form of knowledge largely based on trivia, but it was, nevertheless, a mark of cultural distinction. In the *Breakfast Show*, Evans presided over what we might define as a subculture of 'taste', with a preference for slightly more authentic forms of music, and an ability to distinguish between the 'naff' and the 'cool'.

Evidence of this is most clearly provided in phone calls to the programme from listeners. For example, at the end of his show on 28 April 1996, Evans had time for four quick calls before he was due, at 9 a.m., to hand over to Simon Mayo. In the event, by luck or by design, these were arranged in ascending order of acceptability to the taste culture of the show. Two listeners called to complain, the first suggesting that a track had been played at the wrong speed. It was the dance version: 'Goodbye fool', says Evans. Caller number three, in a falsetto voice, addressing Evans as 'geezer Lord Ginga', requests him to play the theme tunes to three TV police dramas 'in that order', which is acceptably quirky as far as Evans is concerned. The final call, however, is a masterpiece of zoo radio talk. It is remarkably quick witted, it draws attention to the distinctiveness of the show and, I will go on the argue, it anticipates a whole new development in contemporary 'youth talk':

```
Transcript 29:
     CE:    Right we've got one more call and we're gonna leave it to
            a girl Amanda
     A:     Hi
     CE:    How are ya?
  5  A:     Fine thanks
     CE:    What do you want?
     A:     I want to tell you about the confessions thing about that
            erm newsagent er the newspaper boy.
```

```
        CE:      I've got no idea what you're talking about.
  10    A:       The one that you said this morning about that news[paper
                 boy
        CE:                                                          [Jamie
                 'scuse me a minute Amanda can you just excuse me one
                 second Jamie?
  15    J:       [off mike] yea
        CE:      Quiet word
        J:       What?
        CE:      We talked about that an hour and a half ago
        A:       I was trying to get through
  20    CE:      Hang on Amanda don't defend him he's big enough to defend
                 himself
        A:       Okay
        CE:      'scuse me Amanda. What?
        J:       [barely audible] When she hung up I forgot what she
  25             actually phoned up for in the first place
        A:       he he he
        Studio: oooh
        CE:      Jamie
        Studio: Jamie
  30    CE:      I-I'm sorry to interrupt you but we're doing a radio show
                 [here=
        Studio: [oo-h
        CE:      =and we did want a girlie on but we wanted a girlie
                 who had something to say
  35    A:       I have got something to say.
        CE:      Okay Amanda can you change your subject instantaneously
                 please?
        A:       yeh yeh yeh
        CE:      Okay change your subject to something else
  40    A:       I was making my cup of tea this morning and I smashed my
                 Radio 1 mug.
        CE:      Did ya?
        A:       Yeh
        CE:      Oh you don't want a Radio 1 mug anyway [A: ooh] it's all
  45             n- all that stuff's naff (.) That's that's of years gone
                 bye the Radio 1 t-shirts and the Radio 1 mugs [Studio:
                 yeah] Now you get Radio 1 abuse [Studio: heh heh heh]
                 That's far better isn't it? We've got to come into the
                 nineties come on.
  50    A:       Can't you send me Jamie's top?
        CE:      J-no we can send you J-we can send you something really
                 sexy [A:okay] Radio 1 mugs are a thing of the past [A:
                 okay then] What do you want off us? [A:er] You know all
                 the people who work on this show; there's Dan there's
  55             Holly there's me there's Jamie there's Justin there's
                 Johnny boy. Name anything (.)
        A:       I want Johnny boy to come round my house
        CE:      No you can't do [th-
        Studio:                  [heh heh heh
  60    CE:      No we can send you something - we can't send you John his
                 knees are locked up
        A:       [he he
```

```
        Studio: [hah hah hah
        CE:     I'll tell you what we can do for you
65 A:           Okay
        CE:     See Radio 1 mugs are a thing of the past yeh?
        A:      yeh
        CE:     This is the kind of station now that you [studio coughs]
                and you can do the hand over to Simon Mayo [studio: heh
70              heh] Amanda it's you that's going to now hand over to
                Simon Mayo how do you feel about that on a Monday
                morning?
        A:      No-one's going to believe me 'cause they're not going to
                be hearing me 'cause I'm supposed to be at college.
75 CE:          You're on your own
        A:      Can I go and tape it for a minute?
        CE:     No Simon's waiting to do his show
        SM:     And Ama- and Amanda's about to explain about the thing
                that's been nicked from confessions aren't you Amanda?
80 A:           Indeed
        CE:     Oh don't you start retrospecting as well Simon
        SM:     No no I was just allow[ing
        CE:                            [I've just got her off the subject
        SM:     I'm just allowing her to say what she called in for off
85              you go
        A:      (.) I want to say that that newspaper boy is telling a
                load of bull
        SM:     And why is that Amanda?
        A:      Because it was mentioned on your show
90 SM:          That's right (.) And that's where he got it from isn't it
                Amanda?
        A:      No-one will believe me that I'm on the radio now.
        SM:     No well I don't believe you
        CE:     You're not on the radio it's all a dream [music starts]
95              You're a nutter.
```

There are three phases in the development of this call. Initially, following a piece of by-play with Jamie, the production assistant (who is off mike and barely audible), Amanda is requested to change her topic. Instantly and apparently spontaneously, this is achieved (lines 40–1) in a statement which not only breaks the conventional expectations for appropriate topics on radio phone-ins, but also, in its very banality, allows Evans to expound the philosophy of his show. For this, Amanda is rewarded, and the second phase consists of a discussion of what her reward might be. Here, I think it is interesting that one imagined possibility is that John, the show's producer, might pay her a visit (listeners know that the reason John's knees are 'locked up' is because he ran the London marathon the day before). Ultimately Amanda's prize is that she will take over the show's presentation; temporarily, she is to be recruited into the production team. This gives rise to self-reflexive metacomments about being on the radio, but finally, with Mayo's assistance, Amanda gets to say what she came on to say at the start.

To appreciate what is going on here, it will be helpful to recall Horton and Wohl's theory of 'para-social interaction'. In its classical version, that theory assumes a non-reciprocal, and thus 'quasi', interaction at a distance, between the audience member and the 'persona' of the presenter. Something like the on-air personality of Tony Blackburn, as discussed by Brand and Scannell, is what is envisaged here. However, in zoo radio, additional possibilities for mediated interaction are being created, in an imagined studio space which links broadcasters and their audiences. As we have discussed, all listeners are given imaginary access to this space in the 'double articulation' of the presentation, but, as this call illustrates, some audience members (with the right credentials) are also admitted to it. And as the exchange between Amanda and Evans also begins to suggest, this space then takes on a peculiar ontological status.

To try to define this, let us begin by recognising that, at some level, the space of the studio is 'real'. That is to say, if zoo radio constructs its show as a daily soap opera – this is a drama which is largely unscripted and in which the characters are 'real people'. They do mundane things like eating biscuits and having a chat. It is this 'reality' that allows Amanda to ask for Jamie's top and that Johnny should come round to her house. However, this is not Amanda's *real* reality. Without the inverted commas, her reality is that of a college student who is missing her classes. The 'reality' of the radio studio, with its reciprocal interactions and relationships, is then an imagined 'reality', an ideal world.

It is, however, a world where anyone can enter the media and, like Amanda, have their fifteen seconds of fame. It is a world where ordinary people interact with media personnel, and, by extension, the mediated community of mini-celebrity which they inhabit. Para-social interaction assumes our distance from this world, but zoo radio offers, through our access to the backstage of the studio, at least an imaginary entry into it. It is the prize certain listeners are presented with when they pass the subcultural test – they too can become members of the gang. It is not surprising therefore that this structure might particularly appeal to the adolescent imagination. I think it also prefigures the kind of 'reality' offered to participants in TV shows like *Big Brother*. It is a 'reality' where all the world's a stage, where the distinction between frontstage and backstage has collapsed, and where everyone and anyone is a potential performer.

7 Ordinary Talk

1. Being ordinary

With her book *Ordinary Television*, Frances Bonner (2003) has made a significant contribution to the literature of media studies. She points to the lack of critical attention previously given to a whole area of programming, which has become ubiquitous in the competitive, multi-channel TV industry. This area includes game shows, lifestyle TV, 'time-of-day' magazine and chat shows, and the talk shows that will be the focus for this chapter. Bonner is absolutely right to say that these formats have been relatively marginalised by the attention previously given to TV drama, news and documentary. By comparison, 'ordinary' television seems trivial and ephemeral, filling in the spaces between the 'flagship' programmes, whilst very rarely being elevated to that status itself.

It is also the case that much ordinary television is founded on the pleasures of talk. As Bonner points out, this is talk which is conversational and sociable, with no purpose other than to be entertaining. Much of it is unscripted, so it appears to be spontaneous and 'lively'. It also, massively, involves audience participation, of the sort we started to look at in Chapter 4. That is to say, on ordinary television, 'ordinary' people come to have central roles, and Bonner calculates that British television, for example, requires over 6,000 non-professional participants per week in speaking roles or as studio audience members. It seems possible then to conclude that, for all its apparent diversity, there are three common ingredients in ordinary TV programming: its 'central characteristics include direct address of the audience, the incorporation of ordinary people into the programme and the mundanity of its concerns' (2003: 3).

Certainly, ordinary people doing ordinary talk in programmes of this kind has to be a key concern in the analysis of media talk, and we have already looked at some examples in phone-ins and debates. However, before we advance further, some methodological clarification is necessary. One problem with Bonner's discussion, as it proceeds, is that it becomes increasingly difficult to determine the boundaries of the field of 'ordinary television'. In fact she makes several different attempts to define this category. Thus, they are said to be 'mundane' not only in their concerns but also in so far as they are vital to daily schedules and thus to the embedding of television watching in the routines of everyday life. They are also 'uneventful' and therefore have to be distinguished from media events and other forms of 'special television' (43). On this basis Bonner excludes news and sports from her definition of ordinary television, but, as we have seen, both of these genres also feature people doing 'ordinary' talk.

Ultimately Bonner opts for a discursive definition of ordinariness, but it is the approach she takes to this that is at issue. Her approach, which is very common in media and cultural studies, defines 'discourse' as ways of speaking about topics, such as the family, sexuality, race, law and order. Ordinary television has its own ways of speaking, or not speaking, about such things; some discourses are dominant, whereas others (or the topics of which they speak) are absent, or disguised. 'Ordinariness' is thus a kind of ideology, which foregrounds topics like consumption, the family, sexuality and leisure, but not, because of its inclusive sociability, problematic issues like race and crime (law and order). Immediately, however, Bonner is forced to admit one huge exception to this generalisation, for many talk shows, a major genre of ordinary television, do precisely focus on such issues; indeed Oprah Winfrey wouldn't be where she is today if she had not talked about them.

As a category then 'ordinary television' is very slippery, and one finds oneself constantly questioning Bonner's judgements. Clearly, as she recognises, ordinary television is itself not a genre, but neither is it very stable as an ideological field of 'discourses'. But perhaps the problem here lies in the fact that this is not a distinctive *category* at all. It is, rather, a practice in all forms of broadcasting (some admittedly more than others) where 'ordinariness' is displayed in the talk that is produced. In these terms there couldn't be anything more ordinary than a news programme which uses conversational direct address to explain to consumers how to save money on electricity bills. For ordinariness is not a distinct field of 'discourses', it is a *discursive practice*; not a way of 'speaking about' but a way of speaking.

To clarify this methodological shift, it is helpful to recall the pioneering lecture by Harvey Sacks 'On doing "being ordinary"' (Sacks 1984). From his CA perspective, Sacks takes an ethnomethodological approach to ordinariness. In his argument it is not that certain categories of persons, or experiences (or we might add TV programmes) are essentially ordinary, but rather that 'being ordinary' is something that has to be worked at to be achieved. Overwhelmingly in everyday life, people practise being ordinary in order to appear no different to anyone else. People might have extraordinary experiences, such as encountering police with guns at the entrance to a supermarket, or witnessing a terrible crash on the motorway, but when they come to report these to their friends, they characterise them as experiences which anyone, in these situations, would have.

For Sacks doing 'being ordinary' is both a cast of mind and a form of talk. As a cast of mind, it never occurs to the woman at the supermarket that the police are doing anything other than sorting out a problem and protecting the public, including herself, an innocent bystander. Sacks speculates whether she would have had the same level of blissful confidence had she been black and not white (a black woman was involved in the incident she relates). As a form of talk, 'being ordinary' places a particular value on having an experience. Experience is unique to the person who has it; it is not transferable in the way that information can be shared. It can be told, however, and routinely the telling of an experience involves attending to what is ordinarily appropriate. For instance, it is sad to see a terrible crash on the motorway, but telling others of this should not involve the same levels of sensitivity and grief as if a close relative or mutual friend had died.

In this chapter I want to look at how people do 'ordinary talk' in talk shows. That is to say, in telling whatever it is they have to tell, how do they come across as ordinary, just like anybody else? Since talk shows are performed with studio audiences, are there more or less successful ways of being ordinary, reflected in audience approbation? These are particularly interesting questions for some kinds of talk show which feature uncon-ventional people, with so-called 'deviant' forms of behaviour. Constructing these people as 'ordinary' requires special kinds of work. Sacks's point, however, is that we all, routinely, present ourselves as ordinary because we all want to be accepted as such. In a forum like a talk show this is evident in the participants' verbal performances, orchestrated by the host and judged by the studio audience.

2. Moral evaluations

On an edition of the American talk show *Sally Jesse Raphael*, entitled 'I want you back!', Dave is seeking a reconciliation with his estranged wife, Beth. As is conventional for the genre (Hutchby 2001) he, the complainant, gets to speak first, establishing a context which is mildly hostile to Beth, before she then makes her appearance. In the space of three minutes however, the tables are turned and it is Beth who gains the audience's support. How she achieves this might be seen as an object lesson in doing 'being ordinary':

```
Transcript 30
    SJR: Dave has a seventeen year marriage to Beth (.) When it
         ended he says that it destroyed his world so he's come to
         the show to ask for her forgiveness (.) By the way she is
         backstage and she will hear what he has to say (.) Tell
5        me about your marriage you have children together how
         many?
```

```
      D:   I have four children
      Aud: [oooh
      SJR: [ok:ay (.) sixteen thirteen five and one
10    Aud: ooooooh
      SJR: So in- two years ago things must have been pretty [good=
      Aud:                                                    [eh eh
      SJR: = because there's a one year old child.
      D:   yeh
15    SJR: ok:ay what happened t- you met when she was you were both
           sixteen years of age
      D:   yeh erm we got together when we were really young we were
           just children ourselves and erm it was really something
           special and she's the only girl I've loved in my whole
20         life [erm
      Aud:      [aaaaah
      D:   I er I erm things was really good we had a great thing
           going erm we had our ups and downs er we had a run of bad
           luck my father died we had some tax problems er but
25         together it seemed like we we were able you know to
           overcome anything and then erm we then had a lot of
           stupid fights started up and the next thing one thing led
           to another and erm she walked out (.) took my children
           and she never looked back.
30    Aud: ooooh ooooh
      SJR: Do you feel you were a good husband and father?
      D:   I made my mistakes I-I've done a lot of things that you
           know I wasn't proud of I-I've done a lot of childish
           things erm you know but she's made mistakes too I'm sure
35         she can you know come up with a lot of things but I
           thought that together we could work out any kind of
           problems we had.
      SJR: So yes you were a good husband and father?
      D:   I do believe so I made my mistakes but (.) I tried
                        [one minute omitted]
40    SJR: Beth (.) you heard what Dave had to say about your
           marriage
      B:   Yes I did
      SJR: Okay can we hear your side of it?
      B:   Erm I was together with him for seventeen ye:ars erm he
45         controlled every aspect of my life [I=
      Aud:                                     [oooooh
      B:                                              =I couldn't I
           wasn't allowed to (.) get my hair cut I couldn't go out
           with any of my fri:ends
50    Aud: [oooooh
      D:   [that's not true
      B:   Everything had to be approved by him. He did what he
           wanted to do. I- if we made plans it w- it was his plans
           it was never (.) mine erm
55    SJR: But two years ago things must have been all right
      B:   Erm no actually they weren't. I er I love my youngest
           daughter tremendously I would never trade her (.) but I
           was told by two or three different doctors not to even
           try to get pregnant I'd had some health problems. He
```

```
60        didn't erm [SJR: okay] he didn't seem to care he wanted
          to have another kid [and
   Aud:                       [oooooh oooooh oooooh
   D:                         [oh that's untrue (    )
   SJR: You say that Dave was abusive to you for seventeen years,
65        how did you finally, verbally abusive or physically
          abusive or both?
   B:   Well there was some physical violence in our relationship
        [D: oooh] but the majority of it was mental abuse.
   SJR: What did he do to you?
70 B:   Erm he would call me stupid and fat and [erm=
   Aud:                                          [oooooh
   D:                                            [Oh Beth
   B:   =and things you know if I did something (.) that he
        didn't think was good he would he would just go aaah
75      [he was always
   SJR: [With four children how did you get- how did you get away
        then if this is true?
   B:   Erm the last incident occurred over a coupon he got very
        angry because he couldn't find this coupon he started
80      taking it out on (.) at that time our son was fifteen he
        started taking it out on him and I jumped in and erm (.)
        things were said and he finally told me to get the hell
        out and take my four brats with me.
   Aud: [oooooooooooooh
85 D:   [Oh no no. Noooo
   B:   You wouldn't even let me get my purse the daiper bag
        bottles [Aud: oooooh] the police were called. They had to
        let you let me in the house to get my purse so I had some
        ID. I had twenty dollars in my wallet. He went to the
90      bank immediately following that and wiped out our bank
        ac[co:unt=
   D:     [No no
   Aud:   [ooooh
   B:                 = took every dime there was. Erm I had four
95      kids nowhere basically I went to my parents house. Erm we
        had to walk we had plenty of vehicles but I wasn't
        allowed to take one.
   D:   No no Beth this is not true [the facts (.) look
   B:                               [How can you say this is
100     untr:ue?
   D:   My son was destroying the house he kicked in a big
        [screen TV knocked over a stereo
   B:   [Why? Because you pushed him (    ) because you told him
        to kick the TV.
105 D:  No I said Beth please don't. Calm down (.) Come back when
        you're more calm that's what happened
   B:   Oh that's a lie [I'm sorry. You're lying. You are lying.
        I am not lying.
   Aud:                 [oooooh oooooh oooooh
110 B:  [I am not lying.
   D:   [How can you do this?
   SJR: Have you (.) Has he paid his child support?
```

```
   B:    He did pay child support for three months erm I've been
         gone since June twenty sixth (.) with four kids to
115      support.
   SJR:  Would- is there any chance that you'll take him back?
   B:    There (.) there is no chance [that I will take him back.
         No chance
   Aud:                              [eeeeeeaaaaaahhhhhhxxxxxxxxx
         xxxxxxxxxxxxxxxxx
```

What establishes Beth's credibility with the audience as they cheer and applaud at the end of this sequence? There are, I think, two main factors. First, there can be no denying that her version of these events conforms to some general expectations about heterosexual relationships and dysfunctional families. In these terms, it is common sense to assume that the man is more likely to be violent, or at least controlling to the point of demeaning his wife's personality. Equally it is easy to envisage the wronged wife as victim, and Beth paints an affecting picture of herself and her children, with little money and no transport, forced to walk the streets. Closer inspection perhaps suggests that these matters were not entirely one-sided, for Beth admits that she herself contributed to the escalation of the fight. Who said what to whom as far as the son was concerned is also not entirely clear. But these possible inconsistencies do not diminish Beth's credibility because ultimately it is not founded on logic. We can imagine how both parties might have been interrogated in a court of law to try to determine the truth, but that is inappropriate here. The overriding factor is how each guest performs, and the credibility of their performance is to do with the way they produce their talk.

At this level, from the moment she makes her entrance, Beth appears to be making more of an emotional investment, in this occasion, than Dave. He admits to being broken hearted and that his working life is now a mess, but he speaks of this in generalisations and euphemisms: like the 'ups and downs'/'run of bad luck' in lines 23–4, or his gloss on the incidents that led to the split, 'one thing led to another', in lines 27–8. In contrast, Beth embarks on a complex pattern of speech which includes echoes of formal rhetoric, shifts into escalating sequences of argument and, crucially, involves fragments of narrative. It is through these that we can trace her growing credibility with the audience leading up to the final outburst of applause.

The key to understanding this performative factor is, I believe, to examine the moments of interaction between the guests and the studio audience which regularly (every ten lines or so) punctuate the talk. On *Sally*, and in similar talk shows, the studio audience is encouraged (sometimes by prompters in the production team) to express its alignment to what is said, not only through laughter and applause, but also in collective exclamations: 'aaah', 'ooooh' and the like (note that 'ooooh' here has a flat or

falling intonation, signifying general disapproval). These occur at particular
points in the performance, much in the way that 'clap-trap' operates in
political speeches (Atkinson 1984). The term I shall use to define these
moments is 'evaluation', which I have derived from the model of oral
narrative first proposed by William Labov (Labov 1972). To appreciate how
this works, it is necessary briefly to summarise Labov's account, which will
also enable a clearer understanding of the structure of narratives in talk
shows.

The oral narratives analysed by Labov were produced in sociolinguistic
fieldwork interviews with black youths in New York City. Labov observed
that some respondents were highly skilled practitioners of this speech
genre, especially when telling of topics like 'near-death experiences' or 'the
worst fight I ever had'. According to Labov's model, a well-formed oral
narrative consists of a series of clauses, minimally comprising (1) a section of
'orientation' in which background details are provided, (2) 'complicating
action' which recounts the main events (including, sometimes, dialogue
spoken by the characters involved) and (3) a 'coda' which reiterates the
overall conclusion to the story (or 'the moral' that it teaches). Also, because
oral narratives require one speaker to dominate the floor for their duration,
an initial 'story abstract' or preface ('have you heard about x?') may help to
clear the way. However, there is more to a good story than a series of details
and incidents. For its telling also contains suggestions of how these should
be interpreted, what the point of the story is, or (to use an old term from
media studies) what its 'preferred reading' might be. This is 'evaluation'
and it is scattered throughout the sequence of clauses that comprise the
narrative:

> That is what we term the *evaluation* of the narrative: the means used
> by the narrator to indicate the point of the narrative, its raison d'etre:
> why it was told and what the narrator is getting at. There are many
> ways to tell the same story, to make very different points, or to make
> no point at all. Pointless stories are met (in English) with the withering
> rejoinder, 'so what?'. Every good narrator is continually warding off
> this question. (Labov 1972: 366)

And Labov goes on to suggest that evaluation amounts to a 'secondary
structure' superimposed, as it were, on the bare bones of the story.

Now, to return to Transcript 30, I want to use this concept of evaluation
to analyse the interactions that routinely occur at those moments where (in
these 'interview' segments of talk shows) the guests and the studio audience
interact. Note that these moments often involve the production of overlapping talk and exclamations. In this way, the audience becomes complicit
in the production of evaluations (which is not the case, obviously, in Labov's
interview data). In Beth's performance, in particular, there is a pattern where

she says something that triggers an audience response ('ooooh') which Dave simultaneously contests (lines 50–1, 62–3, 71–2, 84–5, 92–3). This is because the audience is warming to Beth's evaluation of her experiences, producing preferred readings which compromise Dave's prior account.

These are not just narrative evaluations in the form described by Labov. In fact Beth does not begin to embark on a narrative until line 78, and then, because of the interruption in lines 84–5, it is briefly diverted into an argumentative escalation sequence which shifts to the second person (lines 86–8). Argument returns again in lines 99–108; so we have to recognise that, in this confrontational context, speakers are not always given the space to produce 'well-formed' narratives according to Labov's model. But again that is not the point: Beth's credibility is not dependent on her being a good story-teller. Rather it is achieved by various sorts of evaluative utterance which add that additional dimension to what she has to report.

Let us look closely at how these utterances are constructed. In the fragment of narrative that starts on line 78 they involve, first, animating something of what was said (in lines 82–3, but this stops short of becoming fully fledged dialogue) and, secondly, a figurative exaggeration of the complicating action (lines 90–4: 'wiped out ... took every dime'). These are classic instances of Labov's narrative evaluation which introduce a dramatic import to the events of the story. However, other evaluations are triggered by the rhetorical delivery of Beth's argument. In lines 50–1, the audience response and Dave's immediate denial interrupts her production of a list of three; and there is substantial audience reaction to the metastatement on line 60, 'he didn't seem to care'. We should also observe that the audience evaluates Dave's contribution precisely at the point where he too produces a list of three (lines 28–9). But this happens less frequently with Dave and he does not add the narrative dimension.

In these ways, talk show talk demonstrates an orientation towards moral evaluation. This is apparent, not only in evaluative statements made by audience members and sometimes by the host (which the next section illustrates) but also in the co-production of evaluative responses, of the sort considered here. Furthermore, to link with our earlier argument, there is an interesting way in which the utterances which trigger these responses reproduce the perspective of 'being ordinary'. This is something of a paradox: what Dave allegedly said to Beth (lines 82–3) is *not* what might be ordinarily expected of a husband talking to his wife. 'Wiping out' a bank account is not an ordinary occurrence. But the fact that these actions transgress the norms of 'being ordinary' is precisely what justifies their moral condemnation. The co-produced moral evaluation thus performs an act of solidarity, in which the reaction of the audience confirms the ordinariness of the victim.

3. Self-transformations

In her overview of the genre, Louann Haarman has identified three subcategories of talk show. These are (1) the audience discussion format (such as *Kilroy*); (2) social issues in a personal perspective; and (3) personal and social issues as spectacle (Haarman 2001). In this schema, *Sally* would fall into the second category, but it is debatable whether the issues that it currently deals with can be called 'social'. In fact Haarman's example of this is *The Oprah Winfrey Show* which, as we noted above, has featured such issues, establishing new areas for debate on American television. As it has developed, however, this subcategory has become increasingly preoccupied with personal problems. There are perhaps some 'social issues' embedded in these, such as gender politics, but, as several critics have observed, both the specific instance of the problem and its suggested resolution are couched in personal, not political, terms (Peck 1995; Cameron 2000).

This 'personal problem' format for talk shows involves two levels of discursive practice. The first level, as we have seen, revolves around moral judgement and the co-production of evaluations by participants and the audience. Thus some participants are cast sympathetically as suffering through no fault of their own, whereas their antagonists are castigated and morally condemned. Even the most tortuous personal problems tend to be judged in this way, so that the evaluations often do little justice to their complexity. However, these serve as a necessary springboard for the next level of activity where both the victims and the perpetrators of such problems are offered the opportunity to 'work them through'. Victims are offered support and counselling. Perpetrators are confronted by the necessity of therapeutic intervention.

In the now substantial academic literature on talk shows this element of self-transformation has been hotly debated. Particularly in work which takes a feminist perspective, there is one view that talk shows are positively therapeutic, and a counter-argument that emphasises their conservative moral agenda (for a summary, see Tolson 2001a). On the one hand there is positive endorsement of talk shows for taking on some feminist concerns, but on the other it is much less clear that they contribute to the empowerment of women (Shattuc 1997; Dovey 2000). Taking a broader view, it seems clear that this kind of talk show is one mechanism for the popularisation of 'therapy talk', alongside the proliferation of self-help and 'life-skills' advice in contemporary popular culture (Cameron 2000). In Dovey's view, this is part of a modern 'neo-liberal' consensus, which links the transformation of the self to a consumerist vision of the 'good life':

> There is an astonishing concurrence between dominant ideologies of late twentieth-century capitalism and narratives of personal recovery and growth. Is it any surprise that an economic system that offers us

personal power only through consumer choice should also offer the often unattainable goal of personal liberation through 'quick-fix' psychic solutions ... Narratives of personal change are the only narratives that the television of neo-liberalism can offer. (2000: 121)

In this way, some of the critique of talk shows connects with Fairclough's argument about the 'authority of the consumer'. It is suggested that an ideology of consumerism is driving both the increasing 'conversationalisation' of public discourse and the narrative focus of much 'ordinary television'.

Dovey also points out that in what he calls 'first person media', the complexity of the therapeutic process is highly condensed. However, his notion of the 'quick-fix' solution does not really apply to personal problems in talk shows. Of course, it is evidently the case that a televisual format of this kind cannot fully display the personal sensitivities of counselling or therapy, so that the possibility of self-transformation has to be presented in a symbolic form. On many talk shows, their problems having been morally evaluated, this takes the form of offering participants the opportunity for counselling or therapy to which they are expected to show a personal commitment. The mechanism by which this commitment is performed is very interesting, from a discourse-analytical point of view.

For example, at the end of *I want you back!* viewers are introduced to Sally's 'after-care specialist', Pat Ferrari. Beth and Dave are shown in the backstage area, still arguing with each other, when Ferrari makes her entrance with their teenage daughter Crystal, who has previously been featured in the show. The importance and necessity of counselling is taken for granted, but Ferrari transfers this from the parents to the child. It is now Crystal, not Beth, who is the ultimate victim of the marital break-up, and both parents are expected to demonstrate their commitment to her welfare. In fact Crystal, who appears to be traumatised by the whole experience, fails to respond to Ferrari's insistent offers of 'after-care', but her parents, or at least Dave, understand what is required. To show willing, Dave performs a gesture of hugging Crystal, simultaneously expressing his love. And despite the fact that Crystal shows no enthusiasm at all for this, Ferrari nevertheless gives it her full approval:

```
Transcript 31
    B:   For five years I begged you (.) to go to counselling with
         me and to get some help. And you ignored me I kept
         telling you over and over again that you were pushing me
         out of the [door
                    [PF enters backstage area with B & D's daughter Crystal]
 5  PF:                [All right hold on no more no more arguing
         here. Here we go here we go okay now, if you want to hug
         your dad hug your dad. Dad if you want to give her a hug
```

```
        and kiss hug and kiss her.
        [to parents] She's hurting now and she feels you know
10      she's very upset and I think you need to listen to her.
        It's not about you two any more it's about your children.
        [to Crystal] Okay it's okay [Crystal shakes head] You're
        hurt [to Dave] she's hurt.
    D:  I love you Crystal. I never wanted this to come between
15      you and I. You know you're always my little girl.
    PF: Hug her, hug her, show your feelings
    D:  [hugs Crystal] I love you baby
    PF: That's it that's it. That's beautiful
```

In talk shows, therapeutic self-transformation is condensed into gestures and statements of this kind. The statements function as 'speech acts' of the classical kind, defined by J. L. Austin as 'performatives' (Austin 1962). That is to say, Dave's statement in line 17 is not reducible to an account of his feelings; it is, especially when allied to this gesture, designed to perform an action which is intended to effect a change in the immediate circumstances. It is a way of 'doing things with words'. In the typology of speech acts introduced by Searle (1976) this is a 'declaration' (in this case, obviously, of love) and the evidence that it is treated as such is provided by Ferrari's response. This is not a statement to be questioned or further discussed but simply applauded: 'That's it … That's beautiful'.

Speech act theory is a complicated, much-debated area of pragmatic philosophy (Levinson 1983). For instance, there are arguments which question Austin's original thesis that 'performatives' are a special class of linguistic utterance, for as CA demonstrates, all talk involves social action of some kind. Nevertheless, Austin's original concept of the 'speech act' does seem to apply very readily to the specific type of statement that is required in a talk show, when self-transformation is at stake. The participant is expected to enter, in a demonstration of personal commitment, a kind of contract, that he or she is open to that course of action. The performance of this commitment is then taken as an occasion for applause. To return to Searle, Dave's declaration here also functions as a 'commissive', in that it commits him to try to mend his broken relationship with his daughter.

In Britain, the *locus classicus* for this discursive practice is the long-running talk show *Trisha*. Trisha Goddard herself is a trained counsellor, so she combines the roles of Raphael and Ferrari, changing her footing when appropriate from lay discourse to expertise (Brunvatne and Tolson 2001). Routinely, there seem to be two kinds of therapy talk on offer in *Trisha*, both in the show itself and through its 'after-care'. One form, typically applied to personal tragedies and unconventional (but supportable) life-styles, involves 'coming to terms' with the problem or the prejudice. Applause is given to statements of acceptance in segments of this kind. At the same time, self-transformation is always on the agenda for dysfunctional relationships and lifestyles, and here Trisha, with the support of the studio audience, lectures her guests from her position of expertise.

Transcript 32 contains the final moments of a segment of *Trisha* entitled *I hate having sex with my husband*. This features Janice, a middle-aged woman, who complains that she has lost all desire for her husband Gary, since he has gained excessive weight. Interestingly, and despite its title expressing her point of view, this segment presents another instance where the audience changes sides, from initial hostility towards Gary to some expression of sympathy. Gary displays a sense of humour, which triggers audience laughter and prompts some statements of support for his characterisation of his wife's criticism as 'nagging'. However, he also, crucially, and under Trisha's interrogation, switches to a serious recognition of his unsustainable lifestyle and makes the commitment to change. Here, the critical speech act is finally delivered on line 90, and it is greeted by extended audience cheering and applause:

```
Transcript 32
     J:    You're making a joke of this. It hurts. You don't
           understand what I'm going [through=
     T:                              [What do you mean it hurts?
     J:                                      = when I see you like
 5   that
     G:    I know what I look like
     J:    What has the medical people told [ya
     G:                                      [keep on and on
           [gestures] [nag nag nag nag nag
10   J:               [no what [has what has
     Aud:                      [hahahahahaxxxxxxxxxxxxx
     T:    Hang on just a minute. Let's get- yes what did you want
           to say?
     W1:   I think what you've obviously got here is a self
15         perpetuating problem because you're comfort eating and
           you're not helping him because you do keep nagging at
           him I think [the pract=
     J:                [Well it's the only way I can get through he
           doesn't listen
20   W1:                         = (   ) to break [that to break
           that cycle you both need=
     G:                                           [It doesn't work
           that way (.) It don't work that way
     W1:                         = to work together and
25   compromise.
     J:    He won't listen
     W1:   You perhaps need to cut down on your weight by going to a
           dietician or something and you need to support him
           through that and help [him. If you work together then
30   it'll work.
     Aud:  xxxxxxxxxxxxxxxxxxxxxxxxxxxxxxxxxxxxxxxxxxxxxx
     J:                          [I've told him I will support ya
```

```
      T:   Erm, yeh hello
      W2:  Er (.) Janice you're obviously not happy with yourself
35         (.) that's why you're taking it out on your husband.
           [That's why he's comfort eating
      J:   [No I'm okay with myself (.) I'm okay. But I'm not happy
           with him.
      W2:  No. You're no happy with yourself first. You gotta look
40         at yourself first that's why you're taking it out on him
           that's why he's [comfort eating
      T:                   [Could that be [part of it?
      G:                                  [That's right
      W2:  When you come on stage you know (.) not being (.)
45         offensive or anything but you looked (.) old
      Aud: [eheheheh
      J:   [I am old I don't mind admitting it I am old
      W2:  You looked an old lady and did you say your husband's
           forty five?
50    J:   Yeh
      W:   Well I-I'm nearly forty five you know you know and
           [looking at you
      J:   [Well would you like to go out with him? Would you like
           him?
55    G:   [You would eh eh eh (.) Give me your number and we will
      Aud: [yeeeeaaaaahhxxxxxxxxxxxxxxxxxxxxxxxxxxxxxxxxxxxxxxx
      W2:  Size is irrelevant you know you married him you should
           love [him=
      J:        [yeh but I can't take this no more
60    W2:  whatever size he is look in his eyes his eyes'll never
           change
      G:   [gestures] look in my ey:es
      Aud: hahahahahaxxxx
      T:   Now look (.) Gary I suspect what is driving your wife
65         bananas is that you don't take it seriously now I wanna
           [remind=
      G:   [Oh I do take it seriously
      T:              = wanna remind you you did have a heart scare a
           [couple of years ago
70    G:   [yes I did
      T:   You've got bad asthma. You're having to sleep upright
           because of stomach ulcers there are a lot of health
           problems and they're probably increasing
      G:   That is right
75    T:   Now (.) away from what you call the nagging [G: mhm] I
           know when you talked to our producers I think you
           actually understa:nd all of those problems and you're
           trapped in a bit of a lifestyle [way of living
      G:                                   [that's right I am yeh
75    T:   You recognise everything that that Janice is telling you
           but you don't need to hear it in the way she's telling it
      G:   I don't like to hear it twenty four seven twenty four
           hours of the day non stop every day [every minute
      J:                                       [You're not with me
85         you're not with me twenty four hours a day
      G:   Well when I come home from work I am
```

```
    [42 seconds omitted: Trisha makes plea to Gary's workmates]
    T:   We'll put him in contact with the dietician [G: okay] but
         there's no point us doing that
    G:   If I don't stick to it
90  T:   If you don't stick to it
    G:   But I will stick to it
    T:   You will stick to it
    G:   Yeh
    Aud: Yeeeeeeaaaaaaahxxxxxxxxxxxxxxxxxxxxxxxxxxxxxxxxxxxxxxxxx
```

It is interesting that Gary's gesture of commitment is jointly performed with Trisha, through a sequence of six turns (lines 88–93). Initially, Gary completes Trisha's sentence (line 89) and in so doing shifts the focus of her lecture back to himself, in the first person. Trisha co-operatively recycles this intervention, whereupon Gary delivers his promise (line 91). Again Trisha responds with a co-operative prompt for Gary to confirm this commitment (line 93). The audience reaction is equivalent to Ferrari's approval of Gary's gesture in Transcript 31. It confirms this as the symbolic moment, performed here in an interactive ritual, to which this whole segment of the show is geared.

It is also apparent that the studio audience is playing a substantial role. Not only do they collectively react and evaluate particular turns, but also two women in the audience offer their own diagnostic observations. There is a space in the programme at this point for audience members to act as quasi-experts, and I have chosen this extract in particular because it illustrates very clearly what this form of expertise entails. It is Trisha herself who spells out the medical consequences of a bad diet, with which Gary can only concur. The women in the audience, however, understand at a more fundamental level, the communication problems that underlie Gary's recourse to 'comfort eating'. For the first woman (W1) this is a self-perpetuating problem that can only be tackled by 'working together' (cue audience applause, line 31). This is followed by W2's direct contradiction of Janice's self-presentation, in the suggestion that she too has problems that she is failing to confront. This then, despite Janice's protests, becomes the generally accepted view.

What both these women are demonstrating here is the ordinary person's expertise in 'good communication'. This is a theory of communication which can be readily applied to cases like this because it is taken to be the root cause of the problem. It is a theory brilliantly dissected, with reference to the talk show *Donahue*, by Donal Carbaugh (1988) and subsequently related to wider developments in corporate and popular culture by Deborah Cameron (2000). At its heart is a belief that better communication improves relationships because this allows for the expression of the 'true self' (and as W2 suggests (line 60) this is visible in the eyes, as the window to the soul). Conversely, bad practices of communication (like nagging) not only act as an obstacle to self-development, they also indicate that their perpetrators themselves have problems: they are not acknowledging their true feelings or are not 'happy with themselves' (line 34).

There are three consequences of the application of this popular theory of 'good communication' to talk shows like *Sally* and *Trisha*. First, it is now clear why these shows require performative declarations, promises and the like – this is because such speech acts provide evidence of 'good communication' starting to happen. They are a form of utterance which directly implicates the 'self' in a first-person commitment. Secondly, and this is especially clear in the arguments made by W2, 'good communication' is also tied to the moral framework for doing evaluations. Janice's problem with herself is related to her failing as a wife; if she can come to terms with this and learn to communicate better, she will also be fulfilling her moral responsibilities (lines 57–8).

But the third consequence, as I have indicated, is that this kind of talk show permits ordinary people to demonstrate a form of expertise. This is no doubt why these shows are so popular: they provide a daily dossier of 'problems' where precisely this form of analysis applies. Indeed one might say that the problems and the analysis support each other in a circular fashion. Problem? Bad communication. Solution? Better communication. This is what 'talk' means on talk shows. On these shows, ordinariness is not about being humble or mundane, or even making a point based on experience. Rather, it is about being proved correct. For the display of a commitment to self-transformation confirms the prior moral evaluation, as both levels of discursive practice confirm the ordinary theory of 'good communication'.

4. Talk as spectacle

The theory of 'good communication' can also perhaps begin to explain the attractions of that ultimate paradox: the talk show in which key moments of the talk are inaudible. On an edition of *The Jerry Springer Show*, entitled *I will break up your marriage*, Gina confronts Misty, who is having an affair with her husband. Misty says that the husband John has told her he is not married, but it turns out that he has been lying to her. This revelation, however, is only a small part of the show; much more significant and dramatic are the physical fights that occur as guests take the stage. When Misty first appears (line 54) Gina rises from her seat, removes her spectacles and advances towards her with apparently violent intent. This is of course a routine, and bouncers immediately appear to pull the two women apart. Meanwhile what they are saying, or shouting at each other, is either edited or bleeped out, or is drowned by the cheering and chanting of the audience:

```
Transcript 33
    JS: Hey welcome to the show my guests today say they will
        stop at nothing to destroy a loved one's marriage (.)
    Aud: oooooh
    JS: And they're here to tell them no matter what you do I
5       will break up your marriage
    Aud: oooooh
    JS: Please meet Gina. She says her husband met his mistress
        on a Tuesday left her and their new born baby and was
        living with her by Thursday (.)
10  Aud: aaaaah
    JS: What's going on?
    G:  Well (.) I'm here I'm not here to talk I'm here to
        [edited out]
    Aud: YEEEEAAAAAHxxxxxJERREE JERREE JERREE JERREE JERREExxxxxx
15      xxxxwoahhhhh
    JS: But this (.) this is a talk show
    Aud: hhhhhhhh
    JS: Ah okay first of all when er (.) how long have you been
        with this man?
20  G:  About two years [JS: t-] we've been married two months
    JS: But you've been together two years=
    G:                            [we have a five month
        old baby together
    JS:                              =[and you have a five
25      month old baby
    G:  Yes we do
    Aud: aaaaah
    JS: How did she get into the picture?
    G:  I guess he met her at work (.) the pig that she is
30  Aud: oooooh
    JS: So he's now with [his mistress
    G:                   [He's with his pig yes
    Aud: hhhhhhhh
    JS: Ah where does he work at a zoo? I mean
35  Aud: hahahahahaxxxxxxxxxxyeeeeh[xxxxxxxxxxx
    G:            No eheheheh
    JS:                          [Do you still (.) do you still
        have (.) but does he still [are you still
    G:                             [He still loves me (.) He says
40      it all the time
    JS: D-d-are you still intimate with him?
    G:  (.) He wants to be. He says it all the time to me
    JS: He wants to have sex [G: yeh] with you still [G: mm] even
        though he's living with her now?
45  G:  yeh
    Aud: oooooh
    G:  He says he's using her (.) He's coming back home to me
        and his son (.) Now I'm going I'm here to give him an
        ultimatum he either comes home with me or he stays and
50      lays with [bleep] pig
    Aud: YEEAHWOOAHxxxxxxxxxxxxxxxxx[xxxx
    JS:                            [All right well here she is
```

```
        Misty
   Aud: AAAAHWOOOOOxxxxxxxx
55                      [scuffles, bleeps etc]
   Aud: JERREE JERREE JERREE JERREE JERREE JERREE JERREE JERREE
        xxxxxxooooh
   JS:  Ah how long have you been with this fella?
   M:   Erm we've been together a month
60 JS:  A month?
   M:   Mhm
   JS:  Did he tell you he's with her? What does he tell you
        about her?
   M:   Erm he tells me he hates her and that he loves me and he
65      even deni:es being married to her
   Aud: ooooh
   G:   [shaky voice] Then why is he coming back? [edited out] he
        loves me [edited out] back home
   JS:  (.) What do you want what do you want to say to her?
70 G:   And he is married [bleep] you can go [bleep]
   Aud:                               [oooohWOOOAH
        [bleep] xxxxxxxxxx
   G:   [(   )
   M:   If he loved you then he wouldn't be with me
75 Aud: yeeeeaaah
```

There is a wonderfully ironic moment here when in response to Gina's statement that she is 'not here to talk' but to do something we are prevented from hearing (line 13), Jerry reminds her that 'this is a talk show' (line 16). But what kind of talk show exactly? Clearly this has some of the personal confrontation and familial conflict found in other kinds of show, and some of the audience response is appropriately evaluative (lines 27, 30, 46). However, there is another level of interaction where the participants are functioning at the very edge of articulacy, threatening to violate the norms of ordinary conversation, and where audience reaction takes the form of cheering and ritual chanting. The transgression from talking to fighting transforms the occasion into a spectacle of confrontation. At these moments it is not important that we hear precisely what is said. It is enough that we witness the spectacle of verbal and physical violence.

There has been some debate about the possible therapeutic value of this kind of confrontation talk. But if this is a kind of therapy, it clearly does not require the intervention of the host as a counsellor or provider of 'after-care'. Rather as Greg Myers has noted, the spectacular events of The Jerry Springer Show are subsumed into the homily Jerry delivers, as his 'final thoughts' (Myers 2001). This is recorded after the show and only addresses the domestic viewer. On the show itself, Jerry does not intervene, and Myers takes his statement 'I'm out of it; you guys argue' as indicative of his overall stance. Myers also notes, however, that the show provides an environment for emotive 'flooding out', where emotions seemingly overwhelm the speaker. Lunt and Stenner (2005) have suggested that the show constitutes an 'emotional public sphere' where, in a safe environment guaranteed by the presence of the bouncers, the inarticulate guests experience 'a controlled decontrolling of emotional controls' (2005: 77).

Certainly *The Jerry Springer Show* seems dedicated to demonstrating the difficulties of ordinary talk. Its moments of high drama are impossible to transcribe with a guarantee of accuracy as any vestige of a 'systematics' of turn-taking breaks down. And if that were not bad enough, the editors then insist on removing utterances (obscenities) which they consider unbroadcastable. It is as if the emotional states of these participants cannot be put into words, or, as Gina says, they are past talking. Surely, however, and this is underestimated in some academic accounts, it is a key factor in the show's appeal that it is not meant to be taken seriously? Jerry's urbane and ironic persona confirms this. Jane Shattuc has made an interesting interpretation of the generic influences here:

> These shows deny restraint; they are more extravagantly theatrical and self-conscious than any nineteenth century melodrama. They are closer to the highly controlled game shows or World Wrestling Federation (WWF) matches in their excessive style, emphasis on ritual, and, most important, audience participation. Roland Barthes writes that the attraction of wrestling was once the 'spectacle of excess' evoked by means of grandiloquent gestures and violent contact ... Like wrestling, talk shows celebrate the self-consciousness of the drama where the performance breaks through the orienting boundaries of stage theatrics into the audience. (Shattuc 1997: 159)

Shattuc provides detailed evidence of a shift in the production format for talk shows. The emphasis on spectacular confrontation in shows like *Jerry Springer* and *Ricki Lake* was designed, in the mid-1990s, to appeal to a new audience demographic. To the traditional target audience, defined principally as 'housewives', was added a new conception of youth attracted to 'the pleasures of youthful rule breaking' and the 'sheer pleasure of breaking social taboos' (139). Now, having identified some of the key ingredients of youth radio in this same period, we are able to add a bit more substance to Shattuc's point. For it is not simply that the behaviour exhibited by the participants is excessive, and it is not just that it has a melodramatic appeal; it is also that the programme is prepared to challenge the communicative ethos of broadcasting. Like zoo radio, there are aspects of the production that appear to be unintelligible, or perversely not intended to be heard. On this level, the edits and the bleeps are not simply there to disguise obscenities – they add to the entertainment.

It can also be argued I think, that *The Jerry Springer Show* offers a spectacle of 'bad communication'. This flatters the audience, who recognise its limitations. Shattuc talks about the high level of self-consciousness in this form of drama; I think this revolves around an awareness that the participants in shows like this are flouting the norms of ordinary talk. The knowingness of the youthful audience for these shows extends to recognising the bad acting, speculating about 'fake guests', and generally feeling superior to the 'trailer-park' behaviour on display. Perhaps this is a dubious attraction, and it has been widely criticised as 'trash TV'. But it can also be argued that the spectacle of bad communication provides an extreme version of the general effect of talk shows, because the display of dysfunctional and deviant behaviour confirms 'being ordinary' as our everyday normality.

8

Celebrity Talk

1. Forms of celebrity

As he begins to outline the conversational practices that constitute 'being ordinary' Sacks identifies a category of people for whom this is at best problematic, perhaps impossible:

> Now it is the case that there are people who are entitled to have their lives be an epic. We have designed a series of storyable people, places and objects, and they stand as something different from us. It may be that in pretty much every circle there is somebody who is the subject of all neat observations, as there are, for society in general, a collection of people about whom detailed reports are made that not merely would never be ventured about others, but would never be thought of about others. The way in which Elizabeth Taylor turned around is something noticeable and reportable. The way in which your mother turned around is something unseeable, much less tellable.
> (1984: 419)

So it is not that you do not see your mother turning round, it is that this action, being ordinary, does not constitute a topic of conversation. In contrast, the actions of film stars, of the stature of Elizabeth Taylor, are always, in Sacks's term, 'tellable'; and it is the conversational practice of 'reporting' that confirms this noticeability.

Such distinctions, between the ordinary and the 'epic', are firmly rooted in the literature of media studies, particularly in discussions of film stars. In this account, the status of stars is confirmed by their 'charisma' (Dyer 1979) sustained first by a finite number of screen appearances and second by our knowledge of their highly glamorous and extravagant lifestyles. It is the job of the subsidiary publicity industry to circulate reports and images of this, as well as to use star images in the promotion of films (Ellis 1982). Further research has demonstrated the fascination of fans with this glamorous imagery, heightened, for much of the last century, by a perception of their distance from the deprivations of everyday life (Stacey 1994). For many commentators, stars as celebrities have been taken to personify the 'American dream' within a consumer culture dedicated to acquisitive individualism (Ewen 1988; Rojek 2001).

In other accounts, the legitimacy of this culture is supported by a broader 'system of celebrity' (Marshall 1997). Here, film stars sit at the top of a tree whose supporting branches are filled, not only by commentators and publicists but also by less-exalted media figures, particularly television 'personalities'. In the influential work of Langer (1981) and Ellis (1982) such personalities are distinguished from stars precisely by their relative proximity to 'ordinariness'. TV personalities make regular and frequent screen appearances, they address the viewer directly using conversational forms of talk, and crucially they insist on their co-membership of a common, usually national, 'imagined community'. Their world is not glamorous or exotic, but familiar and relatively mundane. Partly, however, they function to confirm the exalted status of the stars, especially when the latter make their rare appearances on the talk shows which the TV personalities host.

One corollary of the distance between stars and ordinary people is our preoccupation with the question of what the former are 'really like'. To some extent this is simply an interest in the public figure's private life, which it is the function of subsidiary print media and gossip columnists to cater for. More significantly, however, Richard Dyer (1991) has discussed a 'rhetoric of authenticity' which involves making judgements about star performances. He points out that aesthetic criteria for judging qualities of acting have changed from classical assessments of conformity to convention to modern notions of 'truthfulness', 'that is, true to the true personality of the performer' (133). Psychological realism becomes a significant criterion in method acting, for example. By extension from this, fans scrutinise performances in various media for glimpses of the essence of the star persona. This may be revealed in the unique gesture, the catch of the voice, or in moments when the star appears off guard (138–9) .

Because of the importance of this concept to many subsequent accounts (including this one) it is important to be quite clear what this 'rhetoric of authenticity' assumes. It does not assume that the essence of the 'real person' can ever be captured once and for all. By precisely defining this as a *rhetoric*, Dyer is pointing to a strategy of interpretation which has a figurative, not literal, relation to its object. It is a semiotic strategy, which involves reading certain signifiers (body, voice, movement) as signs of 'authenticity'; but Dyer himself notes that there is an inbuilt instability to this, in so far as 'yesterday's markers of sincerity and authenticity are today's signs of hype and artifice' (137). In this chapter, and the next, we will look at how certain types of media performance, displayed in forms of broadcast talk, might be read as 'authentic'. This will extend Dyer's concept beyond film stars to the broader world of media celebrity and to forms of talk now routinely performed by ordinary people.

This continued interest in 'authenticity' as a criterion for media performance will also necessitate a step beyond, or perhaps back from, other kinds of discussion of celebrity culture (including some I am responsible for myself). In particular we will be putting to one side the recent interest in types of celebrity performance which appear to be deliberately inauthentic, ironic and designed for sceptical audiences. Gamson's (1994) research documents the emergence of ironic celebrity where it seems that any story the celebrity tells, or any 'tellable' feature of celebrity, is perceived as just another performance designed to sustain the hype. 'The private self is no longer the ultimate truth. Instead, what is most true, most real, most trustworthy is precisely the relentlessly performing public self' (54). Given this, what emerges in Gamson's audience discussions is some residual fascination for the authentic star persona, but also a growing attitude of postmodern cynicism together with compensating pleasures of gossip and detective work. For these consumers, Madonna was admired precisely because her persona was constantly changing, its artifice was apparent, and she appeared to be in control. The question of the 'real' or 'true' Madonna was irrelevant.

These issues have also been reflected in the academic literature on celebrity talk in 'chat' shows, with which this chapter is partly concerned. Originally John Langer, in keeping with the rhetoric of authenticity, argued that it was the prime function of chat shows to reveal something of the 'real person' in the public figure or celebrity, and that this was the focus for 'disclosure' as a key feature of the chat show interview (1981: 361). In his account, personal disclosures had the ideological effect of humanising the public sphere. Bell and van Leeuwen (1994) updated this somewhat by suggesting that 'chat' is not so much a revelation of the real person as a fascination with the role of celebrity, from the ordinary person's perspective. But this is still seen as 'wide-eyed' rather than cynical, and it is the role of the host to orchestrate that kind of fascination.

In Tolson (1991) and Montgomery (1999), however, a rather different account was given of a subgenre of chat show which began to emerge in both the USA and Britain in the 1980s. In *The David Letterman Show* and on *Wogan* the main requirement was not so much disclosure as banter, or the play of wit between guests and hosts. In this format, the guests were licensed to transgress their pre-allocated role of interviewee, to ask questions and initiate changes of topic. The performance frame was so marked that the question of the 'real person' could only be provisional: what might be an authentic statement might also be a playful gesture. In Britain, such developments culminated in a form of comic chat show, *The Dame Edna Experience* (1987) where the host was a pantomime dame (a familiar comic character played by the Australian comedian, Barry Humphries) and where the guests were routinely subjected to face-threatening jokes (Tolson 1991,

1996). By 1995, this subgenre had taken a further twist in the form of *The Mrs Merton Show*, where this time the host was a middle-aged, working-class, northern woman played by the (much younger) comedian Caroline Ahern. Her performance was a kind of satire on the ordinary fascination with celebrity, and certainly not meant to be taken seriously – see Montgomery (1999) and the next section of this chapter.

But I now think Dyer was correct to emphasise the instability of the rhetoric of authenticity, just as Gamson has illustrated the different possibilities for its interpretation. There is no necessary teleology here, where earlier forms of naive humanism are simply replaced by postmodern irony. For one thing, a version of the rhetoric of authenticity still survives in Britain in *Parkinson* (as we shall see). This veteran chat show host re-established his popularity in the 1990s, precisely at the time Mrs Merton was in the ascendant. Furthermore, I shall argue in this chapter that a discourse of 'authentic celebrity' has been given another twist, an added impetus, partly following the death of Princess Diana in 1997. What that moment came to represent, and what she has come to personify, is a post-ironic rehabilitation of celebrity in the service of good causes. Princess Diana did not start this trend – arguably in its modern form of highly visible, global charity work, it began with Bob Geldoff's Live Aid in 1985. However, this now offers a new kind of credibility for contemporary celebrity, not in terms of the authenticity of the 'real person' but as the representative embodiment of a collective moral conscience.

2. The limits of irony

Some of the instabilities of the ironic take on celebrity discourse are evident in an interview on *The Mrs Merton Show* in 1997 with Chris Eubank, the former world champion boxer. Following his defeat by Steve Collins and subsequent retirement from boxing, this interview was one of a series of media appearances, including appearances in ad campaigns and reality TV documentaries, designed to rebrand Eubank as a middle-ranking transferable British celebrity. In this context, Eubank has cultivated an interesting persona, adopting the dress and style of an aristocratic 'dandy' whilst acting as a spokesperson for traditional patriarchal moral values. His apparent eccentricity is compounded by his seeming to take himself very seriously. The question of the real Chris Eubank is therefore intriguing; but this was not about to be revealed on *Mrs Merton*, where the serious side of his personality clashed with the premises of the show:

Transcript 34

```
    MM: Tell me this now who's the best British boxer [then
    CE:                                                [the best
        British boxer
    Aud:                                                [Chris
 5      Eubank [xxxxxx
    MM:        [oooo would you say that's true Chris Eubank
        you're the best British boxer?
    Aud: Noooo
    CE: No I'm not
10  MM: What about the guy wh-who beat you last time?
    CE: Statistically he's obviously a better fighter than me
    MM: Do you think so?
    CE: Statistically
    MM: Were you as surprised as we all were when he came from
15      behind and he he licked you in the ring?
    Aud: ehehe
    MM: [Were you surprised
    Aud: [eheheheheh
                           (2.0)
20  MM: The thing about (.) were you?
                           (3.0)
    MM: The thing about Steve Collins he's Irish in't he and they
        are great fighters aren't they the Irish? Had he had a
        drink? [or not?
25  Aud:       [eheheheheheheheheheheheh
                           (2.0)
    MM: Oh come on Chris. Chris Eubank COME ON. It's a chat show
        [eheheh
    Aud: [eheheheheheh
30  MM: T-What did you feel about that? I don't want to bring
        back unhappy memories
    Aud: woooaaaah
    MM: (.) You're going to punch me eheheh [aren't you
    Aud:                                    [ehehehehehehehxxxxxx
35      xxxxxxxxxxxxxxxxxxxxxxxxxxxxxxxxxxxxxxxxx
    MM: Are you? (.) What are you thinking of [hhhh
    Aud:                                      [ehehehe[heheh
    MM:                                              [Oh Chris
    CE: I'm thinking well you've not given me any question I can
40      answer. All you've done is made a statement [and the
        statement is not correct
    MM:                                      [okay how did
        you feel how did you feel when Steve Collins (.) he sadly
        (.) beat ya. How did ya feel?
45  CE: How did [I feel?
    MM:         [as it happened
    CE: Well how I felt was like this. In life you win and lose.
        You win some you lose some. I've won forty three [MM:
        yes] lost two and drawn two. Erm it happens to be (.) one
50      of these erm happenings in life and basically you've got
        to take it like you take the victories. You've got to
        treat it the same.
```

In some ways this extract illustrates the same sort of problems as the Peter Sissons interview with Margaret Rhodes previously considered in Chapter 3 (Transcript 8). Once again, it is not clear that the participants share the same understanding of what is appropriate – the conversational 'frame' in Goffman's terms. There are several signs of trouble, principally CE's failure to respond to MM's questions from lines 16 to 38, with lengthy pauses accompanied by audience laughter as he declines to take his turns. (It might be added that throughout this sequence he holds his right hand, cocked, in front of his chin, whilst fixing Mrs Merton with a stare.) Following the third lengthy pause MM produces an increasingly urgent prompt followed by a metastatement about the frame. Her laughter in lines 28 and 33 is hearably nervous, though the audience, through their laughter and applause (lines 34–5) continue to treat this as a piece of theatre. Finally Eubank is prompted to offer his own gloss on the proceedings.

Clearly he is no linguist, for MM has not been making 'incorrect statements'. Rather the interactive trouble has been caused by implicatures in her questions. At the root of this is what Montgomery (1999), in his analysis of this show, calls a deliberate 'category mistake', that is, a failure to make appropriate cultural distinctions. In Montgomery's example, Mrs Merton implies that Lord Lichfield, the royal family's portrait photo-grapher, might be a member of the paparazzi. Here, she fails to make the distinction between professional boxing and street fighting, reproducing in the process a familiar stereotype of the Irish. The resulting implicature is an insult to Eubank's professional integrity. But this is a routine feature of the show, and generally the effect of the face-threat is mitigated by the character she is playing.

To appreciate fully the levels of irony here, some cultural knowledge is necessary. The 'northern-ness' of Mrs Merton, with its straight-talking vulgarity and cultural naivety, is a parody of a claim to authenticity which is deeply rooted in British popular culture. The industrial 'north' (of England) has long been associated with a gritty realism of setting for claims to moral virtue (Shields 1991). In this version of ordinariness, a stoicism in the face of material deprivation, and a 'down-to-earth' communal identity, is deeply suspicious of 'airs and graces' or indeed any other kind of middle-class cultural pretension. This has been a staple diet in British comedy and soap opera, and has been personified in media personalities from Wilfred Pickles to Cilla Black (Scannell 1996). As a caricature of this, Mrs Merton displays the ordinary person's fascination for celebrity on the basis that celebrities too are ordinary. And ordinary people get into fights.

The refusal of Chris Eubank to play along with this raises an irresolvable question. It is just possible of course that his refusal to answer these questions, together with the posture he adopts, is itself part of the act. For the ordinary view of fighting as a natural, uncontrolled way of responding to personal insults is paradoxically confirmed by his unwillingness, as a professional boxer, to react. But as Montgomery's work shows, the celebrities who appear on *Mrs Merton* routinely display in one way or another (minimally by laughter, or sharing banter) that they see the joke. Eubank is serious throughout this interview, and though irony is constantly thrown at him, he refuses to engage with it. Of course, in the ironic frame nothing is serious, as the audience laughter attests. But we are also left with the possibility that Eubank's 'seriousness' might have been really serious after all.

2. Exemplary human beings

Meanwhile, as I have suggested, a more traditional approach to the performance of celebrity has continued. In this approach, to adapt Dyer's (1986) discussion of stardom, celebrities 'articulate what it is to be a human being in contemporary society' (8). Celebrities personify contemporary beliefs and concerns about the human condition and their talk, in this context, is designed to construct them as representative of this. I have to say that, for all the theorising of celebrity as the embodiment of consumer capitalism, conspicuous consumption is not a dominant feature of this kind of celebrity talk. Where this is discussed, it is often in the context of personal problems, addictions and the like. As representative human beings, celebrities today (when they are not being ironic) are much more likely to reproduce a motivational, even moral, discourse of personal achievement. And here we can see the emergence of a 'middle ground' of global celebrity, which is neither the exotic world of Hollywood stardom nor the mundane ordinariness of the TV personality, but a combination of both.

Oprah Winfrey has been cited by David Marshall as the exemplar for television's construction of celebrity (Marshall 1997). There are certainly some key features of her persona that suggest this. First, Marshall discusses the construction of her show which builds into her familiarity a level of intimacy with her audience and a populist identity as she articulates their concerns. Beyond that, in her ethnicity and her gender, Winfrey has personified some key black and feminist aspirations in contemporary popular culture. According to Marshall, her celebrity 'is built on a reconfiguration of the women's television audience' where 'the real life of the host ... constructed ... as authentic and sincere, is never elided from the stage performance' (1997: 148).

Arguably, however, Oprah Winfrey's celebrity now extends beyond the confines of her TV show. She is no longer simply a 'television personality'. In the USA, she is a public figure who manages credibly to combine her position as a very rich TV executive with being a representative of black womanhood. But she is also a global phenomenon which takes her persona beyond the boundaries of its immediate imagined community. In Britain she is both a famous black American woman and some kind of embodiment of the human spirit (in some ways like Nelson Mandela). At least this was how she was constructed in her performance for *Parkinson* in 1999, where, instead of the usual three guests, the entire show was devoted to an interview with Oprah.

This traversed some familiar ground. Though her appearance was ostensibly occasioned by the promotion of her new film *Beloved*, the promotional discourse was given additional authenticity by the retelling of Oprah's life story. The crucial point here is that the story works on two levels. At one level, because the film is set in the American south during the break-up of slavery, Oprah's own past experience attests to its credibility. At another level, however, her personal narrative has universal themes: it is introduced by Michael Parkinson as a classic example of 'rags to riches', but it is also very much about a personal triumph over adversity achieved through dedication and self-belief (and not a unique talent). It is at this second level that the rhetoric of authenticity is not so much concerned with the 'real' Oprah, what she is 'really like', but rather a version of 'what it is to be a human being in contemporary society'. And the focus is not on the fact that she is rich, but on her admirable personal qualities:

```
Transcript 35
     OW:  Just like in the movie I grew up in an environment where
          you know there's a tin tub in in the kitchen, and you
          heat the water from the pump and you take your bath on
          Saturday night and sometimes my grandmother erm because
  5       this is all she knew she would save up the whippings
          until I was naked in the tub and say 'remember Tuesday'
          'remember you did this remember that' so
     MP:  How old were you?
     OW:  I was erm I-I was between er three and six >cos I lived
 10       with my grandmother till I was six< but that's the way I
          grew up that's the way children were handled
     MP:  But I mean would you were also sexually abused
     OW:  And I was sexually abused beginning at nine I was raped
          at nine. And all of that but all of that that has
 15       happened to me I think has happened to make me a stronger
          erm more vital woman who can now obviously share those
          stories in a way that I hope lifts somebody else up to
          say 'look at me I made it, so can you' that to me is the
          whole point of being [famous actually
 20  MP:                       [But all right fine b-but but
          nonetheless it is I mean how do you get out of that? I
          mean most people find themselves most children in that
          kind of trap [don't escape it
     OW:                [You don't get out. You don't get out unless
 25       somebody helps you out=
```

```
     MP:                        [But then y-
     OW:                        =[Nobody gets out alone
     MP:  Then in your case wh-who was it?
     OW:  It wasn't a person specifically. You know I had books (.)
30        and I swear to you that in my hours of great you know as
          a child I really if you asked me what is the feeling I
          felt the most the most overwhelming emotion I felt as a
          child it would be loneliness (.) loneliness. And a sense
          of abandonment. But the only thing that held me together
35        I believe now er were books. I could read stories and
          know that there was another kind of life and another kind
          of life existed and I always believed. That is I think
          the secret if I had one to how I've become what I've
          become. I always believed that my life would get better.
40        I remember one day watching from this back screen porch
          just like Beloved (.) in the movie Beloved and I remember
          one day looking through the screen door through the back
          of the house and seeing my grandmother boiling the
          clothes cause that's how they would would treat the
45        clothes boil them and hanging them on the line. And my
          grandmother said 'You better stand there girl. You better
          stand there watch me. Cos you gotta learn how to do
          this'. And I remember thinking >I stood there cause I
          didn't want a whipping< but I remember thinking hhh I
50        don't have to watch this because I'm not going to be
          doing this.
     MP:  You knew then
     OW:  Yeh I just knew then inside myself I was not going to be
          boi:ling clo:thes and hanging them on the line. I don't
55        know how we didn't er (.) er we didn't even have like
          television. I just knew in my spirit.
```

It is apparent that there are some inconsistent voices in Oprah's account. In particular the voice of therapy talk which she animates on lines 24–7 produces a maxim ('Nobody gets out alone') which sits oddly beside the main theme of self-reliance. In this context, however, the IR is not about to probe such inconsistency, particularly when confronted by an IE, who, despite the cultural distance, continually assumes a common ground. The collective, indefinite use of 'you' at the start of this extract, is reinforced by the repeated sympathetic circularity ('you know') in lines 29–30. Thus the setting may (to a British public) be unfamiliar, but the narrative – books and education as a legitimate means to escaping poverty – is not.

And the power of Oprah's message is further reinforced by her use of anecdote. We have seen how oral narrative can work to package ordinary experiences for moral evaluation. As a distinctive speech genre, anecdotes are exemplary narratives where the evaluation has the force of an indisputable truth (Tolson 1985, 1990). In chat shows, this ranges from stories told about other famous people, on occasions which confirm the essence of their characters, to personal exemplary incidents where life-changing lessons are learned. Oprah's anecdote, though short, is skilfully told. Again it conforms to Labov's model for oral narrative, consisting of orientation (the screen door/boiling the clothes), complicating action (what the grandmother said and Oprah's response), some evaluation (of the poverty and ignorance of this situation) and the coda, 'I just knew in my spirit.' When Oprah speaks her grandmother's words, she puts on her 'black voice'. This is the same voice she uses in the movie, in which this scenario might have been a symbolic moment.

Thus, anecdotes confirm absolute truths about people and about 'life'. These often take the form of moral imperatives (the moral of the story) which are sometimes expressed as maxims or proverbs. Here, then, the construction of a common ground through sympathetic circularity and the narrativisation of experience is raised to a higher level of moral consensus. Whereas oral narratives generally invoke ordinary common sense, anecdotes articulate a 'philosophy of life'.

There is, however, another feature of Oprah's performance in this extract which is worthy of some comment. This involves a very interesting exploitation of 'footings'. When Oprah speaks her grandmother's words, of which she is not the author, in a voice which is not her own, this is clearly a quotation, and a conventional footing shift. (It is the same move that George Bush makes, in Transcript 12, when he animates his plan). But consider now what happens here in line 18. In this footing shift Oprah is quoting herself, as a famous person: 'I made it, so can you'. However, she is not simply speaking her own words, for herself; in an ambiguous grammatical construction (line 17) these words are also spoken by 'somebody else'. Thus we might say that this utterance, of which Oprah is animator and author, has two principals – it is spoken on behalf of herself and somebody else simultaneously. These are the words of a famous person which carry a resonance not only for herself but also as a public utterance for everyone.

4. Celebrity rehab

Clearly there is a strategy here, in choosing Oprah Winfrey to be the voice of contemporary celebrity. I want to show that there is some space, in conventional chat shows such as *Parkinson*, for celebrity talk to claim a moral 'high ground'. Here, narratives of personal experience, retold as polished anecdotes, carry the conviction of general human truths. In her distinctive shift of footing, Oprah speaks both for herself and for other people, and what she articulates is not just a personal philosophy but a moral imperative. Her story is not so much 'rags to riches' as the virtues of self-improvement.

Furthermore, this message is seen as the justifiable point of 'being famous'. Oprah's celebrity now lays claim to a broader ideological legitimacy of which she seems certain and in control. It is also apparent that one aspect of the legitimacy of this kind of celebrity discourse is that it provides a point of reference for the focus on self-transformation in 'ordinary' talk. Oprah's celebrity persona is explicitly supportive of the philosophy of 'good communication' – not only because she herself hosts a talk show but also because her narrative is about confronting and overcoming personal problems. In this way forms of ordinary talk and celebrity talk (of this sort) echo each other, and it also helps that celebrities like Oprah are able to animate the voice of the ordinary person when it suits them.

Further evidence for this link between celebrity and ordinary talk is provided by Transcript 36, in which Michael Parkinson is interviewing Elton John. At this point in his career (1999) Elton John was speaking publicly about his history of drugs and alcohol abuse and his current commitment to rehabilitation. Again *Parkinson* provided an appropriate forum for this, but without the ideological confidence exhibited by Oprah. It is evident that this interview is more of a co-production, with MP prompting EJ to disclose his personal problems, and where both parties display a high degree of mutual solidarity. In fact this part of the interview is based on the premise that MP and EJ have a long-standing mutual acquaintance:

```
Transcript 36
     MP:  hhh but but but I mean I suppose that was looking for for
          some cure was it?
     EJ:  Well you know drugs and alcohol are really er an escapism
          from what's troubling you I mean erm I'm not very good
5         with confrontation I'm not I wasn't very good at
          expressing how I felt so drugs were an escape. And of
          course then when you're on drugs you think you're being
          so fabulous and truthful you kn- I love you I really love
          you you know you're the best person >well you wake up
10        next morning, you invite people for dinner and you stay
          in bed 'cos you don't want to see em<
     Aud: hhh
     EJ:  It's that syndrome you know it's the bullshit syndrome
          [MP: mm] So erm I've learned since to er (.) confront
15        people and say how I feel it's it's something I've never
          been very good at ever since I was a kid.
     MP:  The th th th what was I found difficult to understand was
          was that you also had this kind of low esteem this low
          self-esteem [EJ: yeh] and that was the basic problem. And
20        you said you felt unattractive as a kid [EJ: mm] and all
          that. And yet there you were, this hugely glamorous
          superstar of pop you walk out and there's eighty thousand
          people in the audience going crackers [EJ: yeh] you know
          for two and a half or more hours you had 'em in the palm
25        of your hand you had all that adoration and adulation (.)
          you had all the money in the world (.) anything you
```

```
              wanted and you came off and you felt worthless [EJ: mm] I
              mean I just thought and used to watch you and I just
              thought what is what's the problem?
    30  EJ:   Well I think I hh I think that's true of a lot of
              entertainers (.) I think they know how to be comfortable
              on stage but they don't know how to be comfortable off
              stage [MP: mm] and I think it was it was very difficult
              for me to er live my life off stage and know what a
    35        balance was in my life or a happy medium or whatever erm
              and drugs were certainly the wrong way to go but that's
              the w- route I chose and er and er and that's the way I
              think a lot I can name you so many performers >but I
              won't because they'd probably sue me< [Aud: hhh] that are
    40        very comfortable and very happy on stage and come off and
              they're some of the best performers in the world and they
              don't know how to live their life [MP: yes] It's that
              seeking of adoration and then not knowing what to do with
              it erm I don't know it's just silly.
```

Evidently the talk here is peppered with markers of mutual affiliation. These include the frequent 'back channel' utterances (lines 14, 19, 20, 23, 27, 33, 42) and the markers of sympathetic circularity ('you know', lines 3, 9, 13, 23). Both parties modulate the force of their utterances using the marker of sociable argument ('I mean', lines 1, 4, 27–8). It is apparent that MP is committed to hedging anything that might be taken as face threatening (for example, '*kind of* low self-esteem', line 18; 'I *just* thought', lines 28–9) and that his question deliveries are characterised by extreme hesitancy (lines 1, 17). In short, this is a very supportive environment.

Furthermore, both parties are constructing a common 'lifeworld'. Elton's excessive behaviour may have been extraordinary but it is not presented as such. His use of the generalised 'you' represents his drug abuse as experiences anyone might have. His dramatic shift of footing as he animates his former self (in lines 8–9) reinforces this effect, as does his use of a colloquial expression to define it ('the bullshit syndrome', line 13). This is drug abuse from the perspective of 'being ordinary' where instant recognition of the syndrome is assumed. The perspective of the ordinary person is also reproduced in MP's lengthy question delivery in lines 17–29. However, this is not so much the 'wide-eyed' fascination for celebrity described by Bell and van Leeuwen (1994), but more a perplexed bemusement that common expectations of fame and material success have clearly been unfulfilled.

As such, it is also evident that both parties have recourse to the ordinary answer to such problems. Elton's unhappiness may have focused on the difficulties of reconciling his public and private identities (the front and back regions of performance) but they were also rooted in a failure to 'express himself' and to confront them. In other words, bad communication.

A further, predictable dimension is then provided by MP's suggestion that this might be related to his childhood experiences of 'low self-esteem'. What is now in place is precisely the lay person's expertise in personal problems and their solutions familiar from talk shows. EJ's testimony, delivered with MP's supportive prompting, provides yet another instance of its 'truth'.

In this interview Elton John also began to sketch a number of pathways to self-improvement. Again with Parkinson's prompting he spoke (with all due modesty) of his work for AIDS charities. A most interesting development was the documentary film he made with David Furnish, *Tantrums and Tiaras* (1997). MP glosses this as 'a man confronting his demons', so winning the respect of the British public. EJ claims that the purpose of the film was precisely to explore beyond the performativity of pop stardom, to an area where 'I was being truthful' and 'that was the real me'. It seems clear from this that such levels of 'truth' and 'reality' can be especially problematic for some celebrities, possibly because they are being explored in public. As the next section of this chapter illustrates, Elton John is not the only celebrity to take the documentary route towards this claim to a new authenticity. At the end of the process, however, it is assumed that a newly rehabilitated celebrity persona might emerge, ready to use its fame in productive ways and as a force for good – just like the exemplary Oprah Winfrey.

5. 'Being yourself'

Whether or not *Tantrums and Tiaras* truly gave us the 'real' Elton John can only be a matter for conjecture. Again, we have to remind ourselves that the *rhetoric* of authenticity bears a figurative relation to that which it describes. Possibly, however, Elton was referring here to a further development in celebrity talk, which is associated with the increasing variety of formats in which it is displayed, including documentary and 'reality TV' formats, as well as the ubiquitous chat shows. It is a development which is glossed, by professional broadcasters and celebrities, as the notion of 'being yourself'. The goal here seems to be a type of media performance which is not perceived as such, but rather taken as a display of authentic personality. In the course of his discussion of Erving Goffman as a media theorist, Espen Ytreberg (2002) comments on this notion:

> Today's radio and television provides a glut of informality, which displays all the hallmarks of a dominant discourse. Notions of 'speaking from the heart' and 'being oneself' have been thoroughly appropriated for strategic purposes by the broadcasting industry ... A host of notions of 'being genuine' and 'being yourself' dominate the legitimating rhetoric of the broadcasters. They provide a yardstick for success and

a rationale for the star system of celebrity hosts, anchorpersons and reporters. (2002: 492–3)

Taking up Ytreberg's suggestion, it is instructive to examine this type of celebrity performance, using Goffman's theoretical concepts. Indeed it is intriguing to explore what 'being yourself' entails – what exactly is this form of 'being', what ontological space is defined? In Ytreberg's account, it is a notion which seems to combine the authenticity of the self with a professional, public role. However, such is its claim to legitimacy that it is no longer confined to the dominant discourse of broadcasting; rather, it has become a mantra of everyday life. Ytreberg's discussion echoes my previous account of this phenomenon, where I first gave some examples of the professional ideology and, secondly, explored its take-up in another celebrity documentary (Tolson 2001c). Here I will reprise, briefly, some aspects of that account, which analyses a film made about the ex-Spice Girl Geri Halliwell, in which, in its opening sequence, she announces her intention to 'be herself'.

Crucially for the overall argument of this chapter, Molly Dineen's film *Geri* (1999) was part of a public relations strategy of redefining her celebrity persona (just as *Tantrums and Tiaras* had attempted for Elton John). In this, Halliwell was to escape the confines of her previous incarnation as 'Ginger Spice', setting out not only on a solo recording career but also on an Oprah-esque moral crusade. Dineen's film charts how Halliwell became, for a time, a 'goodwill ambassador' for the United Nations, with a brief which focused on women's reproductive health. However, the really interesting thing about the film is that it shows us how a celebrity persona is formed in this context, and specifically how 'being yourself', as a species of public talk, is performed.

There are two moves essentially, in this film. The first involves taking us 'behind the scenes', beyond even the backstage areas of performance, and into the private sphere. Here Halliwell is filmed in big close-up and without make-up, and the talk she produces conforms precisely to the practice of 'disclosure' which John Langer (1981) took to be the defining feature of the celebrity chat show. However, in this context, Geri's discourse is charac-terised by ambiguity, amounting to a paradox. On the one hand, in practices which are now familiar, she displays her 'ordinariness', whilst on the other hand her discourse becomes an extended meditation on the impossibility of the celebrity 'being ordinary'. Indeed she seems to be trapped in precisely that situation described by Sacks, that whatever she does is reportable:

Transcript 37
```
   GH:  You know everything's going right (.) but then (.) you
        know I was thinking oh maybe I haven't got any friends is
        that what it is (.) you know and I have got some really
        nice friends you know but I've I've three four I don't
5       know and my sister's there and Alastair's there and it's
        great and whatever but I've just got this massive (.) you
        know I don't mind working hard all week but at the
        weekend I think oh it's kind of an anti-climax at the
        weekend happens to me (.) 'cos I know there's nothing
10      there (.) do you know what I mean? When the work stops
        I'm like oh like that every weekend I start crying hh erm
        [cut]
   MD:  Would you describe it as a void?
   GH:  I don't know. I think everyone's got a void to a degree
        if we really set down (.) the unconnection with God or
15      with the world but then maybe I was thinking maybe it's
        something more simpler than that maybe I just want
        someone to love in my life [cut]
        But the thing is I can't just go and have a fickle
        flippant snog with someone because there's no point
20      because (.) it'll get blown up out of p-proportions (.)
        you know the whole media thing do you know what I mean?
        The consequences the repercussions are not even worth it
        (.) Do you know what I mean? I can't go [cut]
        You know when you have a fling you think 'oh god why did
25      I do that?' Then you forget about it. You get a real
        [shakes a piece of paper] 'WHY DID I DO THAT?' Do you
        know what I mean? So it's just like 'oh I'm not even
        going to go there it's not even worth it' so I'm feeling
        really lonely hh (.) [cut]
```

The paradox of Geri's discourse is that she speaks of the impossibility of leading an ordinary life in very 'ordinary' ways. Here, the possibility of her having some 'love in my life' is immediately segued into its colloquial reformulation as a 'fickle flippant snog'. There are the shifts of footing where she proceeds to animate what anyone who had a fling would think. There is also the characteristically modern, youthful way of not simply reporting or narrating personal experiences, but rather dramatising them in dialogical expressions ('So it's just like ...' line 27). This dialogical use of the discourse markers 'like' and 'so' assumes the affiliation of co-participants, as of course do the more traditional markers of sympathetic circularity, 'you know' and 'do you know what I mean?' In the next chapter I will explore some differences between these expressions, in terms of the kinds of solidarity they construct.

So Geri demonstrates her ordinary credentials, even as she asserts their inappropriateness for her. This, I want to suggest, marks a key dilemma in contemporary celebrity talk. Of course, it is possible to avoid seriousness altogether and retreat into realms of irony and playfulness, and there are still chat shows which cater for that. But suppose, like all my examples in this chapter, the preferred strategy is to link fame with some sort of moral purpose, where the celebrity persona achieves some sort of authenticity? Geri is casting doubt on the possibility of celebrities like herself really 'being ordinary', despite her evident ability to perform ordinary talk. So the authenticity of the celebrity cannot be that of the ordinary person. The question is whether another kind of authenticity is achievable – which is where, I think, the notion of 'being yourself' comes in.

Dineen's film illustrates how Geri successfully achieves this kind of authentic performance, at least in the eyes of her sponsors. In Goffman's terms, it involves a further footing shift, beyond that of 'being ordinary'. In this case, it requires the celebrity to take on an institutional role whilst at the same time making it seem that she is the author of its discourse. It thus involves investing the institutional principal with 'fresh talk', which, according to Goffman, 'commonly presents congruence among animator, author and principal' (Goffman 1981: 229). In fact, in this footing, two principals are invoked simultaneously: the institution on behalf of which one speaks, and oneself, as its authentic representative. In professional media talk, this makes it seem that the animator is also the author of the discourse (Ytreberg 2002). In political talk, the animator comes across as having the 'courage of her convictions'.

When she arrives at the UN, Geri is filmed first in a backstage setting, rehearsing her lines. Here it is apparent that the two principals of her discourse, the political and the personal, do not coincide, as she continuously shifts her footings:

```
Transcript 38
     GH:  My main mission my main plight can I use the word
          plight?=
     MD:            Erm
     GH:              =Give me another word my main
  5  MD:  Objective?
     GH:  My main objective oh that's too big a word my main
          objective is to er(.) bring awareness to reproductive,
          for the need of reproductive health (.) care (.) for
          undeveloped country-countries (.) [cutaway]
 10  MD:  Miss Halliwell are you in favour of abortion yourself?
     GH:  I'm in favour of, choice (.) I think that's a very
          personal decision and you can never say never erm (.) I'm
          in I'm in favour of, healthcare (.) So I'm in favour of -
          this is such a delicate situation I was going to say I'm
 15       in favour of pro-choice and pro-life (.) Apparently, pro-
          life is the name of er-erm a real anti-abortion activists
          out here I didn't know that so I was going to blurt it
          out and then all the all the nutty real pro-activists
          would have gone yeh she's on our side.
 20  MD:  Don't you find the biggest nightmare is you're having to
```

```
        tread so [carefully=
   GH:            [yeh absolutely
   MD:                        =in front of all these people that
        could take offence?
25 GH:  Yes absolutely I'm just going to say well actually you
        know it's down to the individual woman (.) and I don't
        know, I don't know what my opinion is [cut]
```

   Geri's initial approach to this assignment is to treat it as a script to be performed. That this is clearly not a discourse with which she is comfortable is indicated by two things: first, the high degree of hesitancy (pauses and false starts) that characterises this performance and, secondly, the frequent recourse to a footing shift in which she expresses her personal doubts. There is an institutional, opinionated voice which she is required to animate, but this does not coincide with an authorial voice in which she expresses confusion and doubts what her real opinions are. Interestingly in this extract, these two footings are given different identities, as Geri first has a go at speaking as 'Miss Halliwell' and then resurfaces as herself to question what Miss Halliwell was about to say. It is also apparent that pressure is added by the fact that this is a public performance, and Geri is about to make a contribution, as a celebrity, to the public sphere.

   But in fact, at the subsequent press conference, Geri appears quite fluent with her opinions, and her performance is described by one UN official as a 'breath of fresh air'. This is because the animator and author footings, which appeared quite distinct in Transcript 38, now begin to converge. This convergence is achieved by three strategies which together construct an 'authentic' voice for Geri to adopt. First, there is an agenda-shift away from the specific politics of population to a more general endorsement of the 'empowerment of women'. Here an ideological argument trips neatly off the tongue: Western women/under-developed countries/freedom/the right to choose. Secondly, Geri herself can now appear, not simply as a spokesperson, but as an embodiment of this ideology, insofar as this is consistent with the 'girl power' slogan previously promoted by the Spice Girls. Thirdly, particularly in the second extract below, Geri's ownership of the discourse she speaks is reinforced by its fluent, colloquial delivery. And she takes on a celebrity persona which we have met before:

```
Transcript 39
   GH:  I think they're all (.) inter-related you know
        population, erm, but I think the thing that inspires me
        most is empowerment of women. I believe that the western
        world women in the last hundred years have come a long
5       long way and I think women in under-developed countries
        deserve that same you know freedom and ability to have
        the right to choose. And in- on a bigger scale that's
        going to benefit our world as a whole.
```

```
          Well I think at the end of the day I am famous okay lots
   10     of people know who I am and I'm damn well gonna use my
          fame positively. You know if I can bring aware- if I can
          save one person's life just by awareness I'm gonna damn
          well do it I don't care what you know, you know whether
          I'm famous enough. If just one person recognises me and
   15     thinks well actually you know that's gonna bring
          attention that's good enough for me.
```

It is surely not necessary to elaborate on the features of ordinary talk which Geri uses here. There are markers of sympathetic circularity ('okay' is used in this way, as well as 'you know') and there is the colloquial emphasis ('damn well', lines 10 and 12–13). Again there is a hint of that peculiar construction where the celebrity animates the ordinary person thinking the celebrity's thoughts (lines 15–16). The key point is that this way of talking reinforces the claim of the celebrity to speak for everyone. This claim is given further legitimacy by its attachment to a global humanitarian project, and, interestingly, this is a form of politics that seems to transcend the conventional public sphere. No longer simply a matter of political debate or opinion, where Geri is floundering, it is now the focus of a higher moral conviction. I will return to the implications of this in the conclusion to my final chapter – but for the moment let us note that it has become the rationale for some forms of celebrity talk. And let us not be too cynical when we recall that Geri's adoption of such an exalted persona lasted for about a year, after which she reverted to her former career as a fairly average pop star.

9 Talking to Big Brother

1. Approaches to reality TV

Not surprisingly, given its rapid growth, 'reality television' has been the focus for increasing debate in the recent literature of media studies. Initially some of the discussion was concerned to compare and contrast reality TV with more conventional documentary formats (Kilborn 2003). It has been suggested that reality TV is indicative of a 'post-documentary' culture in which traditional concerns for social or public issues no longer apply (Corner 2002). Subsequently, other writers have discussed the affinities between some reality TV formats and naturalistic drama (Piper 2004), whilst it has also been recognised that the application of generic definitions may be problematic in this ever-diversifying field (Holmes and Jermyn 2004). Thus the term now seems to apply, not only to documentary formats with an emphasis on 'real lives', nor simply to lifestyle makeovers of various kinds, but also of course to 'created for TV' shows, the game-docs and survival programmes, which have enjoyed international success. In these shows, where participants are placed in artificially constructed environments and required to perform extraordinary tasks, the question of what 'reality' might possibly mean is at stake. This chapter makes some preliminary explorations of this question, by focusing on aspects of the talk in the widely successful format of *Big Brother*.

Big Brother is indeed the reality TV programme that has so far received the greatest attention. I want to start, perhaps provocatively, by making a distinction between two types of academic approach to its analysis. The first approach takes the programme to be symptomatic of a crisis in the public sphere. Thus Van Zoonen (2001) in a commentary on the European success of *Big Brother* speculates that it might be indicative of a challenge to the traditional bourgeois distinction between public and private life (and thus, at some deeper level, consistent with feminist concerns). Van Zoonen's positive endorsement of this is at odds with, but strangely in the same territory, as Corner's conclusion that such 'documentary diversion' might represent a deepening 'crisis in the very idea of the public' (Corner 2002: 265). A common theme in much academic commentary is that this crisis in the public sphere relates to emerging dynamics of consumerism; and this is given a further, sinister twist by Andrejevic's (2003) argument that reality TV programmes function as a metaphorical representation of a new kind of customised consumer economy characterised by increasing levels of surveillance. Here, before the omniscient gaze of Big Brother, individual self-expression is realised, via consumer choice, in self display. This again connects with Dovey's suggestion that 'first person media' operate within, and work to support a 'neo-liberal' economic formation (Dovey 2000).

These are all suggestive accounts, but at this general level they do not begin to engage with the specific dynamics of reality programming. Andrejevic's account can be taken as a case in point, because it does begin to touch upon some of the concerns of this book. Thus Andrejevic points out that a concept of authenticity, and indeed the notion of 'being oneself', was part of the professional ideology governing the production of the American show *The Real World* (2003: 104). It is not clear, however, beyond broad references to 'self-expression' and 'self-validation' how this translated into the performances of ordinary people who were neither professional broadcasters nor (yet) celebrities. To British eyes, Andrejevic's account of the US version of *Big Brother* makes for depressing reading. Apparently the American audience was split between a 'savvy' minority attuned to the show's manipulative construction and a naive majority who voted off all the 'actors', thus reducing its entertainment value (2003: 129). In this chapter I hope to show that the UK *Big Brother* (BBUK) has succeeded in creating a form of entertainment out of ordinary people 'being themselves' in ways which are not perceived as acting.

A second approach, which does begin to engage with some of the appeal of reality TV programming, starts with a foundation in audience research. In the UK, to date, there are two studies of the audience for BBUK which have raised interesting questions about viewer engagement. The first of these, the survey reported by Annette Hill (2002) suggests that of the various sub-genres of reality TV, 'created for TV' is the least popular generally, partly because many viewers are critical of participants overacting for the camera. This connects with the theme of 'performativity' identified by Corner (2002) as a key feature of the new factual entertainment. More significant, however, is the finding that it is 16–34 year olds who are least worried by this (they are of course the target audience) and in this connection Hill argues that *Big Brother* presents the engaged viewer with a challenge:

> The focus on the degree of actuality, on real people's improvised performances in the program, leads to a particular viewing practice: audiences look for the moment of authenticity when real people are 'really' themselves in an unreal environment. (2002: 324)

Of course the inverted commas in this quotation again beg the question of what 'really' being yourself might mean, but what Hill's research does deliver is a sense of active interpretation and qualitative judgements of contestants' performances. In a further study, Janet Jones (2003) has given further insight into what these judgements might entail. Fans of BBUK are described as 'using the vicarious experience of watching others to help them make sense of their lives' (407). Crucially this involves judgements of 'worthiness', or moral judgements, as one fan is quoted as saying: 'I feel that watching and commenting on *Big Brother* tells us a lot about ourselves: how we judge people, what our values are in relationships' (408).

From her findings, Jones starts to map out some key criteria for making judgements of moral 'worthiness' in BBUK. A clear distinction is made between those contestants who are honest, genuine and 'themselves', as opposed to those who are apparently 'two-faced, devious etc., and/or are too intent on playing the game in a manipulative fashion' (413). Herein lies the basic paradox of this particular reality TV format. It is a game which involves nominating other contestants for elimination in order to win a cash prize. However, the virtues which are most highly rewarded by the audience have nothing to do with any skills one might have as a game player (indeed they involve the suppression of these) nor do the winners display any special talents or knowledge as would be required in a more traditional game show. Rather, in BBUK, contestants appear to be successful in so far as they offer an effective performance of 'being themselves' which is understood in terms of moral 'worthiness' by the *Big Brother* audience.

Now it will be clear from the previous chapter that I think the methodology of broadcast talk has the potential to probe more deeply into this territory. In fact, the analysis of talk is particularly relevant here because that is precisely what the contestants do for most of the time, and indeed *Big Brother* has been described as a 'gossip community' (Scannell 2002). In this chapter then I propose to investigate how moral worthiness might be performed in the way contestants talk, with the further assumption, taken from the audience research, that the contestants who have been judged most 'worthy' are likely to have been most successful. Having said that, there are two caveats. First, I think the audience research of Jones, in particular, fails to investigate fully other possible motivations for watching *Big Brother*, such as voyeurism (Goode 2003) or a desire to be entertained by spectacular conflicts as per Jerry Springer. BBUK caters for several tastes, and it also, in any single episode, produces vast amounts of different forms of talk, much of which is untranscribable. There is then a doubly selective approach taken in this chapter, to one aspect of the interactional dynamics of *Big Brother* and to a particular setting for the talk. I shall look at some examples from the 'Diary Room' of BBUK5 (2004), to determine what is at stake in talking to Big Brother.

2. Enforced Sociability

I am assuming that the format for *Big Brother* is familiar to readers of this book and therefore only a brief résumé of its basic structure is necessary. Essentially this involves an interplay between three spaces in which the contestants are observed. The first, the most fluid and the largest source of footage, focuses on the interactions between contestants in the living areas of the house. The second space is the Diary Room, which contestants enter, usually individually, at their own request or at the behest of Big Brother, to offer observations on the interaction, to make nominations for eviction, or personal, sometimes emotional, statements. There is a sense in which these first two spaces operate as 'frontstage' and 'backstage' areas of activity, in so far as the statements made in the Diary Room are confidential with respect to fellow contestants. The third space is the studio to which contestants are admitted on leaving the house, and where, to considerable fanfare, they are interviewed by the show's presenter.

For present purposes, I have chosen to focus on the Diary Room. To use Paddy Scannell's phrase previously discussed (in Chapter 5) this space involves a 'double articulation'. That is to say, contestants enter to speak to Big Brother, but they also speak directly to the overhearing audience. This directness is intensified by the fact that, although contestants are overheard talking to Big Brother, they are observed by a single camera which they often address directly. Visually at least, the viewer is aligned with Big Brother here. Contestants then proceed to offer metastatements on developments in the house and/or to disclose their personal feelings. Thus, though there are opportunities to make judgements of 'worthiness' in all spaces of the format, the Diary Room counts as a privileged space for the performance of a persona styled for direct consumption by the viewer.

By Day 61 of BBUK5, there were six contestants remaining in the house. The script for the week involved each contestant being shackled to another housemate of the opposite sex and being required partly just to live, but also to complete set tasks, with this handicap. The set tasks in BBUK often take the form of games, associated (in British memory) with game shows of the most traditional kind: for instance the contestants were required to throw a pot, on a potter's wheel, using one hand apiece, and to write a short story, typing one letter each. Because contestants were bound together they had to appear in the Diary Room in pairs. In Transcript 40, Shell and Stuart, who finished fourth and fifth in the final vote, have been invited to comment on the situation. To understand some of this fully, it is necessary to know that the couples were attached by different parts of their bodies — ankles (Dan and Nadia), hands (Michelle and Jason), hips (Stuart and Shell):

Transcript 40

   V/O: Stuart and Shell are in the Diary Room talking to Big
         Brother
   BB: How did you find your first night chained up together?
   Sh: Fine
5 St: Yeh I slept all right [Sh: yeah] I think we kind of got
       the best deal out of everyone just because we can kind of
       roll
   Sh: And move around rather than having to keep a hand in one
       place or a leg in one place [cut] I mean it's not as
10   perfect a sleep you might have if you were sleeping on
       your own but I think we definitely got the best deal so
       yeh it was absolutely fine.
   BB: How do you think the other pairs are coping with being in
       such close proximity to one another?
15 St: Dan and erm Nadia are like the comic relief pair [Sh:
       yeh] just as in the most erm flamboyant erm sort of
       almost a bit of a kind of mismatch in like her little
       steps his big steps [he's so big and yeahhhh
   Sh: [Yeh and sort of insulting each other
20   all the time and stopping to put on each other's mascara
       and moisturiser [St: yeh] and one takes it too far for
       the other one and then they're in a huff which is even
       funnier=
   St: [yehhahaha just sort of
25 Sh: [='cos you're still chained to each other which
       is really good but erm
   St: The Michelle and Jason and the hand thing I think it's a
       problem of kipping [Sh: yeh] but everything else is fine.
   Sh: Before I think Jay had spent a lot of time with Vic when
30   he kept himself to himself sort of you know having wee
       chats with himself (   ) and it's quite nice 'cos he's
       good craic when he's around. When he laughs he's really
       really funny to have around so it's nice. I think he
       enjoyed it last night 'cos he was forced to sit and have
35   a beer with us [you know
   St: [It might it might make things easier as
       well for the rest of the week [Sh: yeh] cause he'll just
       feel easy [easier
   Sh: [Yeh he'll feel easier about sort of joining
40   with everyone if he wants to although he'll be able to
       have his own space if he wants so maybe he can have the
       best of both now [cut]

Now I am going to suggest that one way of understanding much of what happens in *Big Brother* is to focus on different meanings of the word 'character'. There are three possibilities here, all of which are invoked by the programme: first, a character performs a function in a scripted narrative; secondly, being 'a character' is associated with a successful demonstration of sociability; and, thirdly, 'character' is used to describe the moral worth of a person. We will return to the third meaning in the next section. What

```
        Michelle. It's not it's not erm it's not it's not there's
        nothing wrong with that it's just the fact that it's
        occurring in here so just oh I do don't even know- see
10      this is it I don't even know I don't even know what's
        going on in my own sort of (.) 'cos it's such a such a
        unique and s-strange situation (.) And I was I was
        prepared for everything erm (.) like (.) prepared for all
        the crazy games and you know and arguments and everything
15      but I was not I wasn't prepared to become like
        emotionally involved with like a chick in here like I
        just wasn't prepared for that and that's and that's just
        oohharrgh
   BB:  Are you pleased that Michelle's back in the house?
20 S:   Yeh definitely
   BB:  Have you spoken to her at all about how you're feeling?
   S:   No (.) because this is it I don't even I don't even know
        how I'm feeling bec-because I know how I know how I'd
        feel if I wasn't in here uuhh cor blimey
25 BB:  Can Big Brother ask how you would feel if you weren't in
        here?
   S:   Erm no I can't I'm afraid I can't tell you that Big
        Brother. Not for your ears I'm afraid.
```

It is apparent that Stuart uses several strategies here to display his emotional distress. His speech packaged with multiple markers of disfluency, such as high levels of hedging ('sort of', lines 5 and 11; '(kind of) like', lines 6 and 16) and hesitant repetition ('it's not' line 7; 'I don't even know', lines 9–10 and 22). In line 9 hesitancy is intensified by the fact that it is preceded by a strongly marked false start ('just oh') and there are further markers of frustration in the exclamation in line 18 and in the colloquial 'cor blimey' (line 24). At this level, Stuart presents a persona which is barely articulate or in control, apparently overwhelmed by the emotional difficulties he is facing.

Looked at carefully, however, Stuart's lengthy turn which begins in line 3 does have an interesting structure. Three propositions are made, and each follows a pattern of alternation in which a positive and emphatic point is followed by an observation which is more negative and hesitant, as follows:

1. I'm really enjoying my time here but
   I'm unclear about my relationship with Michelle
2. There's nothing wrong with that but
   I don't know what's going on in my mind
3. I was prepared for everything (sociable) but
   I was not prepared to become emotionally involved

It is the second part of each proposition that is the more heavily marked by hedging and disfluency. The effect of this is to introduce each point of difficulty, which is potentially problematic for relations in the house, on the back of a positive statement which reaffirms his commitment to the norms of sociability and moral decency. In this way, Stuart mitigates the potentially disruptive effect of his Diary Room appearance, not only by his use of discourse markers and exclamations, but also by a propositional structure which displaces each problematic point.

Now contrast that with a Diary Room appearance by Victor, on the same day of BBUK5. If Victor had read Jones's audience research he might have thought twice about presenting this persona, though he was reasonably successful in terms of the vote, finishing seventh overall. From the start, however, Victor characterised himself as a calculating game player. There are two difficulties with this persona: first, of course it involves the overt betrayal of fellow housemates; but secondly, as a calculated stance, it precisely does not allow for the kind of mitigation and hesitancy displayed by the individual in distress. The context, however, for this appearance in the Diary Room by Victor made it especially shocking. Emma, a vulnerable female contestant, had been removed by Big Brother earlier that day following a particularly violent altercation with Victor himself. On this occasion, return to a sociable consensus was impossible, but Victor represented this, not as a loss, but an opportunity:

```
Transcript 42
   V:   Erm got the laminate today, this evening saying Emma's
        not returning erm (.) hh can't say I'm not happy about
        it. I'm happy that she's not coming back but I'm unhappy
        that she didn't get to leave during the right process.
5       Like I said everybody deserves (.) their erm to leave
        through the front door not the back door you know it's
        not right [cut]
        Everyone's just rebuilding old bridges and forming new
        ones forging new ones so to speak which is quite
10      interesting in here you know all of a sudden like within
        Marco's harem and that which now consists of Michelle,
        Nadia and Marco there's three of them now. They're now
        making an effort to get to know people they didn't want
        to know before like Ahmed, Vanessa, Shell and Dan (.)
15      It's just even give them their mourning time you know
        give them the space you know mourn the loss of their
        friend and then I'm going after the rest of them. If
        they'd come in this place for a laugh they f- they
        shouldn't have wasted their time they should have gone to
20      the fun fair you know this is a game. You can't you can't
        knock people for having a game plan if you're in a game
        you know. There can only be one winner (.) And I'm trying
        to give myself the best possible chance for that to be
        me. Let this be (.) the first time the bad guy wins [cut]
```

For the present purposes, the main conclusion to be drawn from the comparison of these two transcripts is about the way personalities are performed in Diary Room talk. Contestants not only make their observations and present their problems, they also construct different sorts of interactive relationships with Big Brother and, by extension, the overhearing audience. In this respect, the feature which clearly differentiates Stuart and Victor is their use of sympathetic circularity. It is the difference between 'just kind of like you know' (transcript 41, line 6) and 'you know' (transcript 42, lines 10, 15 and 16) where the former is hedged and the latter is not. As we have seen now in many examples, hedging expresses hesitancy and modifies the modality of a statement, whereas the unembellished use of 'you know' is more categorical. Victor thus appears altogether more confident in his position – as he then proceeds, with the generalised 'you' to articulate the assumed rules of a game show. The problem is, given the type of game show this is, such a strategy is ultimately fatal.

Now I hope, as we near the end of this book, that I may be allowed to develop a more speculative argument relating to these points. The starting point for this is the concept of 'sympathetic circularity' itself. As noted above (Chapter 2), Montgomery (1986a) introduced this concept as a feature of spoken discourse, which he had derived from the work of Basil Bernstein. Bernstein (1971) was mainly interested in social class variables in language use which, using the sociology of his day, he related to different patterns of social relationships in middle-class and working-class communities. Sympathetic circularity was a feature of working-class speech because it expressed the values of solidarity and shared life experience enshrined in traditional working-class communities. These social values and shared experiences were taken for granted and incontrovertible, so speakers could be confident of a cultural consensus.

It seems to me that 'just kind of like you know' backs away, a little, from that degree of confidence. Clearly Stuart's relationship with Michelle is common knowledge but what he might say about it, especially given the contradictory position he is in, is not. My suggestion is that the use of 'like' is crucial here for it transforms the assumption of a shared social world into a scenario (this is what it's like) which the recipient is invited to recognise. There is only one shared social world but, by implication, when boy meets girl, there are several possible scenarios: so 'like emotionally involved with like a chick' is orientated towards not our unquestioned solidarity but our sympathetic understanding. This is where (to use the colloquial phrase) Stuart is 'coming from', and there are links here to the dialogical use of 'like', noted in the previous chapter, where such scenarios are dramatised: 'and I'm like', 'she was like…' etc. Identities are not being assumed here so much as negotiated. This dialogical use of sympathetic circularity is a distinctive feature of contemporary youth talk and it is in dominance on *Big Brother*.

4. Nadia's triumph

There cannot be many British readers of this book who do not recall that BBUK5 was won by Nadia Almeda, a 27-year-old transsexual from Portugal. Nadia's overwhelming victory was widely acclaimed as the culmination of a series which revitalised the format, achieving the second highest audience ratings in its history. The final night won a 48 per cent share of the UK TV audience. But quite apart from Nadia's popularity, there are other reasons why she was a very interesting contestant. In relation to our previous discussion, Nadia was the first contestant explicitly sanctioned by Big Brother to be 'two faced', in so far as her medical history was revealed to the audience from day one, but was kept hidden, with Big Brother's blessing, from her housemates. This took her performance to another level of interest, for it was no longer just a test of her sociability, or her ability to come across as a decent, genuine person. It became a question of whether she would 'pass' as a woman with her fellow housemates and whether they would ever guess her secret.

In this respect, Nadia's predicament reproduced, almost exactly, one of Garfinkel's classic studies in ethnomethodology, the case of Agnes (Garfinkel 1967). Agnes was a 19-year-old transsexual who presented herself at UCLA's Department of Psychiatry in 1958, as part of her campaign to secure a sex change (male to female) operation. Garfinkel uses her case to show how 'passing' as a woman becomes a practical accomplishment, which involves learning a whole new set of social behaviours (including practices of talk) and reconstructing her biography (which involved staying silent on certain issues). Garfinkel shows how this identity had to be negotiated in different ways with those who knew Agnes's secret (for example, the psychiatric and medical staff) as opposed to those who did not (her friends). His general point was that gender identity (which he calls 'sexual status') is not an incontrovertible given, even if it is treated as such by most people in most social circumstances. As the case of Agnes demonstrates, gender can be thought of as an ongoing performance, orientated towards mutual confirmation in everyday social interaction.

Now the only real difference in BBUK5 was that Nadia was a post-operative transsexual. Otherwise the scenario was uncannily similar, as we, who knew of her history, watched how she would pass with her housemates, who did not. Furthermore, as the series progressed, it became clear that if Nadia were to win *Big Brother* this would be taken as a popular endorsement of her identity. This is how she began to present it herself, in a guarded way, to fellow housemates, who were left in no doubt that Nadia would regard victory as a vote of confidence. The stakes were high therefore, and there were some scary moments as it seemed that Nadia's secrets might be revealed. For instance, on one occasion, a group of housemates with Nadia herself in attendance held an extensive conversation about the anatomical details of sex-change operations. After this, Nadia locked herself in the toilet for several minutes, her behaviour attributed by the others to an unsatisfied craving for cigarettes. On Day 61, during another cigarette break, Nadia and the other housemates overheard shouts outside the *Big Brother* compound. To the TV audience these were indistinct, but Nadia herself was clear that they contained references to her gender, and this occasioned another visit to the Diary Room:

```
Transcript 43
          (6secs)
    BB:   Evening Nadia
    N:    Hello
    BB:   How are you this evening?
 5  N:    mhm you tell me
          (13 secs)
    BB:   What is it you'd like to discuss with Big Brother this
          evening?
    N:    What I've just heard
10        (6 secs)
    BB:   What have you heard [Nadia?
    N:                        [hh Big Brother you know (   ) about
          what I heard. I'm just wondering what is going on(7 secs)
          ooh (5 secs)
15        I am not a man. Just for the record. And what I heard was
          Nadia is a man. Are you satisfied with that?
          (2 secs)
          And you I'm not going I'm not going to cry about it do
          you know what I mean I'm going to it's just like I'm just
20        like shocked (.) I wasn't expecting it. I mean I'm
          actually quite surprised it took this long hh I don't
          know exactly what they heard and I think they've heard or
          just they can't handle it or I or I d-now I'm like in a
          position that I don't know what how to sort of justify
25        myself. I don't know what to do.
          Either they heard it and they're not telling me or they
          did not did not hear it and I'm compl-completely paranoid
          about it (.) So wh-what am I supposed to do now I don't
          know (.) I just I I'm not I cos I've forgotten about it
30        so well the it kind of it makes me more vulnerable
          because I c- I-I don't know how I'm how I'm going to deal
          with it 'cos I'm=
                         (5 secs)
                         =kind of like I'm not sure if I'm going
35        to be that strong for confronta- to confront it justify
          to them why exactly I haven't told them (   ) I'm not
          that strong right now 'cos I haven't been thinking about
          that it has it hasn't been part of me (.) whatevoooh hh
          (.) I think it's all my fault because I actually said to
40        them let's go and have a cigarette we'd've been in bed by
          now. Oh my god it's like sort of fate or destiny whatever
```

```
that is. I don't know I don't know I'm just I'm just a
little bit scared right now I'm just a little bit scared
hh [cut]
```

In this extract, Nadia engages with one of the basic concepts in ethnomethodology (and thus the methodology that informs this book), namely, *accountability*. Her immediate concern is how she will justify herself if she is found out (lines 24–5, 35–6) for, by not being straight with her colleagues, she can be accused of flouting Grice's maxim of Manner. Moreover being found out might well lead to a further spiral of accounting, because she will be obliged to explain, not only her immediate behaviour, but also a past history which has involved 'breaching' one of the most fundamental 'natural-moral' institutions of everyday life (Garfinkel 1967). Note also how, as a consequence of the conventions for talking to Big Brother, Nadia's appearance is, from her point of view, unhelpfully one-sided. Big Brother is not about to answer her questions or provide any kind of reassurance – a point which is evident in Nadia's rhetorical responses (lines 5 and 16). Nadia is therefore put in the position of displaying her anxieties to a non-reciprocating interlocutor and, by extension, overhearing audience. It is almost as if we are positioned as witnesses to an ethnomethodological experiment.

In this context, Nadia can only do what any 'good contestant' on *Big Brother* would do, and that is to perform her distress. What may not be particularly evident from the transcript (though the false start on line 35, 'confronta-', is indicative of this) is that, despite her insistence that she is not going to cry, she is on the verge of flooding out. The difficulty of this whole exchange with BB is further illustrated by the lengthy pauses between turns. Initially BB demonstrates a reluctance to respond to Nadia (lines 6 and 10), and she then prefaces her key declaration ('I am not a man') with a double pause (lines 13–14). In the lengthy turn that follows this, Nadia escalates the evaluation of her distress from being '<u>shock</u>ed' (line 20) to 'paranoid' (line 27) to 'vulnerable' (line 30). This whole turn becomes a performance of vulnerability, and it is not until she produces the formulaic *Big Brother* exclamation 'Oh my god' (line 41) and the de-escalation 'just a <u>little</u> bit scared' (lines 42–3) that she seems ready to move on.

Throughout, Nadia also employs the type of youthful approach to sympathetic circularity discussed in the previous section. Here it is apparent that the initial appeal to a common ground ('do you know what I mean?') is immediately hedged and modified ('its just like', 'I'm just like') on lines 19–20. The point made previously about scenarios is most clearly illustrated in lines 23–4: 'I'm like in a position'. This is Nadia's position, not ours, but we are being invited to recognise and affiliate with it. This is different from the use of hedging to mitigate the force of certain words – '*sort of* justify

she was, like Agnes in Garfinkel's account, resolutely conservative, invoking the natural-moral order that equates gender identity with being essentially female. In her persona, however, and in her mediated performance, Nadia was something of a radical. Her excessive display of femininity in her sociable moments, together with her self-reflexive negotiation of 'passing' as female, indicated a self whose gender identity was in transition. One thing *Big Brother* dramatises, at this level, is a complex politics of 'doing being gendered'. For several contestants conventional expectations, in this and other areas, are under negotiation, and the trick is to reconcile that with a coherent self-presentation.

The suggestion that this amounts to a 'politics' needs some consideration. This is not a politics of ideological belief or commitment to a cause: Nadia was no sexual politician, and neither are the majority of contestants on the show. But nor is this, I want to emphasise again, a complete abandonment of politics in the pursuit of hedonistic consumerism and 'lifestyle'. As the audience research shows, there is a moral concern for the 'worth' of a person related to perceptions of how they are engaged with the performance of identity. All of this has much in common with the sphere of 'life-politics' outlined by Anthony Giddens (1991) and, in the reflexive restructuring of her gender identity, Nadia can be taken as an exemplary case for one aspect of the politics he outlines.

In *Modernity and Self-Identity*, Giddens distinguishes between two kinds of political formation. 'Emancipatory politics' is concerned with life-chances and opportunities, combating forces of discrimination and inequality. This politics is socially engaged and seeks access to the public sphere. It is what has often inspired the documentary movement, in its traditional forms, as outlined by Corner (2002). In contrast to this, 'life-politics' is concerned with lifestyle, but in a broader sense than simply the consumption of commodities. Life politics focuses on identity formation, the self-reflexive 'trajectory of the self', in a social context characterised by the availability of choice. Such choice is not limited to the conventional parameters of social 'mobility', it also extends to what one might 'make of oneself', including one's gender identity:

> What gender identity is, and how it should be expressed, has become itself a matter of multiple options – ranging up to and including even the choice of whether a person remains anatomically of the same sex into which he or she was born. The politics of self identity, of course, is not limited to matters of gender differentiation. The more we reflexively ' make ourselves' as persons, the more the very category of what a 'person' or 'human being' is comes to the fore. (Giddens 1991: 217)

Characteristically, Giddens proceeds to totalise this account, seeing life-politics as a symptom of 'late modernity'. Here, life-politics presents a programmatic engagement with the 'abstract systems' that govern the globalised world order, like the ecology movement, moral dilemmas around genetic sciences and concerns for the welfare of animals. But the kinds of media talk we have considered in this book, particularly in its last three chapters, do not necessarily operate at that level. They may do – as, for example, when celebrities associate themselves with global humanitarian causes, or seek a purpose for themselves in fronting up for charities. However, underpinning all of that is a mundane circulation of ordinary talk, dominated by the ideology of 'good communication', where all kinds of people, interactively, 'work' on themselves.

In this respect our study of media talk in this book has taken us beyond the terms of its starting point. There, the reader will recall, the claim was that talk was central to the way broadcasting works and in particular that the study of broadcast talk can illuminate the ways in which TV and radio communicate with their audiences. That, I hope, has been achieved; but at the same time a more general set of cultural questions has emerged, where talk on radio and TV engages with, and participates in constructing, some key preoccupations of modern everyday life. Central to these is a concern about the 'presentation of self', that, however flexible they may be, lifestyles should ultimately cohere as morally defensible identities, demonstrated in authentic performances of 'being oneself'.

It is crucial to note, however, that such concerns are not only discussed in much contemporary media talk, they are also dramatised by it. To a large extent, media talk might indeed be responsible for their intense interest, particularly in programming targeted at young people. For here, media talk dramatises the moral concern for 'being yourself' in a problematic performative context, where conversational forms of talk are displayed as mediated quasi-interaction. Nadia's problem with Big Brother is precisely emblematic of this key point: that the identities performed in media talk, for an over-hearing audience, are not directly reciprocated. In ordinary conversations participants co-operatively confirm their mutual understandings in face-to-face interaction. In media talk, such confirmation is impossible and the identities on display are always therefore fluid and provisional. The self is performed in a context where, as a para-social construct, it is always in a state of uncertainty, subject to capricious tests and unknowable moral judgements. In this respect *Big Brother* is such an effective TV format because it dramatises the very essence of media talk, and the lesson that it teaches. For as Nadia clearly understood, and demonstrated in her moment of triumph, she could only confidently be herself when the audience had cast its vote.

References

Anderson, B. (1983), *Imagined Communities: Reflections on the Origin and Spread of Nationalism*, London: Verso.

Andrejevic, M. (2003), *Reality TV: The Work of Being Watched*, Maryland: Rowman and Littlefield.

Atkinson, M. (1984), *Our Masters' Voices*, London: Routledge.

Austin, J. L. (1962), *How to Do Things with Words*, Oxford: Oxford University Press.

Bakhtin, M. M. (1986), 'The problem of speech genres', in *Speech Genres and Other Late Essays,* trans. V. W. McGee, Austin: University of Texas Press.

Bell, P., and T. van Leeuwen (1994), *The Media Interview: Confession, Contest, Conversation*, Kensington: University of New South Wales Press.

Bernstein, B. (1971), *Class, Codes and Control,* vol. 1, London: Routledge & Kegan Paul.

Bonner, F. (2003), *Ordinary Television*, London: Sage Publications.

Boyle, R., and R. Haynes (2000), *Power Play: Sport, the Media & Popular Culture*, Harlow: Longman.

Brand, G., and P. Scannell (1991), 'Talk, identity and performance: *The Tony Blackburn Show*', in P. Scannell (ed.), *Broadcast Talk*, London: Sage, pp. 201–26.

Brown, P., and S. Levinson (1987), *Politeness: Some Universals in Language Usage*, Cambridge: Cambridge University Press.

Brunvatne, R., and A. Tolson (2001), '"It makes it okay to cry": two types of "therapy talk" in TV talk shows', in Tolson, A. (ed.) (2001a), pp. 139–54.

Cameron, D. (1997), 'Performing gender: young men's talk and the construction of heterosexual masculinity', in S. Johnson and U. Meinhof (eds), *Language and Masculinity*, Oxford: Blackwell, pp. 47–64

—— (2000), *Good to Talk?*, London: Sage Publications.

—— (2001), *Working with Spoken Discourse*, London: Sage Publications.

Carbaugh, D. (1988), *Talking American: Cultural Discourses on Donahue*, Norwood, NJ: Ablex.

Cardiff, D. (1980), 'The serious and the popular: aspects of the evolution of style in the radio talk 1928–1939', *Media, Culture & Society*, vol. 2, pp. 29–47.

Cardiff, D. (1988), 'Mass middlebrow laughter: the origins of BBC comedy', *Media, Culture & Society*, vol. 10, pp. 41–60.

Carpignano, P., R. Anderson, S. Aronowitz and W. Difazio (1990), 'Chatter in the age of electronic reproduction: talk television and the "public mind"', *Social Text*, vol. 25, pp. 33–55.

Clayman, S. (1992), 'Footing in the achievement of neutrality: the case of news interviews', in P. Drew and J. Heritage (eds) (1992), pp. 163–98

Clayman, S., and J. Heritage (2002), *The News Interview: Journalists and Public Figures on the Air*, Cambridge: Cambridge University Press.

Coates, J. (1989), 'Gossip revisited: language in all-female groups', in J. Coates and D. Cameron (eds), *Women in Their Speech Communities*, London: Longman, pp. 94–122.

—— (1993), *Women, Men and Language*, 2nd edn, Harlow: Longman.

—— (1996), *Women Talk: Conversation between Women Friends*, Oxford: Blackwell.

Corner, J. (1995), *Television Form and Public Address*, London: Arnold.

—— (1999), *Critical Ideas in Television Studies*, Oxford: Clarendon Press.

—— (2002), 'Performing the real: documentary diversions', *Television & New Media* vol. 3, no. 3, pp. 255–69.

Corner, J., and J. Hawthorn (eds) (1993), *Communication Studies: An Introductory Reader*, London: Edward Arnold.

Crisell, A. (1994), *Understanding Radio*, 2nd edn, London: Routledge.

Crystal, D., and D. Davy (1969), *Investigating English Style*, London: Longman.

Dahlgren, P. (1995), *Television and the Public Sphere*, London: Sage.

Dovey, J. (2000), *Freakshow: First Person Media and Factual Television*, London: Pluto Press.

Drew, P., and J. Heritage (eds) (1992), *Talk at Work: Interaction in Institutional Settings*, Cambridge: Cambridge University Press.

Dyer, R. (1979), *Stars*, London: BFI.

—— (1986), *Heavenly Bodies: Film Stars and Society*, London: Macmillan.

—— (1991), '*A Star Is Born* and the construction of authenticity', in C. Gledhill (ed.), *Stardom: Industry of Desire*, London: Routledge, pp. 132–40.

Ellis, J. (1982), *Visible Fictions*, London: Routledge.

—— (2000), *Seeing Things: Television in the Age of Uncertainty*, London: I.B. Tauris.

Ewen, S. (1988), *All Consuming Images: The Politics of Style in Contemporary Culture*, New York: Basic Books.

Fairclough, N. (1989), *Language and Power*, Harlow: Longman.

—— (1994), 'Conversationalization of public discourse and the authority of the consumer', in R. Keat et al. (eds), *The Authority of the Consumer*, London: Routledge, pp. 253–68.

—— (1995a), *Critical Discourse Analysis*, Harlow: Longman.

—— (1995b), *Media Discourse*, London: Arnold.

—— (1998), 'Political discourse in the media: an analytical framework', in A. Bell and P. Garrett (eds), *Approaches to Media Discourse*, Oxford: Blackwell, pp. 142–62.

—— (2000), *New Labour, New Language?*, London: Routledge.

Feuer, J. (1983), 'The concept of "live television": ontology as ideology', in E. A. Kaplan (ed.), *Regarding Television*, Los Angeles: American Film Institute, pp. 12–22.

Foucault, M. (1979), *The History of Sexuality*, vol. 1, London: Allen Lane.

Gamson, J. (1994), *Claims to Fame: Celebrity in Contemporary America*, Berkeley and Los Angeles: University of California Press.

Garfinkel, H. (1967), *Studies in Ethnomethodology*, Englewood Cliffs, NJ: Prentice Hall.

Garnham, N. (1986), 'The media and the public sphere', in P. Golding et al. (eds), *Communicating Politics*, Leicester: Leicester University Press, pp. 37–53.

Giddens, A. (1990), *The Consequences of Modernity*, Cambridge: Polity Press.

—— (1991), *Modernity and Self-Identity*, Cambridge: Polity Press.

Goffman, E. (1959), *The Presentation of Self in Everyday Life*, New York: Anchor Books.

—— (1967), *Interaction Ritual: Essays on Face-to-Face Behaviour*, New York: Anchor Books.

—— (1974), *Frame Analysis: An Essay on the Organization of Experience*, New York: Harper & Row.

—— (1981), *Forms of Talk*, Oxford: Blackwell.

Goode, I. (2003), 'Value and television aesthetics', *Screen*, vol. 44, no. 1, pp. 106–9.

Greatbatch, D. (1986), 'Aspects of topical organisation in news interviews: the use of agenda-shifting procedures by news interviewees', *Media, Culture & Society*, vol. 8, pp. 441–55.

—— (1992), 'The management of disagreement between news interviewees', in P. Drew and J. Heritage (eds), *Talk at Work: Interaction in Institutional Settings*, Cambridge: Cambridge University Press, pp. 268–301.

Grice, H. P. (1975), 'Logic and conversation', part reprinted in A. Jaworski and N. Coupland, *The Discourse Reader*, London: Routledge, 1999, pp. 76–88.

Haarman, L. (2001), 'Performing talk', in Tolson, A. (ed.) (2001a), pp. 31–64.

Hall, S., and P. du Gay (eds) (1996), *Questions of Cultural Identity*, London: Sage.

Harris, S. (1991), 'Evasive action: how politicians respond to questions in political interviews', in P. Scannell (ed.), *Broadcast Talk*, London: Sage, pp. 76–99.

Hendy, D. (2000a), *Radio in the Global Age*, Cambridge: Polity Press.

—— (2000b), 'Pop music radio in the public service: BBC Radio 1 and news music in the 1990s', *Media, Culture & Society*, vol. 22, pp. 743–61.

Heritage, J. (1984), *Garfinkel and Ethnomethodology*, Cambridge: Polity Press.

—— (1985), 'Analyzing news interviews: aspects of the production of talk for overhearing audiences', in T. van Dijk (ed.), *Handbook of Discourse Analysis*, vol. 3, London: Academic Press, pp. 95–119.

Heritage, J., and D. Greatbatch (1991), 'On the institutional character of institutional talk: the case of news interviews', in D. Boden and Zimmerman (eds), *Talk and Social Structure*, Cambridge: Polity Press, pp.93–137.

Hill, A. (2002), '*Big Brother*: the real audience', *Television & New Media*, vol. 3, no. 3, pp. 323–40.

—— (2005), *Reality TV: Audiences and Popular Factual Television*, London: Routledge.

Higgins, C., and P. Moss (1982), *Sounds Real: Radio in Everyday Life*, St Lucia: University of Queensland Press.

Holmes, S. (2004), '"All you've got to worry about is the task, having a cup of tea, and doing a bit of sunbathing": approaching celebrity in *Big Brother*,' in S. Holmes and D. Jermyn (2004), pp. 111–35.

Holmes, S., and D. Jermyn (eds) (2004), *Understanding Reality Television*, London: Routledge.

Horton, D., and R. Wohl (1956), 'Mass communication as para-social interaction: observations on intimacy at a distance', *Psychiatry*, vol. 19, no. 3, pp. 215–29.

Extracts included in J. Corner and J. Hawthorn (eds), *Communication Studies: An Introductory Reader*, London: Edward Arnold, 1993, Ch.18.

Hutchby, I. (1996), *Confrontation Talk*, Mahwah, NJ: Lawrence Erlbaum Associates.

—— (2001), 'Confrontation as a spectacle: the argumentative frame of the *Ricki Lake* Show', in A. Tolson (ed.) (2001a), pp. 155–720.

Hutchby, I., and R. Wooffitt (1998), *Conversation Analysis: An Introduction*, Cambridge: Polity Press.

Jaworski, A., and N. Coupland (1999), *The Discourse Reader*, London: Routledge.

Jones, D. (1980), 'Gossip: notes on women's oral culture', in C. Kramarae (ed.), *The Voices and Words of Women and Men*, Oxford: Pergamon Press, pp. 193–8.

Jones, J. (2003), 'Show your real face', *New Media & Society*, vol. 5, no. 3, pp. 400–21.

Kilborn, R. (2003), *Staging the Real: Factual TV Programming in the Age of* Big Brother, Manchester: Manchester University Press.

Kuiper, K. (1996), *Smooth Talkers: The Linguistic Performance of Auctioneers and Sportscasters*, Mahwah, NJ: Lawrence Erlbaum Associates.

Labov, W. (1972), *Language in the Inner City*, Philadelphia: University of Pennsylvania Press.

Langer, J. (1981), 'Television's "personality system"', *Media, Culture & Society*, vol. 3, pp. 351–65.

Lee, D., and J. Peck (1995), 'Troubled waters: argument as sociability revisited', *Language in Society*, vol. 24, no. 1, pp. 29–52.

Levinson, S. (1983), *Pragmatics*, Cambridge: Cambridge University Press.

Livingstone, S., and P. Lunt (1994), *Talk on Television: Audience Participation and Public Debate*, London: Routledge.

Lunt, P., and P. Stenner (2005), '*The Jerry Springer Show* as an emotional public sphere', *Media, Culture & Society*, vol. 27, pp. 59–81.

Marriott, S. (1995), 'Intersubjectivity and temporal reference in television commentary', *Time and Society*, vol. 4, no. 3, pp. 345–64.

—— (1996), 'Time and time again: "live" television commentary and the construction of replay talk', *Media, Culture & Society*, vol. 18, pp. 69–86.

Marshall, P. D. (1997), *Celebrity and Power: Fame in Contemporary Culture*, Minneapolis: University of Minnesota Press.

Meyrowitz, J. (1985), *No Sense of Place: The Impact of Electronic Media on Social Behavior*, New York: Oxford University Press.

Montgomery, M. (1986a), *An Introduction to Language and Society*, London: Methuen.

—— (1986b), 'DJ Talk', *Media, Culture & Society*, vol. 8, pp. 421–40.

—— (1999), 'Talk as entertainment: The case of The Mrs Merton Show', in L. Haarman (ed.), *Talk about Shows: la parola e lo spettacolo*, Bologna: CLUEB, pp. 101–5.

—— (2004), 'Broadcast news, the live "two-way" and the case of Andrew Gilligan', paper given at Ross Priory Seminar on Broadcast Talk, University of Strathclyde.

Moores, S. (1995), 'Media, modernity and lived experience', *Journal of Communication Inquiry*, vol. 19, pp. 5–19.

—— (2000), *Media and Everyday Life in Modern Society*, Edinburgh: Edinburgh University Press.

Morse, M. (1983), 'Sport on television: replay and display', in E. A. Kaplan (ed.), *Regarding Television*, Los Angeles: University Publications of America, pp. 44–66.

Index